Ho Tactics:
How to MindF**K A Man into Spending, Spoiling, and Sponsoring

GOLD EDITION

G.L.
Lambert

Cover Design by Cornelia G. Murariu

For more information visit:
FarFromBasyc.com

$***$

THE GOLD STANDARD: THROUGHOUT THE PANDEMIC THAT CHANGED HOW PEOPLE DATED AND SOCIALIZED, ONE THING REMAINED STRONG, MEN SPENDING MONEY! IN HONOR OF THE WOMEN WHO WROTE ME SUCCESS STORIES AND THOSE WHO ASKED QUESTIONS, I'VE UPDATED HO TACTICS TO BETTER ADDRESS THE WORLD WE NOW LIVE IN.

IT DOESN'T MATTER IF IT'S ONLINE DATING APPS, ZOOM DATES, OR LONG-DISTANCE MARKS; THESE TACTICS HAVE PROVEN TO BE PANDEMIC-PROOF! IT DOESN'T MATTER WHO THE MAN IS, HOW MUCH MONEY HE HAS, OR WHAT AGE HE IS, I HAVE COACHED COUNTLESS WOMEN ON HOW TO SECURE THE BAG. FINALLY, IT DOESN'T MATTER HOW YOU LOOK OR HOW OLD YOU ARE SO LONG AS YOU ARE WILLING TO TAKE THIS BOOK SERIOUSLY, PLAY THE ROLE, AND MOVE WITH CONFIDENCE!

23-YEAR-OLD GIRLS TO 60-YEAR-OLD WOMEN, HAVE MADE THIS BOOK WORK FOR THEM, SO THERE IS NOTHING STOPPING YOU, BUT YOUR OWN HESITATIONS. TAKE NOTES, HIGHLIGHT, AND GET READY TO DIVE INTO HO TACTICS WITH A FEW SLIGHT TWISTS…

Table of Contents
Part One
Secrets of the Smart Ho

Table of Contents
Part Two
The Power of Sex Magic

Bonus Chapters

Foreword

I was given *Ho Tactics* after G.L. made me cry. It was October of 2014. I attended a seminar in London centered around the book *Solving Single*. Being literally his biggest fan, I had to attend despite currently being in a relationship with no need for advice. I was so wrong. After the event, I was granted time to talk with G.L. in private. What began as praise and admiration slowly turned into a teary-eyed confession. My boyfriend had cheated on me twice. He did not have a job. He would stay in my flat during the week promising to look for work. On the weekends he would run off with his brothers, or so I hoped. As I ran down my basic bitch ways, G.L. listened patiently. At the conclusion, he didn't so much as rip into me but read my entire story back in a way that made me feel like complete shit. He has a knack for doing this. As the other women stared daggers waiting for me to get the hell up so they could have a turn, he hugged me, went into his bag, and retrieved a copy of *Ho Tactics*. It was his last copy, reserved for someone else, but he felt I should have it. That was the start of the new me.

I thought that a woman should never ask for things. If a man wanted you to have it, he would surely offer. My father and mother had a relationship that was more like Servant & Homeowner. Mother took care of the house. Father paid the bills. Maybe this is why I took care of my last two boyfriends instead of been taken care of by them. I was trying to earn their affection by being a wife in training. The hustles in *Ho Tactics* felt so daring yet so far away. I convinced myself that this was for American girls with fearless attitudes and hourglass bodies. Not a girl from the UK that wore a coat to cover her enormous ass even when the weather didn't call for it. I reached out to G.L. and asked if he remembered me and embarrassingly he mentioned the crying. I wrote back about *Ho Tactics* and asked if it pertained to someone such as myself. He didn't see the awkward, insecure girl who hid her ass and spent hours in the mirror obsessing over blemishes; he saw what could be. G.L. told me that I had the body and face that could hook any man if I stopped focusing on the negative. I had always been able to get male attention, but it didn't boost my self-esteem. Boys will bed anything. Still, hearing someone say these things with nothing to gain made me give the book a go. G.L. states that you must be clear on your goal, aim for something tangible. I wanted money to pay my rent for one month. That was my aim. Small, I know, but I was being realistic. I met a gentleman who courted me in all the ways I wished my ex-boyfriend had. Passed my "headphone test". Then eagerly provided rent money when I said I was in a jam. By the next month, I began to cool on him, but low and behold he showed up to pay it again, this time without asking! I cried, but this time they were tears of joy.

I didn't believe in myself and couldn't believe in myself until I had proof. *Ho Tactics* provided that and fundamentally changed my way of thinking. When I visited the States and met with G.L., he told me that he would be updating *Ho Tactics*. I had not worked a mark since my initial experiment. I found the Spartan road of *Men Don't Love Women Like You*, a better fit for my ultimate goal, but I begged G.L. to let me write this introduction. There are women who have gotten much more than I have, as well as those that are still in the thick of it who have achieved greater results, but I am proof of the indirect power of the book. I found confidence by exercising my will, and that has made me rich in spirit and wealthy in life experiences. I no longer wait, I take action. I no longer hope and pray, I make things happen. I get my way whereas before I let everyone get away with devaluing me. It's not always well received, but fuck'em, it's my world. They're just living in it ☺

-Spartan Eva

Preface

Why can't I find a man with money? The first time I heard that, I was sixteen years old, dropping fries in the back of a fast food joint. The twenty-something lead cashier was leaning against the counter, cheeks puffed with bitterness moments after her mousy best friend had been chauffeured through our Drive-Thru by her Lexus pushing new boyfriend. "I look better than her! Y'all tell me I don't look better than her?" She peeped through the burger slide, flashing her baby blue eyes, waiting for me and the rest of my teenage burger flipper crew to hop on her clit with a unanimous, "you are prettier!" The truth was that she was more physically attractive than her best friend, but having seen both of them in the restaurant palling around; the difference in personality superiority was obvious. My co-worker was what the pre-ratchet world referred to as redneck white trash. She was overly loud and mannish, flirted with everyone, and had a reputation for telling her business and the business of those close to her for the sake of attention. If I had the wisdom back then, I would have chimed in, "Sure you're prettier, but those set of lips aren't worth the trouble if the other set won't shut the fuck up." It was my first experience with a woman thinking that men are completely driven by looks, and this rule that pretty gets pampered… but it wouldn't be my last.

    Why can't I find a man with money? The first time I read that was a few weeks after *Solving Single* came out, and I was doing the first round of advice emails. This young lady listed several qualities that she possessed that made her better than the rest. She had a Master's degree, was in a supervising position at work, no kids, just bought her first new car, and was working on saving money for a home. The first half of her email was an angry response to all the black men that had used her, passed her over, or played games in the 29 years she had been alive.

The second half was a tirade on "Hoes[1]" as she called them. She did everything that men say they want from a wife in the making. She held them down with home cooked meals, understood when they didn't have money, gave out loans, and sacrificed dates for in-house chilling because that's what her mother did for her dad. What set her off was her cousin's best friend. At first, she assumed that this well styled, yet unemployed girl was walking around with fake handbags. When she came through with a new BMW, she assumed this girl was borrowing someone's car. Finally, when she had a New Year's Eve party at a home bigger than the one her parents owned, she realized she wasn't a fraud. This girl was winning with men on a level that she couldn't reach with her degrees, career, and nurturing love.

Why can't I find a man with money? Why do I only meet men who need me to sacrifice or be a team player? Why can't a good woman get spoiled too? That was the exact ending of this woman's email. I imagine the reason this bothered her so much was that when she went home alone after that NYE party and laid in her cold bed, she realized that playing by the rules of her mother, the rules of society, and the rules of so-called good girls had not made her "Wifey Material," it left her as "That bitch that doesn't mind going Dutch." For all of those positives she bragged about, she was nearly 30 and dating on the level of a 19-year-old college student. As I began to think about what I should write back to her, I realized that what I had to say wouldn't be short, and it wouldn't be what she would consider fair.

Unlike most men, I can freely admit that I love Hos. I believe a woman that can get a man to pay for her college education is just as smart as the 21-year-old guy that goes to Wall Street and convince men three times his age to line his pockets. I am whole-heartedly a capitalist, and it would be extremely misogynistic for me to not applaud her cousin's

---

[1] A hoe is a garden tool, but this spelling of "Ho" is still relatively popular.

friend over her own effort. **One attacked life, the other complained.** The woman writing me was an educated fool who placed all her faith in outside forces, while the alleged Ho she was slandering manifested her own destiny. As an educated woman, she should be able to win on the highest levels, but knowledge without the courage to apply it is worthless. This emailer and that cashier from years ago represent two schools of thought. The first being the extremely attractive woman who has nothing of substance inside feeling as if her Maxim looks should be enough to get the highest caliber man. The second being the career woman who feels as if her education, professional ambition, and niceness should be enough to inspire men to wife her. Both women were wrong because neither understood what truly excites men. The purpose of this book is to fully explain what drives males and how to weaponize it to your advantage.

When it came time to focus on how to get this message across in regards to the practical use of female power, I choose to break down Hos because they use their power in the simplest and most efficient way. It isn't the lies and deceit that I respect. When it comes to Hos, I respect their uncompromising confidence. For those of you who read *Solving Single*, you know that I coined a term for those women that have ultimate confidence and aren't held back by what society thinks of them — **Spartans**. The difference between a Spartan and Ho is that one is after genuine love, respect, or partnership while the latter is after money, material goods, or status. That's it! Neither of these women play by the rules nor put other people's needs ahead of their own. The end goal is the only thing that makes one seem Positive and the other Negative. Spartans are just as ruthless as Hos are, but they are loyal and have a code of honor (which you can read about in *Men Don't Love Women Like You*) where they don't need to lie to get things from a man. At first, I was going to do a Spartan Tactics book, but I felt that most of the ideas and concepts would seem too abstract, and most women looking for direct examples on how to pull it off would crumble as soon as they were rejected by a man.

Reaching Spartanhood is simple yet seems advanced because weak women with zero understanding of power think of it as magic. Typical Basicas[2] that have lived in a city or town their entire lives will complain about men not dating, or how they need to move if they ever want to find love. A Spartan woman can be dropped in any city and come away with a date by the end of the week. I've actually seen this happen with different women that I've given advice to who happen to cross over into each other's cities. The Spartan proves the weak woman's theory wrong by winning in her own backyard. The excuse then becomes that the Spartan got lucky. Luck is a myth, and there is no real excuse these Basicas can make because all women are created equal. What's the difference between a Type A and a Type B female? **Confidence**! A confident woman doesn't look for excuses; she doesn't get discouraged by rejection, and she never gets flustered when results aren't instant. A confident woman has faith that she's the best there is and sees every setback as a chance to improve upon her greatness and attract an even better man. That's knowledge I've shared for years, but when a woman with false confidence goes out and tries to live the Spartan way, she fails because she doesn't have the stomach for winning, she wants safe, and playing it safe is the DNA of losers.

Spartan women are honorable, and their intentions are pure. Hos are opportunist and their intentions are selfish. Both know how to get what they want, and both win more than they lose. Neither woman is better than the other because what's right and what's wrong is up to the individual to decide, not you. One of the women interviewed for this book told me that

---

[2] Basica is a term I coined to describe Basic Bitches, those women who act cliché and exhibit conformist stances in regards to personality or fashion.

being a Ho is the best path to evolve into Spartanhood. She may be right, but for others, graduating from the naive world of being a sweet doormat into being a Spartan Queen may be a smoother transition because they never have to feel guilt or fear karma. Either way, Spartanhood is the ultimate achievement because money is not the end all be all—Love is now, and will always be the greatest thing you can attain. One day Hos will learn that lesson, but for now, they are *Moneyvated*, and that fire they have for finance or fame, if used correctly, is unstoppable. I used the Ho example for this book over that of the Spartan because it is something any woman can grasp onto and apply in a practical method.

Hos have an advantage over normal women because they aren't confined by honesty or loyalty. Thus, they can stoop to a level that a classy lady would never stoop to, they can say things that a girlfriend would be ashamed to say, and they can do things sexually that a woman that's looking to become a wife won't be comfortable doing until she has a ring. How can you compete with someone that is willing to break the rules? You can't! **A man will pick a Ho 9 out of 10 times because men cherish excitement over stability**! Look at you, sitting there with all this ego and lists of things you don't do. Look at her sitting there with her hand on his knee, telling him to order more shots because she's ready to be bad. Hos make a man's choice easy because they aggressively lead him to his most savage urges. The greatest misconception is that a Ho is doing this for the love of penis. Some of these girls are just looking for sex, but the Hos that I know and that I outline in this book are not what I call sluts, fast, or freaks looking to get laid. They are smart, and <u>Smart Hos</u> are flirty, forward, and manipulative for one non-sexual reason: Any man with a hard dick is her Aladdin's Lamp.

This book isn't meant to make women go out and play games with men, it's meant to shed light on the fact that women will always be the most powerful creatures on this earth. The reason "Hos be winning" has little to do with looks, looseness, or how they perform in the bedroom. Like the Spartans they may one day transform into, Hos understand that Pussy Power is real! The only thing separating a 29-year-old woman that goes Dutch from a 29-year-old woman that gets her entire lifestyle paid for by a member of the Miami Heat is ruthless aggression. This book will lay out step by step how to get anything you want, but it isn't a magic pill, it does take one conscious bit of effort to make all of this work—Confidence. Confidence is a word that will pop up in every chapter, and not by coincidence. No matter if you're reading this to get a little more insight on how to get treated by the man you love or if you're looking to score a sponsor that can change your fortune, none of this works without you taking control of your own fears and anxiety.

What makes this book different from these generic "Gold Digging 101" books is that it isn't about sex! Nor am I talking about finding an old fat bald guy and making him think you like him for a few months to get a handbag or pair of shoes, any dumb stripper can get that. This is exact science on how to combine womanly charm with verbal aggression in order to win the lottery—literally. No matter what race you are or what age you are, these tactics prove that tricks, treats, and sponsors come in all shades and sizes, and all you have to do is use your BRAIN to get whatever you want. The economy may be down, but men are still making money, and as long as they are making it, you can be taking it. Right is a direction, not a state of living, so leave all of your judgments at the door and take thorough notes because this book is about to change your entire life.

Part One:
Secrets to Being a Smart Ho

*"Give a girl the right shoes,
and she can conquer the world."*
-Marilyn Monroe

#1
Ho World Order

When was the last time a man gave you a Christmas gift that took your breath away? Where is that epic Valentine's Day gift that you can show off and make every girl on Facebook jealous? Can you post a birthday picture on Instagram of you on a vacation that cost you $0.00? I don't want to hear barbwire lined excuses about shallow corporate holidays or how you would rather sit home and cuddle than go on bae-cations. Don't sidestep the question with that "it's the thought that counts" bullshit. You have entertained grown men, given them your time, energy, and affection...yet, in the end, you get the short end of the stick in exchange for the shiny end of the dick. If you publicized what you had to show for your last two relationships the same way you publicize pictures of your food, you would be the laughing stock of the internet. **Add up all the free pussy you have given up to men who turned out to be assholes.** Men have undervalued you your entire life and they will continue to do the least for the most going forward. You're not content with that treatment, you're angry, but you don't know how to change those results, so you bottle it up and go on the defensive.

It's not you; it's them, right? Men today don't know how to court, how to date, how to treat, blah blah blah! But you fuck them, you fall in love, and you cry over those same men you complain about. Your love life is a math problem that will never be solved because you refuse to look at why the numbers aren't adding up. Why do you always manage to get involved with men who are between jobs or who don't believe in that "man pays" tradition? Why can't you look through your phone and point out one non-family member that could give you, not loan you, a thousand dollars by the end of the day if you were in need? Your pussy is tight, your personality is bomb, and your heart is good, yet you have never been truly treated by a boyfriend or even tricked on by these clowns who stalk and flatter you. Men buy you with words and compliments, and you pretend that's all you need. No woman is born low maintenance, she's shamed into that role. And here you are, happy that a man wants to half-ass date you. Where's your sense of value? It's locked away under this notion that "a good girl takes what's given and doesn't ask for extra." These men aren't too shy to ask for sex, but heaven forbid that you ask to be taken out and treated to a romantic night. Year in and year out, you prostitute your body for men that are only pretending to want your heart. It's time to wake the fuck up and stop being so foolish!

Why are you getting used instead of spoiled? It's the men, right? Times are tough, jobs are few and far between, and guys do not have it to give in this day and age… However, when you look online or are out in public you still see women who don't have half your class or looks, being spoiled by good looking and affluent men. Go to any restaurant, and you will see that couples dominate the tables. Go to a tropical resort, and you will see that couples dominate the grounds. Men are still treating women by the millions, so there goes your theory that on average males are broke or refuse to court anymore.

Weak women blame to explain, strong women who are looking to better themselves do the math no matter how much the truth hurts. Her 1 is the same as your 1, yet she ends up doubling her value, and you end up getting subtracted to 0. You don't have the power to do what she does, but you don't know how to admit that, so you soak in that pool of animosity every time you see a woman sharing vacation pictures. Let's keep it real, you are a woman that has dealt with splitting checks, paying your own way, driving your own car to places, and while you say that you don't mind, it does bother the fuck out of you. You're not a hater; you're not disgruntled, but you know that you deserve to be spoiled too. You can go out and get your own, but that want to be appreciated remains, and nothing about it is anti-feminist. **It's not about being dependent on a man; it's about being valued!** You are a queen, but that doesn't mean you ever grow out of being pampered like a princess.

Seeing other people who you feel aren't as deserving win is a bitter pill to swallow. I don't care how pious you try to be; you don't think it's fair, and you find it very confusing. How do you deal with these feelings besides repress them and say, "My time is coming"? What do you think when you see men and women pass you in the mall with arms full of bags? Your mind decides that all of those men are dumb, and all of those women are selling pussy for Balenciaga. A bunch of high-class prostitutes and johns... meanwhile, you're too much of a lady to sell your soul so you'll go back to eating Chipotle with Dennis your friend with benefits who doesn't even have his own place. While you're eating that $5 burrito your mind is racing with bullshit affirmations: *God will reward a good woman in the end, my prince will come, those guys probably cheat anyway.* Countless women are going through these "why can't that be me," emotions and the only way to keep sane is to make up excuses, but why hate when you can participate?

I recently spoke to nearly a dozen women that live or have lived a life where men literally took care of them, and I can honestly say that more than half of them were getting Celine bags, red bottoms, even cars leased, without ever sucking a dick or riding one. The men who do these things are from all lifestyles, not just the wealthy. Look wise they also run the gamut, so you can't chalk it up to, "only ugly men trick." The identities of men who break women off would shock you in the same way females who walk into strip clubs for the first time are surprised at the quality of men throwing racks for a dance they could get for free. These women I interviewed aren't chasing old guys and fat boys; they are getting in the pockets of guys who you would probably fuck off appearance alone. *Tricks, Treats, and Sponsors are hidden all around you*! These men aren't hard to get to if you know what to look for and how to set your value. You've probably been in relationships with tricks, but you never saw that side of them; instead, you had to watch as the girl that came after you milked him. It's time to stop thinking, "That should have been me," and make it you! I can't tell you personally what you do wrong and why these men don't spend on you because I don't know your story nor have I been on a date with you. However, I can show you exactly what other women do that you do not, and from their **Hoexample**, maybe you can step your cookies up.

Any woman can get at least one thing she wants from a man, yes, even that broke dude that just popped in your head. Feminine wiles aren't reserved for women with coke bottle shapes or girls with flawless magazine faces. **The art of seduction can be mastered by any woman with half a brain because the allure of new pussy is timeless.** I want you to get rid of your preconceived notion that certain men are Hoexempt.

Some men are harder to crack than others are, but none are Hovincible. With any new knowledge that seems too good to be true, your first instinct will be to create a laundry list of excuses as to why it won't work for you. You aren't the kind of girl that can pull this off, and the men you come across aren't those kind of men that will fall powerlessly to these methods… stop doubting! This will work ten out of ten times, on any straight male, and if you do falter, it's because you didn't follow the steps. This guide is practical, kind of like putting together an Ikea dresser. You can get frustrated and fuck this up, but it's not because the pieces weren't in the box, it's because your fast ass didn't follow each step! Don't race to the last page of this book if you don't understand certain things, re-read until it makes sense. It's important that you don't just inhale this like a trashy ratchet sex novel that you finish in one day. This guide is meant for you to study and absorb <u>slowly</u> because it can literally lead to a better life if done correctly.

***

To most "Ho" is an interchangeable term used to describe a loose woman that fucks any and everybody. If you define a Ho as simply a dick thirsty woman, then you're about to land in India; that's how far off the map you are. Semantics; depending on where you live definitions vary. For example, the word "bitch" can be offensive, empowering, a replacement for "sis", or the act of complaining. Meanings destroy perceptions and reshape language. Which is why we're going to take the art of being a Ho and forge it into a weapon not an insult. There are women society has labeled as sluts because they treat sex the same way most men treat sex—a physical release that they want to do with someone attractive. Sluts fuck to cure their physical lust or emotional loneliness and sex is no big deal. Hos fuck for status, money, or goods to cure their financial limitations, and sex is expensive. The key difference is one has sex for attraction alone the other has sex for materialistic gains.

I only use these derogatory terms to make it easy for those reading to grab on to a label that can be referenced. I do not think any woman should be boxed in generically. Like all human beings, women are complex, and within every "good girl" is a "bad girl." At some point in life, you may do something another thinks of as slutty or Hoish. In the bigger picture, it doesn't matter what people think because your opinion is the only one that matters. Women have the right to have sex with whomever they want to regardless of the reasoning. This is *Ho Tactics*, which means that we are using my definition, not your Uncle's theory of what a Ho should be. This isn't *Slut Steps* or *Groupie Guides*, and it has nothing to do with sex as sport or celebrity chasing. These are techniques utilized by real women that get status, money, or goods as opposed to an orgasm from a cute man or relationship from a famous guy.

I break Hos down into categories. **<u>Dumb Hos</u>**, who are usually low class and fuck for Olive Garden and T-Mobile bills. **<u>Basic Hos</u>**, who are usually of a higher class, but don't have the sense to hustle for more than free entry to parties and an occasional handbag. Finally, **<u>Smart Hos</u>**, who have reached the upper echelon of seduction and have fully mastered the art of "Give me because it makes you feel good to see me smile." Smart Hos are the most hated women on the planet because they don't use ass and titties; they use their brains to turn men into tricks without them even realizing they are tricks.

The girls I talked to while researching this book get condos, cars, tuition, and whatever else they need to live. Smart Hos know how to use their pussy like a Green Lantern ring; all they do is focus on what they want, and shit falls out of the sky. This guide is for Smart Ho usage. If you want to shortchange yourself for a Michael Kors bag and a trip to Jamaica, that's fine, but the message throughout will be, aim high or don't aim at all.

The first part of this book is sex free, so don't think you will have to fuck to make any of these tactics work. *What, I can get my rent paid without fucking, boy you lying*! If that amazes you then you have a very low opinion of yourself and have no clue of your power and I advise you to go read my other books over and over until you graduate to the first level of Spartanhood. If you're not using sex, you'll have to use something else—your words. This book will teach you the hypnotic way to turn a man out verbally. Sometimes you will tell them what they want to hear, other times you will tease them into a frenzy by dangling their deepest desires like a carrot. It isn't about a lack of consciousness, it's about exploiting male psychology in the same way retail stores do market research to exploit the wants and needs of shoppers. You're not stealing, you're not taking, these men will GIVE GIVE GIVE because they want to.

"You have to be heartless to manipulate a man," false! You don't have to be cold hearted or a sociopath to pull this off, but you must be a sales woman that isn't afraid to open her mouth. Nothing about these steps are malicious or evil, it's a safe blueprint for making sure you get the highest value for your time. Not your body, your time! If you're too soft and the thought of leading a man with your words and verbally seducing him scares you, then go back to your Applebee's two for $20 dates. Keep being content with watching Netflix while some loser tries to get your bra off. Allow yourself to stay that sweet shy girl who thinks being nice will pay off. Men today are savage, they're unapologetic, and they feast on basic bitches like you who don't have the heart to be hard and use the power of her pussy. <u>Final warning:</u> These tactics aren't for insecure women. You can get anything you want, and you will get anything you want without spreading your legs, but it does take one skill many of you don't have, unwavering self-confidence.

#2:
Why Men Love Hos

The first thing that crosses a man's mind when he meets a new woman is how she looks. Before you stop reading like, "I knew there was a catch, I gotta look like Beyoncé and shit," calm the fuck down and let me continue. Guys react to beauty but looks alone do not enchant. When a man meets a new woman, he unconsciously judges her level of pretty. She's sexy, cute, okay, or ugly. I'm not going to sugar coat that because it is just the reality of how male brains work. Of course, having certain body features make women more attractive. For example, I once watched how my friend started talking to the more classically beautiful of two friends while sitting in a hotel lobby. The moment the less attractive friend got up to go to the bar, his eyes lit up at the sight of her ass. Once she came back, my friend immediately switched his focus to the donkey booty girl—her ass upgraded her beauty over that of her friend's face. Breast upgrades, legs upgrades, even hair upgrades. Doesn't matter how fake any of it is, men don't really care where it came from as long as it looks good in motion! There is something even more powerful than blemish free skin, D-cups, Malaysian hair, and an ass that you can sit a Ciroc bottle on, it's called charm.

To engage a man and flirt with him in a way where you stroke his ego will always win him over. Charming a snake is similar to charming a man, you hypnotize them into a comfortable state, and from there you can do with them what you will. Compliments, flirty sass, and sexual body language will bring a man to his knees. Keep in mind that men don't know for sure that you're attracted to them, they assume it. No matter how cocky he acts, he still craves the ego stroke of your attention. To confirm your attraction under the pretense of flirting, will put the biggest Kool-Aid smile you've ever seen on his face. We will get into the ins and outs of flirting later, but for now, let's focus on the psychology because you should never test these things out without first understanding what's mentally at play. **Hos have mastered the art of flattery and that, more so than their appearance, makes them sexy.** A woman who looks like Mila Kunis[3] can walk up to a guy and start a conversation where she doesn't really engage, just answers straight, and any man with eyes will like her, but he probably won't ask for her number because the vibe is mixed, and he doesn't want to get rejected. A woman that doesn't look half as good as Mila can walk up to a man, make eye contact, compliment his smile, and give off crazy body language, and magic happens. This man's brain transforms her from a seven to a nine because she's being nice, showing interest, and filling that insecure hole that all men have. That's called charm.

The strippers that make the most money aren't necessarily the prettiest; they're the ones with the best conversation, the ones that put a man at ease, and that make him feel handsome. They charm the money out of his wallet for longer than that one song he swore he wasn't going to go past. There are corny strippers who are happy to take their clothes off

---

[3] Mila Kunis is the brunette bombshell best known for *That 70's Show*.

and ask guys if they want a dance, but they're lap-dancing like they're shadow boxing, numb to reality and dry as hell in their salesmanship. Let a stripper who comes over with something interesting to say like she's a human being and not just making the rounds, and she's going to force that dude to hit up the ATM. Her bare breast and ass hanging out didn't pull him; her charm pulled him by exploiting a man's need to feel special in a room full of rival males. That's Ho appeal! These women not only come off as sexy, but also know how to make a man feel like he's the center of the universe.

Charm alone won't captivate a man to the point where he's treating you to Vegas trips just because. Charm alone is an easy way to find yourself in the friend zone unless you have the next ingredient—sex appeal. Hos know what men look for in a woman physically and what other women look for competitively. **Master charm and then turn your attention to amplifying your sex appeal.** The thing to focus on is your body, and how the right fashion choices will draw attention in various degrees. If you have a big ass, you wear things that accentuate that ass. However, that ass is a gift and a curse because if you accentuate it too much you draw the wrong attention. For instance, a girl comes to get her son's hair cut at the barbershop I go to, and she always wears shorts that barely cover her ass. Guys look, but then they look at each other in a way that the fellas do, "she's phat, but she looks funky." There are fools who will pursue her because they want to fuck, even if she comes off as ratchet. However, most of the quality men will be turned off because they don't want to be seen walking down the street or cuffing a girl who dresses like a hoochie mama.

As a female looking to win in any field, you have to address your sex appeal in ways that lead to you being embraced first, and then you can unload the big guns. Dressing provocatively will get you hit on, but it's only because guys think you're easy. Leave something to the imagination, not too much, but enough where you will at least garner some respect. Hos spend a lot of time perfecting their appearance because they know other women will try to label them in earshot of men who will then be influenced by, "Your dick might fall off if you put it in that," slander. Dress sexy but not sleazy, because your hustle won't work if a man sees through you, and your top, at first glance.

No matter if you're skinny or fat, small chest with big hips, big tits with no ass, and everything in between—know your body and know what looks good on you. I'm not talking about looking in the mirror and thinking that it matches, go deeper and really focus on your clothes as if you were picking out a Halloween costume. Girls who wear slutty outfits on Halloween are transformed mentally; they feel like that Sexy Officer or that boobalicious *Alice in Wonderland*. Every day you should wear things that give you that same confidence. If you are going to a club or party, dress up and play that part. If you're going to the store to get some hairspray, wear your sweatpants but make sure they fit the right way and that you feel like a goddess in them, not a bloated girl on her period that just found something to throw on.

Every time you step out of the house is an opportunity to attract someone who could change your life, so always look your finest. A thirsty man will talk to any woman; they're just playing the percentages. A pussy hunter will talk to any woman showing skin because men understand that women sex trap for a reason—they want sex. Tricks and sponsors aren't racing after pussy; they're looking for a sign that you're different, that you're quality and not someone that the world has sampled. If you expect a man to treat you like a princess, you can't run around looking like a pauper nor can you go around looking desperate like you stepped out of the brothel. It's a balance of makeup, hairstyle, and fashion and the only way to know that you've gotten it right is to be your own test—*Do I look sexy as fuck today in my messy bun, worn out jeans, and lip gloss? Yes, I do!* Reach that level mentally, and your sex appeal can't be touched.

Men think they know everything there is to know about women because, in all honesty, most women do behave uniformly. I had a discussion with a guy friend who told me, "You can explain how we work to these bitches all you want, but it doesn't matter because girls still fall for game." So how do you standout to a man that's used to charm and sex appeal? What action can you take to register to any man that you are a real-life Unicorn worthy of special treatment? Most men are biased because they have seen how women from different backgrounds all do the same exact things and react in the same exact ways. Females say they are different, but their actions disprove their claim. Girls want boyfriends, even when they say they don't. Girls get mad when you don't call them back, even though they pretend they didn't notice. Girls get jealous if you show another female attention, even when they claim not to care. What separates Hos from this typical passive aggressive, relationship lusting variety of woman is that they don't give a fuck. I'm not talking a ratchet[4], "no fucks given," defensive attitude. I'm talking about a genuine, down for whatever, let's have fun, no stress no mess disposition. Along with <u>Charm</u> and <u>Sex Appeal</u>, there is one last piece of the puzzle—Coolness.

---

[4] Ratchet is a derogatory term used to describe various classless women or trashy behavior.

Ho Appeal

A Ho's attitude is the sexiest thing about her because these girls are all about keeping it light and fun. Hos don't ask questions about love or relationships; they live in the now. Hos don't call to talk about who missed who, they call to talk shit. Hos don't worry about other girls; they point out other girls. This behavior is so unique it confuses a man to the point where he's genuinely amazed. To spend an evening with a girl who doesn't mind referring to him as sexy, who knows how to dress in a way that turns him on without embarrassing him, and who truly could care less about being his girlfriend, is a fun and zero-pressure situation. It tells a man that she wants that dick, yet she's not trying to imprison that dick. That she's freaky but she's not a freak that every dude has probably been inside. Most importantly, it says that she's cool enough to drop his guard around without the worry of offending her with his comments on the attractiveness of other women or confessions about not being ready for a relationship.

A man's biggest fear is commitment, while a woman's biggest fear is never finding commitment. As a woman, you can sit and say you're happy being single and don't need a man, but you will most likely slip up and show things that give you away because most of the time saying you're happy and single is a defense mechanism to prevent being hurt again. "I don't want anything serious," transforms to "what are we," because women are either lying or confused about their wants. Not Hos. Hos don't give ultimatums, nor do they lay claim, they prove they aren't the same as these Title-Chasers by being cool with everything and not reacting the same way other women do.

A good time girl is priceless! I have an associate who lives in LA, she's always on the scene, party after party, pictures with your favorite rapper and TV actor on her Instagram. She once told me how a girl commented on her vacation pic, "you probably don't have any walls," and we laughed because I know for a fact that she's been celibate for over a year. Girls who sit home being jealous assume that a woman has to fuck to get treated—wrong! **Her superpower was Ho Appeal.**

Those celebrities, party promoters, and even myself enjoy having her around because she's insanely fun and doesn't bring any attitude or drama. It's not about sex, it's the rush of your personality that hooks a man. The party is boring, call her to come liven it up. Taking a trip to another city, bring her along because she's going to turn up. Bored driving to work, put her on speaker phone because she's better than coffee. He's not inviting you to the party because you don't dance, you sit and play on your phone. He's not inviting you out of town unless pussy is promised because that's all he thinks you're good for, laying on your back. He refuses to call you just to talk, because you're a buzz kill, not a buzz. Because of this uniqueness, men want to keep women like that on the team permanently and will go above and beyond to make it happen.

Hos win because their cool attitude combined with their charm and sex appeal is Disneyland for dudes. It's a fantasy world where a guy can relax with a girl who doesn't pressure him for anything but a good time and doesn't mind his hand on her thigh. If you give any man a choice of going to school and having to put in real work or going to an amusement park where he doesn't have to do shit but pay the cost of admission and buy a few gifts, he's going to pick the fun expensive option because it's safe, easy, and stress free. Hos are worth that price. They aren't easy sexually, but they are easy emotionally, and that's the riddle that most women can't solve. The average female mind can never understand how scary the concept of commitment is to men who just want to have a good time. Hos understand and turn that desire into currency.

#3:
Being Disciplined
Around Dick

You fuck a man because you think he looks good. Does that make you selective? You spread your legs and let a man inside because he's hung around for 90 days. Does that make you classy? You have sex with men who say the right things, look the right way, or promise the right future. Does that mean you have standards? No, no, and no. The average woman is in denial about why they have sex with certain men faster than others. The truth is that pussy is cheap, easy, and plentiful depending on the man, more so than the standards set by the woman. The majority of women put their pussy on a pedestal, telling anyone who will listen that the combination to her vagina is harder to figure out than a Dennis Rodman press conference. In reality, these women are fronting for other women or attempting to convince the man with his hand up her skirt that she's not that kind of girl.

With her chest poked out, and head cocked to the side, she proclaims to her friends, family, Twitter followers, and Facebook friends, that she's not a Ho, she knows her value and has a list of things a man must prove before she even considers sex. She needs to be in a relationship first. She needs to establish trust. She needs to know that the man she's giving her body to is sincere. Let's keep it real, that shit is an Amazon wish list, not mandatory prerequisites for sex. Of course, there are exceptions to the rule and those women that require a real bond before he can even taste it, still walk among us. However, the thing no one wants to talk about is that the normal American woman is extremely weak when placed in close quarters with a man she likes. A Ho in comparison is more disciplined than a Victoria's Secret Angel trapped inside Krispy Kreme. The first step in building your Ho arsenal is understanding why you can't fight your urges around handsome men.

There are okay-looking guys, good-looking guys, and "damn my titties tingled just because he smiled at me" looking guys. Women not only rank men, their bodies react in ways that let them know which level a guy is on in her book. I've always been conscious that I treat girls whom I'm more sexually attracted to nicer, even if there is no chance that we will ever have sex. I call this "sex bias," and all men are guilty of it no matter if they are single or in a relationship. Women are no different internally from men in terms of lust, but they aren't nearly as bias externally because they have the greatest poker face in history. A woman will hug a man that makes her moist with the same level of intensity that she will hug a man that does her taxes. She will answer the phone call of a guy that sets her clit on fire with the same effort she does when the friend zone guy calls. It's a front females use so they won't play themselves.

To let a man know that you're excited to see him translates into being pressed or thirsty, so guarding lust is taught from an early age. No female wants to be that overeager girl who crushes on some guy that ends up wanting to talk to her friend. Women fear rejection like roaches fear light switches. Therefore, instead of owning up to their sexual nature, exploring these feelings, and learning to separate lust from genuine like, most women bury it.

Real Discipline: *Wanting something, understanding why you want it, and then making a conscious and unwavering decision to abstain because you don't need it.*

Fake Discipline: *Wanting something, not fully understanding why you want it so bad, and trying to hold out using willpower to fight the part of you that must have it.*

Willpower alone can't save you because it often conflicts with the logic of the mind's Pleasure Principle. In ratchet terms, a Welfare Queen who wants a Gucci bag can try to fight off the urge to blow her child's food money on it, but having that bag will make her feel like a boss bitch when she walks in the club. Her mind reinforces with pleasure logic, "Them kids love Ramen noodles and mama deserves something for herself doesn't she?" In non-ratchet terms, it's similar to the way someone on a diet sees a piece of red velvet cake. They shouldn't have it, but their mind is reminding them that one little piece won't make a difference, so they have a slice, and then regret it. Willpower has to be paired with knowledge and understanding or you'll buckle the moment you're put to the test.

If you take that person on a diet, explain what even a gram of that cake will do to their body, they can't logically make an excuse as to why they should have it. With that knowledge now backing that dieter's willpower, they are able to cancel out the Pleasure Principle and discipline themselves from eating even a small piece. Ahh, now it makes sense! **Comprehension is the only path to real discipline.**

Bringing it back to relationships, girls know they shouldn't have sex too fast or commit themselves to one man too early in the game. However, their minds think, "it won't make a difference. If he likes me he likes me" and they break their diet, aka ruin their standards and go for the pleasure. Before you can apply any Ho Tactic, you must strengthen your sexual discipline. Not in the repressive way you've been doing with willpower alone, but in a way that you fully understand why you want that man, and why you shouldn't give in until you get what you want first.

Top Shelf Men

The typical girl doesn't approach men. Instead, she waits for a "Good Man" (handsome and into her), to make the first move. All night she is hit on by 5s, maybe one 7, but when that perfect 10 shows interest, it's like a dream come true, and that girl drops all defenses in an insanely short period of time. What did that man do to make her drop that guard other than look the right way and show a surface level attraction? **This doesn't speak to the guy's game; it speaks to the low quality of men that girl is used to attracting.** Most men win girls over with basic behavior and minimal courting because the sexual attraction is so strong that it makes them perceive that he's doing amazing things. In reality, her defenses are weak because she's rarely been tested by stallions, treated by ballers, or charmed by geniuses.

He took you to the movies, OMG he loves spending time with you. He called you in the morning to make sure you didn't oversleep, OMG he's so considerate. He tried to finger you but stopped when you said, "chill," OMG he's such a gentleman. I'm not exaggerating; women really do see little things as huge character defining traits, based off of one thing—sexual attraction. An ugly guy can do those same OMG things and that fool will be greeted with an eye roll. Every woman needs to understand what's at play when she's overcome by lust if she wants to go forward with these Ho Tactics. You will find yourself face to face with men who are in another league from those you normally deal with, and if your discipline isn't airtight, you'll be eaten alive.

Regardless of how you underplay your feelings for guys you crush on, years of pent up sexual fantasies that you weren't allowed to talk about have made you a sexual powder keg. The butterflies, the nerves, the grinning, it's the result of attractive men striking a match, and it won't take long for you to explode no matter how coy you act. Play it off all you want, but this man has only to ask, and you will give it all to "daddy" because your body is on fire. This is not love; this is a loaded gun called sexual desire that most women misdiagnose as falling in love.

My first question to most women who come to me with guy troubles is, "What do you like about him exactly that makes you want to keep fighting for him?" Most can't really tell me because it's nothing concrete or amazing, they are wide open due to an indiscernible feeling that they don't experience with the average lame. He's above average looking, not above average in his actions, but at the moment of moistness, it all blends, making Derrick the postman into Derrick the perfect man. **You like cute boys, you are turned on by cute boys, and you want to sit on the face of cute boys.** You're horny, and he pushes all the right buttons, that's what you like about him! Ladies aren't allowed to communicate these thoughts because the status quo has determined that a sexually expressive woman is a slut. Instead of saying, "I want to fuck him." A proper young lady is supposed to say, "I want to be his girlfriend." This is slut-shaming 101, brainwashing that makes girls see love when it's only lust.

Due to this emotional girdling, all of that pent up lust eventually erupts, and she will become just another lovesick girl who doesn't understand why she had sex so fast, why she couldn't see that he was a jerk from the start, or why she reacted like a psychopath over a man that she barely knew.

The eruption I'm talking about is the suspension of all standards when faced with a good-looking man or any man that you've emotionally connected with romantically aka <u>Top Shelf Dick</u>. Picture your fantasy man; it can be a tall, dark, and handsome football player, or a bearded outdoors type, whatever gets your juices flowing. Place the two of you in the same room. His voice low and engaging, his hands politely stroking your knee, the sexual tension thicker than Chris Christie in a bubble goose. You can be a moral woman, a church-going woman, or a classy woman. It doesn't matter how you describe yourself, you are still a human being. At that peak moment of attraction, you will become high on that sexual energy and you're most likely going to give into your craving for the physical touch of a man and then hold off on the relationship talk, the trust talk, and the sincerity tests. Willpower versus The Pleasure Principle is like throwing rocks at a tank when you lack real discipline.

You want to see how big his dick is; you want to feel how hard it can get while inside you, and every ounce of your body has already caved in, leaving only one last move to seal the deal—him taking that pussy and you submitting to daddy. Most women pursued by Top Shelf Dick will have sex before they are ready. You couldn't help yourself because your body was tingling, your heart was racing, and your mind gave into this man despite all reservations because he made your body feel amazing. Think about this, as a woman you've spent so many years saying, "No" to men because something about them didn't feel right. A good looking, well spoken, or alluring man feels right physically—holy shit that's the sign you've been waiting for from God. The problem is it isn't a sign from God; it's a sign from your sexually frustrated pussy that you misread and allowed to numb your common sense.

In *Solving Single,* I dug deep into the Come Over & Chill dates, which are cheap dates where men would rather get you in a room alone than take you out in public. It's a brilliant strategic move because men have come to learn that the majority of women who agree to come over do not pass the sexual test. Guys get the pussy without spending a dime, by simply pretending to be interested. Women old and young related with my take on Come Over & Chill because it's an epidemic that speaks to the very sexual repression I just mentioned. Close quarters have a habit of making a girl who wanted a real relationship into just another bitch he easily fucked. Women fall for this hustle not because they are stupid or lack common sense; it's because they want him just as badly and couldn't fight that urge to fuck an attractive guy. Once again, it's that false sign from God mixed with a lack of discipline. Ugly dudes are easy to ignore, okay looking guys who are trying too hard are easy to give excuses to, but men who look like your fantasies or come pretty close to it, you don't want to ruin that so you crack.

A part of you wants to be his girl, part of you wants to be his mother, a part of you wants to be his sister, but every part of you wants to feel him inside you. There is nothing wrong with being horny! When you run from what you want, you lie to yourself. When you lie to yourself, you confuse your mind. When you confuse your mind, you become indecisive and indecisive women are easily manipulated. Men manipulate women into sex because their repressed body is saying yes while their confused mind is saying "maybe." In the end, all it takes is a few reassuring words, "I'm not like that, baby," and her confused mind gives in to her repressed body. Of course, the next day, you feel guilty because you went against all of the things you claimed to want before sex, and you're not sure if that guy who had you gushing on his bedspread was sincere about really liking you because you don't really know him.

I need every woman reading this to come to grips with their sexual nature. Stop lying to yourself about how nasty you are, how freaky you want to be, or how much you fantasize about sex. YOU LIKE TO FUCK. I don't care if you're a virgin or only had sex with two guys. You. Like. To. Fuck! The thought of it excites you even if you haven't experienced it or only experienced it a few times; the need for sexual satisfaction is in your DNA. Grab on to this, accept this, and the moment you find yourself face to face with the sexiest man that's ever held your hand, understand what's happening. That tingling feeling isn't proof that he's special; it's proof that you're not gay. Understanding your sex drive keeps you from losing yourself in the moment, it keeps you from going YOLO[5], and it shows the man that is trying to pass your guard that you aren't like the average woman. Once a man sees that you have discipline and that you don't fall for the typical tricks or lies, then you earn his respect. Any woman can use sex to get what she wants, but my job is to teach you how to use respect to get what you need.

Own Your Sexuality

Hos are overly sexual and comfortable in the face of handsome men. They wear sexy outfits, talk seductively, but they never lose control. Men press hard when they're being tempted and will bribe, promise, and beg for sex. A man who looks good and spends even better usually gets what he wants from women, but Hos shake off male manipulation and use an even powerful tool—<u>female seduction</u>. The lessons I'm going to write about all start with knowing yourself sexually, knowing what turns you on, what type of men you have a soft spot for, and promising to abstain from sex even when pushed to your limit. You will come face to face with men that just want to fuck you, but it will be

---

[5] You Only Live Once = YOLO.

your job to get what you want while making him think that he's on his way to getting what he wants. This sounds simple, but when the legendary "Chris Brown but darker," is offering to book your trip to Bora Bora, there will be a huge part of you that will want to let him unfasten your bra before you even see the ticket. Discipline, bitches! **Realize that the moment you give a man your pussy, your leverage becomes nonexistent.** Leave your ego at the door and never assume that a man can't break you down sexually. Find your weakness, understand it, and reinforce your willpower, because either you're in this for a Coach bag or you're in this for the condo.

Being shy or nervous around a man means that you aren't used to something, that it's a new experience, and you're afraid of what could happen. The more attractive, successful, or charming men you hang around or date, the less nervous you will be. Right now, you most likely deal with bums 85% of the time because they approach you first and try the hardest to hit. When you meet winners, you're a ball of nerves because a man with money, looks, and the gift of gab is a unicorn in your world. I can't drive this in your head enough—understand that your attraction is based on him being different from what you're used to, it's not a divine sign that he's "the one," so check your lust, and listen to your common sense.

What do you have to fear from a boy? Men are boys in big pants, don't ever get that twisted. They talk about sports, cars, girls, and money the same way they did in middle school. They play it cool, and then poke fun at you to show their attraction the same way they did in high school. There is nothing scary about boys. The root of your fear is rejection. You are afraid that you're reading too much into his flirting. You are afraid that he's either after sex or not after you at all. You are a victim of your overactive and unconfident mind. Now that you realize that, control your thoughts. This isn't about if he wants to be your boyfriend or not. Who gives a fuck about his intentions? You have a vagina that he wants to sample, and you are going to use it to get a down payment on your next car. So long as you are female, you will always have something every man wants. In order to utilize these tactics, you must look at all men this way:

A Man's goal is to fuck me. He will be nice to me. He will be sweet to me. If that does not work, he will ignore me. He will threaten me. He will challenge me. He will push me away then try to pull me back. He will even act as if sex isn't important. These are games. His goal is to fuck me.

Memorize the above statement because too many women crack when a man uses reverse psychology. They see him becoming distant and rush to kiss his ass. They see a man playing the victim and rush to throw a tit in his mouth. Don't fall for male manipulation or the player becomes the played! Men use Dick Tactics, but these are not as strong as Ho Tactics because dick will never be as powerful as pussy. You will not be nervous around men. You will not get open off his compliments. You will not fall for the push and pull. All those weak bitch ways that you've been a victim to throughout your romantic life have failed you, so it's time to be reborn. You have become a creature of fear and habit, and there is no room for that thinking if you want to apply these tactics. This isn't about finding a boyfriend; it's about profiting, so do not let the thoughts of him liking you or not liking you cloud your mind or affect your strategy. That little Kitchen Bitch on your shoulder that has been with you since the age of 8 will tell you, "He seems nice. Maybe I should give him a chance and wait to use this stuff on the next guy I meet." There is no next guy! Stay strong and conquer him.

Hosheet

Get Comfortable Talking About Sex: This week I want you to have a conversation with a male about sex. It doesn't matter who the guy is, so long as it forces you to step out of your comfort zone. Ask this male about his favorite positions and then tell yours. Ask this male about oral sex, and how getting head makes you feel. I want you to openly express yourself in a way that takes away all the giggles and discomfort. Going back to being disciplined, some girls get open the moment they start talking to a man about sex because they rarely do it. Guard against this by knowing your way around a filthy conversation to the point where it's as natural as talking about nail colors. If you can't find a boy to talk to, you can do this online, log into one of those anonymous chat rooms and have a few typing sessions where you unleash your inner Jada Fire.

Don't Just Watch Porn, Study Porn: Speaking of Jada Fire, you need to watch porn. Porn movies often use dialogue geared toward the male fantasy. This ranges from submissive, "fuck me, I'm a dirty slut," to dominant roles like, "Your little dick can't make me cum, you're pathetic." Know both sides, and appreciate that these porn stars are truly actresses playing a role. This will come in handy when you begin things like phone sex and date teasing.

An Orgasm A Day Keeps Thirst Away: Remember that scene in *There's Something About Mary* where Ben Stiller is told to jerk off before his big date? That's fantastic advice. Instead of pre-dates, masturbate daily. If you're dealing with a guy you want to fuck, you may crack if the last time you had an orgasm was a year ago. Unleash that sexual tension often; it'll keep you honest.

Learn To Take A Compliment: When a man who you're into keeps filling your gas tank like you're a Range Rover, it may be hard to handle because you enjoy that flattery. For those of you who don't think of yourself as pretty or rarely hear anyone decent admit to it, this could be dangerous. Toughen up by complimenting yourself every day. It will feel weird, and you'll want to call bullshit, but that's the old you, the insecure you, the never been good enough little girl that's holding you back from being a confident tigress. Ride your own clit to the point that you become immune to verbal manipulation.

Don't Let Pride Fuck You: You aren't stronger than sex. Therefore, do not put yourself in the same room alone with a man that you're extremely attracted to unless you have an easy out. Most women go with the flow, they get led, and that's what men depend on. That one last, "please stay another hour" turns into all night. That, "just let me taste it," turns into sex. Stop being led by this sense of pride that no man can break you down or catch you slipping, he can. Before you even begin these tactics, be honest about your limits! You can write it down or just keep it in your head, but based on past experiences and the way you are around someone you see as sexy, you must know where your line is, and be careful never to cross it.

"We'll see" Is Better Than "No": Men love to be challenged, but they hate to be rejected. This means that the word, "no" can lead you into a brick wall when attempting to get a trick open. Understand "we will see" is the better term to use in your daily life. To tell him that you're thinking about it sends a signal to that man that he has to keep working away because he's almost in there. Getting what you want without giving away too much is dependent on the giver believing that they will eventually receive what you have to offer, so straddle the "maybe" fence.

#4:

Pussy Costs

Take a girl out to dinner. Treat her to the movies. Buy her flowers. Pick her up from her place and drive her to his. All of these things require money. A man will do all of these things, one of these things, or none of these things depending on how much he's impressed by a woman. Women tell me that "guys today" don't date, or they date cheaply. They claim that this is not a reflection of their value as women; it's proof that men of the 21st century lack respect for the dating game. I call bullshit. Pussy is recession proof. Pussy's value doesn't fluctuate on the NASDAQ. Every day a new vagina breaks a price record. So why is your stock flat? Pussy hasn't become free in the last 20 years it's become cheap, it's become discounted, and it's being given away by women who think men are hard to find and need to be fucked ASAP. It's been manipulated by men who've convinced girls to buy into this idea that to be independent means to accept going Dutch or submit to Come Over & Chill dates. Your pussy isn't a man's only option, there will always be girls who give it up faster with a lot less effort, but despite what other females are doing, YOUR PUSSY should always remain a luxury item.

Your pussy costs and every man is willing to come out of pocket in one way or another to get your pussy. This is a fact. You can look at your past relationships and point out that no man has ever really felt the need to spend or treat in order to win you over…but you fucked him anyway. Maybe there were men who simply tried a little, didn't get anything, and vanished…but when they came back, you fucked them anyway. You control whom you have sex with, and you dictate who has done enough. Stop pointing to those men who blow you off when they don't fuck you after a month as proof that you have zero value in today's market. Those men are window shoppers. Either they never really wanted your product, or they weren't in a position to afford your product, so they browsed and then exited through the gift shop. These males aren't a reflection of your worth; you will not be everyone's cup of tea nor in everyone's price range so to speak. **Tiffany's doesn't redo its front display every time some broke motherfucker walks by and looks, but doesn't buy.** Throughout this journey, you must keep your value! You shouldn't try to switch up things that are proven to work if one or two guys don't buy into your allure.

The same way Napster fucked up the music industry, simple-minded women who allow men to manipulate them with this, "Oh, I don't believe in dating" rhetoric have fucked up the dating industry for all highly valued women. There will be those who will pass you up because even at dinner and a movie price, you come off as too expensive-- fuck those lames they aren't who you should be talking to in the first place. Men with real money will always be willing to pay full price, so your goal in life, even outside of these tactics, should never be to give yourself away to the cutest guy, it should always be to be shown respect and treated with full value. No matter how cute he is, how nice he is, or what story he has to tell, you do not Groupon your pussy because a man doesn't want to pay full price!

I remind you; I'm not talking about the act of prostituting yourself for dates. The aim is to get value for your time and your time only. After a man has sampled your pussy, no matter how good it is, he's not going to be that enamored where he can't afford to walk away. However, if you get him to see you as extraordinary, sexy, and fun, that's something he'll always want to invest in because most girls are mediocre, stressful, and boring. The cost of getting to know you in the first place should be set at a certain limit, this serves as a fortress wall that will keep broke men, stingy ballers, and con artists out of your face. It's an unwritten rule that the first conversation is free, but the second one costs, stick to that.

Setting Your Price

How much is your pussy worth? Your answer should be, "priceless," or you've already failed. You don't need a man financially; you may want one, but you don't need him. You're a grown ass woman capable of finding a job, earning money, and buying what she wants on her own. At no point in this process should you ever fall into desperation and feel that you should sell your pussy for a fixed price because you have rent due, a lingering bill, or an emergency. This is *Ho Tactics*, not *Prostitute Practice*. You are priceless, act like it, and that power will get you anything you want without ever having to spread your legs. I will delve into seduction techniques later, but I have to remind those simple-minded women reading that this has nothing to do with prostituting yourself, but positioning yourself as an object of worship and desire. How much does your pussy cost? That's a better question. Remember, worth and cost are entirely different concepts. While your pussy appraisal is priceless, you have to give those bidding the appearance that you aren't out of their reach.

If I wanted to take you out on a date, what's acceptable? I'm talking real life, acceptable, not Twitter/Facebook putting on a front acceptable. If I were to call and ask to hang out next Friday, I imagine you would say, "Okay, wherever you want to go is cool with me." That humble and downright sweet response puts the power in my hands. I'm going to take you to IHOP, for a $27 meal for two (tip not included because cheap dudes don't tip), followed by a trip back to my house to watch some Netflix. Even if you don't fuck me that night, I'm sure I will fuck you within the next two weeks, and I will never go over that $27 again. As a man, I've determined the price of your pussy as if it's an EBay auction with no other interested bidders.

Most women who go on a date with a handsome guy who has good conversation and an excellent choice in Netflix movies will give up the pussy without raising that price or demanding anything more than what they get. Why? Because that's what "nice" girls do, they don't ask for shit; they quietly take what they're given and are thankful they're not home alone. Maybe you have other guys taking you out or trying to take you out, but we all know that women who begin to over-like one guy are turned off by multiple suitors because they have tunnel vision. That makes this an EBay auction with only one serious bidder. By the end of the month, you've gone on one real date, two house dates, and have auctioned your pussy off for a grand total of $81 or less. Your pussy may be priceless in your head, but you just sold it for $81. Are you following me?

What's a girl to do, ask for a $200 date the first time out? Recommend going on a yacht cruise to show him you're fancy? Negative! No matter if you want a sponsor, a boyfriend, or just a gift buying trick, you have to start with the same foundation— the sample. Your personality, sex appeal, and conversation are like a shot of top shelf Tequila. It gets a man's blood flowing and puts a smile on his face.

The shot of your personality is free, and thus the first date is free. It's a sample, a way to break the ice and show him how different you are from other women. You can go to IHOP, Red Lobster, or Ruth's Chris; doesn't matter as long as your sample is potent. You do not go home with him. I repeat; you never go home with him or let him come home with you. You're like those little perfume samples that they pass out at Nordstrom's. That fool can rub that scent on him and wear that memory until it washes off, but that bottle costs too much for him to afford at this point. You set your price as priceless on the first date by not giving into your lust. If you can't fight your lust, then I assume you sped through the last chapter on Dick Discipline. If the first date aka "the sample" goes well then you will use the second date to set your price in a way that shows him what level of woman he's pursuing. Here are some things to keep in mind on date two:

♥ **You Are What You Eat**
If you recommend cheap places, you establish that you're basic. You let him play the man and take you out on the first date to a place he established. Maybe he took you somewhere nice maybe he didn't. What's important is that you impressed him enough for a second date. Now you start to set the rules by showing him what's expected going forward. Go for elegance, not expense.

Yelp is your best friend from now on. Look for spots operated by well-known chefs, which have romantic settings. Sexy food, sexy wait staff, sexy date. Everything should scream sex! Wine, small portions, ambient lighting-- you're that kind of girl. There will be no drive thru windows or ordering pizza if he wants to get to know you.

♥ **You Need To Be Showcased**

You're not a Reebok broad, so why are you going on Reebok dates? Fuck going bowling, you need to establish that you're the type of girl that dresses like a goddess and needs to be taken places where he can show you off to envious men. For non-dinner dates, you should look into live music shows or the theater. Not a fake Tyler Perry gospel "play" that's hosted in the local YMCA, but a real theater that has an elegant vibe. The idea is to be able to wear that sexy red dress, show off your heel game, and do your hair in a way that's different from the last time he may have seen it. It's also important to go places where other men will be watching you. Playing on a man's jealousy makes you even more desirable.

♥ **Dogs Get Doggy Treats**

You must reward men for good behavior. Going forward, you won't have to ask for things if you take this time to train him to do good by you. He took you out to a nice dinner and treated you to a bottle of wine. Give him a deep passionate kiss. *Good boy*. He took you out on a unique and romantic date. Play with his dick on the car ride home. *Good boy*. Basic bitches would reward this behavior with pussy or a blowjob, you don't! You give him simple treats that mean little to you, but get him excited at the thought of having you fully.

The key is to not let him lure you into having a nightcap. A man who gets worked up doesn't want the night to end. He will ask to keep hanging out, try to order more food or drinks, whatever—but you must be perceptive. Leave him wanting more by ending the date at a reasonable time. Make sure the last image he sees of you is one where he's hard up after a kiss or worked up after a little fondling. This unattainable desire sends a man into a frenzy, and you are guaranteed to get a call that night and the next morning. His actions during the following week will continue to escalate in hopes that the pussy is around the corner. With each new act of affection, give him a small treat, but never your pussy. This is how you train that dog and set your house rules.

Pretty hurts and pussy costs, so why get all dressed up, waxed up, and made up to go sit in some guy's house? These things establish your value without him ever seeing your pussy. After the second date, he may not want to go out anymore, he'll be through with games, and ready to get you alone. Don't feel pressured. Continue your course as if you don't care if he stops talking to you, this lets him know that you have other options. This is the final stage of knowing your pussy's value…

Limited Supply

When I was dating, I used my apathy as a weapon to get more free pussy than rescue day at Petco. Don't get me wrong, I did care about some of these females. There were girls I liked a lot, others I crushed on hard, and there were even girls who had me thinking it was love. My focus wasn't a relationship; it was seeing how fast I could sleep with them. **Let's face it, a man's intent is sex first and then explore the bond second.** When certain girls wouldn't want to come over, or they didn't want to rush the sex, I behaved myself as if it didn't bother me. This was all a front. When you're immature, the want for new pussy can't be denied, you want what you want, and you're willing to risk what could be a good relationship if you don't get that new pussy on your timeframe. In accordance to my horny nature, I went to war with these women, in a way they never truly understood, but in a way that I will now share.

I was semi in love with this girl; we were good friends in terms of talking about life, feelings, blah blah blah. She didn't want to have sex, she needed more time, so I stopped calling her. I would make up excuses as to where I had to go, and how I wouldn't be able to talk. To prove that I was still into her, I would check in, but only for a minute or two, and then get off the phone before she was ready. This pissed her off, but it didn't say, "he's not into you," it was more of a "you're losing him, you better think of something to get him back." Of course, it was a ploy on my part. **When someone takes away their attention, human beings react the same way; they try to experiment with ways to get it back.** One girl cursed me out and acted like a brat. Another one tried to talk to one of my co-workers to make me jealous. This girl decided to pour her heart out about how much she loved me and missed me. All three of these scenarios using anger, jealousy, and love pleas all ended the same way. The next time I saw the girl, we had sex finally.

I learned that women don't like to be abandoned, and fearing this rejection some use sex to recapture that interest. As men, we push women away and then pull them back as soon as they're ready to give us what we want. The Dick Tactic of Push and Pull is the most used, it's a form of reverse psychology that women fall for because most have this fatal flaw of trying to make it work, make someone like them again, or fix something that's about to break. Men want vagina, women want validation, it's a trade off that leaves the woman used... not anymore.

Now that you understand this concept, I need you to guard against it. You met a guy who really likes you; you've seduced him, you've gone out on two dates, and his mind is blown. Now he's tired of dating, tired of spending money, and wants to get the sex over with the same way he does with every other girl. He didn't break you down with the nice act, so his next move is to stop caring. He now does the same thing I used to do, stop calling, stop being available, and he only hits you up for short spurts, just to dangle that carrot in your face. Instead of falling for this push and pull behavior like a typical bird, turn the tables on him. Let him vanish, and when he comes back around, be busy. Miss his call, then text him, "I'm out with my friend, will call you tomorrow," followed by that flirty kiss emoji. Don't call him tomorrow or the next day.

Wait for him to reach out again, and then suddenly remember him as if his very existence slipped your mind. Shift the blame. Say that you felt as if he were falling back, and remind him that others are always ready to step up to the plate, so you were living life. This shows him that you're not a chaser, and it bruises his frail male ego. **Guys hate when a woman takes away her attention, they are so used to a lady that yells, acts passive, writes long text blocks, unfriends him on social media, etc...** by not caring at all to argue or fight for him, you win! He will bark at first, but then he will rush to see you again, this time without the pressure to have sex—you, my love, have just trained a man to lay off the pressure. You have proven that you are irreplaceable, and unbeknownst to him, you just used your own version of push and pull, and it worked.

There are women who claim they don't chase men, yet their actions suggest all they do is chase men. Don't be the Basica that chases a man because he's done a good job at promoting himself as a baller or a romantic match. This is about establishing value, not "does he love me, does he love me not," bullshit. If a man pushes you, run. When he pulls you back, resist. At this moment, you either win or you win, never feel as if a man cutting you off is a negative. Men only react in TWO ways, they will give up because you're too complicated or they will stop playing games and do things your way. I said win-win because if a man gives you the run around in terms of dating early on, that's a blessing because he exposed that he isn't the type to invest in you, and you don't have time to waste on those.

All the things I'm talking about are literal. If you can't open your mouth and stand up to a man, fake as if you have another date, or go without returning his call for a day or two, then you will fail. The foundation of Ho Tactics begins with being the type of woman that's not afraid to say whatever she needs to say and check a man if he's not reacting in a way that you expect. Typical female behavior is to suppress anger and go along with the flow in the early dating stage because you don't want to ruin it. This isn't a mating call, it's a paper chase, so take the emotions out of it. *Oh, you stood me up for our second date... cool, say hello to the ignore button Mr. I own a chain of Wing Stops, because you are not special nor am I hard up.* Establishing that you have value mandates the ability to be a bitch and prove that you're not going to let a man pick you up and put you down, use reverse psychology, disappearing acts, or threats of other women to check you. Respect isn't given to women, so earn it!

Now that you've shown him that he doesn't mean as much as he thought he meant to you, get back to dating at the same level you left off. The pressure of sex will still be there, but now he's begging, not demanding. Remain strong, because it's time to go in for the kill. At this point in a new relationship, you have all the power. You've proven that you're not afraid to lose him and that other men are always interested. You aren't some EBay bitch with one bidder; you're a pair of Retro Jordan's with a hundred dudes trying to win you. Regardless of his money or his status, he now knows that you can do better and will do better, and he will act accordingly.

#5:

Treats, Tricks, or Sponsors, Who to Hustle

Are you a woman who just wants to be able to date various guys, get taken to nice places, get gifts even when it's not your birthday, and never have to come out of pocket when you're on a date? Then you want to be *Treated*. Being treated is the easiest hustle because you can use it on multiple men at once, ranging from those whom you have no romantic interest to those you crush on. If you don't like the whirlwind of dealing with various men, you can focus your energy and reserve it for that one guy you want to take on as either a boyfriend or friend with benefits that hooks you up on the regular. Think of treaters as starter men when perfecting your game. Treaters aren't necessarily ballers; they are normal guys who don't mind doing what they can, but you can't push them past basic gifts or activities because they literally can't provide luxury things. Most men enjoy showing a woman a nice time, so no matter your confidence level, these men can be your gateway hustle until you muster the courage to get more.

Are you a woman that wants to live an extravagant lifestyle and be spoiled by men with real wealth, then you need a *Trick*[6]. Every woman says she wants luxury, but most should stay on the treated level because they don't have the mentality or seduction skills to impress a man with money. Tricks are usually well traveled, extremely aggressive, and have heard it all before, so you must be on an advanced level to separate them from their paper. This isn't to dissuade you, but to remind you to be realistic in your aspiration. If you're a woman that's simple, homely, and doesn't really want to put a lot of work into perfecting the right appearance and mastering the right conversational skills, then you're not going to reach this level. Tricks have addictive personalities and are usually very busy men who would rather spend money than time. They will give you almost anything you ask for, but they're not trying to keep you on the payroll, it's usually pay for play, not pay to stay.

Are you a woman that needs assistance, not gifts? Maybe your tuition covered, your rent paid up for a few months, a car leased in your name, or business idea funded? If so, you're after a *Sponsor*. These men are usually older and have "I don't give a fuck" money. Sponsors are more concerned with having a fantasy woman at their beck and call than having a trophy on their arm in public. Most of these men have girlfriends or wives, so if you're a jealous type, this isn't the avenue for you. Unlike treaters and tricks, sponsors are usually guys who you won't be physically attracted to or guys you have to play the side chick role for because they have a family. These flaws are a part of their willingness to support a woman financially.

---

[6] Trick is also commonly used to refer to any man that spends money on women, often interchangeable with the term "mark".

Married or men in long time relationships get bored, they see something in you, and they go for it in a very upfront way. Most won't lie about their other life; they'll put it in the open to see if you're okay with being the other woman. Why? Think about how stressful it is for the average man who cheats, having to cover tracks and worry about some crazy woman popping up at his job or his wife's Yoga class with accusations. Adults have affairs, not screaming matches, thus the sponsor will make sure that you're on board before moving forward. It's a business arrangement. **Sponsors are going to take care of you, so long as you are cool with their truth.**

Unlike treaters and tricks, real sponsors aren't Joe Average. To have amassed enough money to finance a woman's lifestyle means he's not just a professional, but one that overachieved. In terms of self-esteem, sponsors who aren't lookers, are usually those men that grew up wanting to fuck the prom queen, but they were never cute enough or popular enough. Money has changed that, and now their one wish is to pay to have the prom queen at their disposal. Don't let this intimidate you. The nerd from 9th grade who became a millionaire is still a nerd, it's in his DNA and he can be seduced easier than you think if you know the right tactics.

Most women say they have a sponsor, but 9 out of 10 just has a trick that is okay with giving her a few hundred here and there. That's not an authentic Sugar Daddy. I know Hos that weekly bank transfers will make you Basicas feel ashamed for bragging about your measly Cash App deposits. If you truly study this book, that's the level I will get you on. Most of the men you meet will be tricks who you have to convert to sponsors. Authentic sponsors aren't usually that social, which is another reason they want to take you away from the real world and set you up in a secluded apartment where they're the only ones with the address, it gives them a safe haven.

Treat	Trick	Sponsor
Hair done Dinner Date	New Handbag Caribbean Vacation	Rent Paid New Car

Take a notepad and draw three columns, and at the top of each column list, Treat, Trick, Sponsor. Write out all the things you want from men, but more importantly, have the heart to go for practically. Some of you want a new car but would only have the heart to get your phone bill paid. Be honest with yourself, you don't have to make some Aladdin's lamp wish list just because you want to front as if you're about that life. **Your list should be practical because this is what you will actually get.** If you want a dinner buddy who takes you out whenever you feel like it, then write that down under Treat. If you want to travel to different countries for free, write that down under Trick. If you need ten thousand to start that cosmetic line you've been dreaming up, write that down under Sponsor.

You're smart enough to know what level of hustle you're trying to pull, and if you get confused think of it like this: $500 and below goes under Treat. $500 to $5000 goes under Trick. $5000 to infinity goes under Sponsor. That's a generalization, remember that the longer you know a man and the more infatuated he is, the more the lines will blur, so it's totally possible for a guy on the treat level to be so taken with you that he breaks you off with a pair of Louboutin's for your birthday. For the purpose of this list, keep it simple, it's just to focus you during the learning stage.

Every hustle has a beginning, middle, and end. None of this is meant to be a long-lasting relationship. You get what you want and then you get out. To get lazy and comfortable leaves you open to exploitation. No matter if he's a treater or trick, once he survives your initial hustle and becomes someone you actually depend on or love, you lose your power and that man can and will reverse rolls and get everything you got out of him back and maybe more. **Don't fall in love with your mark!**

The first step when trying to land one of these men is to put up your walls in order to eliminate broke dudes from your life. The average guy you talk to will be full of shit, they will say they own businesses that don't exist, drive cars that are borrowed, rock watches that are perfect knock-offs, and unless you do your homework, you'll end up like the dumb Hos that travel to NBA All Star Week and end up entertaining some local drug dealer that got fresh for the weekend. Your job is to weed out Mr. Nice Watch from Mr. Fake Watch, to get to the middle game where you're milking this man for whatever you want, and to know when to walk away. This requires you being emotionally strong; this is business disguised as pleasure, so keep your eyes on the prize. You're trying to come up off this dude, not make friends with him! I realize the hardest part will be telling who is real from who is fake, so here are some tips.

♥ **Show Not Tell**
It's easy for a man to talk about what he's doing, what he's done, and what's he's going to do for you. Fuck the talk, where are the fruits of his labor? Forget the kind of car he drives or the jewelry that's blinging off him, only basic bitches would ever equate a luxury car and earrings as proof that this man is legitimate. Where does he live? Not where he stays, or where his mail goes, but the home he can take you to if you were to ask to go

right now. Where does he work? Not what his hustle is, or what business he's in, where does he physically work? Those two things will reveal if you're wasting your time, or if he has potential. Guys who are bullshitting will claim to have multiple homes or name drop an area that he knows people check for like Buckhead in Atlanta. Ask where he works he'll say he's a business owner and entrepreneur, maybe listing something vague like real estate or music. Your job isn't to confront him and challenge his honesty; it's to make him show you in a way where it doesn't seem as if you're testing him.

If you don't think he lives where he says or he's being aloof, ask to come over sometime during that first week that you meet him. **You're not really going to go to this man's home.** You want to see if he's going to invite you to the spot he claimed or if he's going to give you an excuse like, "Um, the house in Buckhead is being fumigated, but we can link at my cousin's crib in College Park." In terms of employment, if he's listing a job that doesn't seem real, again ask the "where" not the what. He has to be working out of somewhere even if he's self-employed. Tell him you'll stop by and bring lunch, then ask for the address and watch for his reaction. If he has what he says he has, he will prove it, so always look past the flash, and ask to see the substance. Housing and employment are two things you can't be afraid to check.

♥ **Burden of Proof (*Headphone Test*)**
No matter if he's a dude who's living large or average, you have to see how willing he is to spend. Just because a man is rich doesn't mean you're going to get in his pockets. There are millionaires who wouldn't buy a bitch a bottle of water in the desert, so don't think because he

has it to give that he will give it. The burden is on you to get proof! There are numerous reasons why men refuse to come out of pocket, maybe their money is tied up in their business, they're going through some kind of financial crisis that you would never know about judging by their lifestyle, or it could be as simple as they don't trust women and see them all as gold diggers.

You don't want to spend your time with "Rich-Broke" dudes or cheapskates. This goes back to the second date. See how he spends on the meal, the type of wine he orders or the seats to the show he splurges on. **During the next week that you're seducing him, ask for something small that he can drop off to you on date #3.** For instance, everyone uses headphones for their phones these days, and they vary in price. During a conversation ask if he could stop by a store and pick you up some headphones as if it's an emergency. Don't specify the brand or the type you want, let him decide and tell him to surprise you with them when you meet up.

If a guy shows up empty handed and says he forgot, then he isn't someone who spends money on women freely, and should be phased out immediately. If a man shows up with a pair of cheap $20 headphones, then he's probably on the Treater level. He will make an effort to give you what you want, but only within his budget. If your date brings you an expensive pair of headphones from a quality brand like Bose, then he put thought into it. Most likely, this is a sign that this man has money and doesn't mind tricking to put a smile on your face. The headphone test is an easy and simple must try with every man. Feel free to substitute headphone for whatever small gift that makes sense in your world, use your own creativity!

♥ **Celebrity Means Nothing**

Some of you live in cities where you will frequently come across celebrities. In LA and New York, it'll be actors and musicians, other places this means pro athletes. Just because you see someone on TV doesn't mean he's rich, he doesn't mind spending, or has it to spend. I knew a guy that spent all his money to keep up appearances and relied on women to pay for his lifestyle. He was a semi-famous dude who used his celebrity to pimp women in the very manner that I'm trying to teach. Understand that the celebrity culture comes with many free perks. They eat free at restaurants because the manager wants to use their business to lure other clientele. They get free jewelry or clothing to promote a company. They get free pussy because some women just want a notch in their belt and brag that they were pretty enough (ha!) to fuck such and such. Due to living in a world where they aren't used to paying, some celebs will treat you worse than a broke dude. You know where they work. You know where they live. They may even pass the headphone test by giving you a pair of their old Beats. The way you test a celebrity Treater, Trick, or Sponsor is different because they are used to Ho Tactics. You see if these types of men are worth your efforts by using reverse psychology.

You don't need anything, and you don't want anything—the first month that is… Go out on those nice dates; be sure he's not shortchanging you as far as courting, and act as if he's replaceable if he tries the push and pull. **The biggest difference with a celebrity is that you pay for every other date.** Let's say you average four dates in a month. Come out of pocket twice, and don't accept a tip either time. This way you show this celeb that you're not a gold digger and establish a difference in your mentality from the token groupies he smashes weekly. During this dating stage, one thing must happen. He has to prove his personality by doing something to compensate for your kindness. For example, he will let you back him down and pay for dinner, but the next day he'll try to rectify it by buying you a gift or over doing the next date in a way that makes up for you paying. He doesn't want to feel like he owes you, and it's offensive for any man with money and class to let a woman grab the check. If he doesn't try to make it up to you, then he's not a spender, he's a taker-- cut him off. If this celebrity does reward you early and often, then he's just like any other mark and Ho Tactics will work.

♥ **Know That World**
Comedian Lil Duval once said, "I have one chick that thinks I'm a Co-Owner of the Jacksonville Jaguars." What made that funny is that it's probably true. There are girls who are very intelligent, yet so fucking dumb when it comes to knowing how a man makes his money. If a guy were living a certain lifestyle, and he were to tell an airhead woman that it was the result of working in some industry she didn't know a thing about, she wouldn't rack her brain thinking about the plausibility or if it were true, she would take it at face value and enjoy the meal because the proof is there. The minute you let a guy bamboozle you, your allure fades. You're still pretty and still an object of desire, but you will never get that respect back. The average non-celebrity, local drug dealer, or weekend baller, relies on dumb Hos who fall for the stories that they're legitimate big shots.

You may think it doesn't matter where he's getting the money to trick on you from, but you should. You don't want to get caught up investing your time with a man who's playing you at the same time. Nor do you want to become linked to a man that's one police bust away from naming you as an accomplice. Don't bury your head in the sand if his story doesn't quite sound right. I've seen a few women in Baltimore have their cars repossessed because they didn't know their sponsors stole the whip or used illegal money to buy it. Some of you live in areas where the only men with money are the D-boys[7], but I strongly advise against trying to turn someone like that into a trick or sponsor. Drug dealers and criminals are some of the biggest marks out there because their egos blind them to sophisticated Hos, and fast money is burning a hole in their pocket anyway. Coke boys, credit card scammers, and all level of thieves love Hos. They will fall for all these tactics, but their lifestyle is a risk and even if you only want to pull a short hustle, it isn't worth the danger. The FBI will take the house and the IRS will come after you if they think that gift money was laundered. Ignorance is never bliss!

Know the industry a man claims to be in, so you can prove to him that you're not a ditz, but it also protects yourself in case of any fallout. Be able to figure out how much money his industry is really paying him. If he's tall and claims to play for the Timberwolves, check that roster. If he's a chubby dude that says he

---

[7] D-boy is slang used to describe a drug dealer. These men are often seen as "Hood Rich," due to having more money than those in the same low-income community; however in mainstream America their level of income would not be considered wealthy or rich.

plays left guard for the Houston Texans, bring up that fool's football card on Google. The music industry is harder, but know what artist he works with and look up credits. If he has a legitimate business, search for records in the state he operates. Don't get so blinded by your hustle that you get hustled yourself.

Oh, did you think this was all about going out, smiling at a guy in a Benz, playing with his dick under the table, and waiting for him to deposit money in your Wells Fargo account? Hoing isn't easy; it takes discipline, knowledge of your value, and the ability to sift through the lies and bullshit of men to determine if they can afford you. Most of you reading this can't tell if a man's lying or not after he's already fucked you, you're smart but not perceptive, no-nonsense yet naïve. This is the big leagues, and there is no room to second-guess yourself, so read the previous chapters several times, and make sure you're ready to proceed with the things you placed on that list.

The deeper you go, the more curve balls these men will likely throw at you. You're always free to email me about specific situations if you sign up for my advice, but I shouldn't be your crutch. Treat, Trick, or Sponsor, each stage will force you to outwit a mark, sometimes on the spot. You must study this foundation and be able to roll with the punches. You wanted to learn how the dark side wins, so don't get scared now.

THE VALUE OF YOUR VAGINA

"I get so lonely, I forget what I'm worth." -SZA

You went to high school together and you know his family—*that deserves pussy?* He pulled your chair out at the restaurant and paid for the meal—*that deserves pussy?* He took you on four dates in one week—*that deserves pussy?* You spent five hours having a conversation in his car—*that deserves pussy?* You used to talk back in the day and now he's back and acting more mature—*that deserves pussy?* You met his mother and she liked you—*that deserves pussy?* He brought you a bag and some shoes the first week of knowing you—*that deserves pussy?* He hoped in your DMs then flew you out—*that deserves pussy?* All the other girls at work want him but he likes you—*that deserves pussy?* He's a student athlete about to go to the league and he's feeling—*that deserves pussy?* He's your platonic best friend and wants more now that you're single—*that deserves pussy?* You've talked to a lot of guys, and his energy just feels different—*that deserves pussy?*

You're too damn old to be falling for basic ass game from these basic ass niggas who's only skill set is telling hopeless romantics what they want to hear. He doesn't like you, he wants to fuck you. He isn't proving consistency by being nice to you for a few weeks, he's chasing ass. Yet there you go, on another date that ends with you letting him go too far or exposed via another house date that proves you aren't as hard to get as your Instagram captions claim you are. **Pussy is priceless. It's rewarded to the best, not given to the latest crush that gets you drunk off brown liquor.** Stop sliding your panties off for these peasants for fear if you don't give it up he'll go find his happily ever after with the next woman. You're competing with time, competing with other women, competing with this idea that you have to hook a man with sex for him to like you. You're the trophy, not him! He should be trying to prove that he values you, that he respects you, that he is interested in getting to know what shaped you and how you think. What is he talking about? What is he trying to do with you? What is he revealing about himself? He's not special, he's just another guy in the race until he proves himself. Reclaim your power by resetting how you think about men in the first place.

Know who you are. This isn't Prostitution Tactics, it's Ho Tactics, a strategy to win without opening your legs. You can't be paid for, and your vagina doesn't have a price tag...

#6:
How to Flirt the Ho Way

Women have become so bad at flirting that men can't tell if the average girl is being nice or if she is genuinely interested. This leaves a huge opening for those who know the ends and outs of flirting to dominate the game on every level. I once spoke to a girl who was frustrated with her inability to get this guy at her son's school to ask her out. They would say "hi" and chat about the weather, but she assumed that he didn't really like her, so she acted sheepishly instead of going after him. I asked if he spoke first or if she spoke first? She said he would initiate most times, once he even chased her down outside to ask about her Christmas since he hadn't seen her in a few weeks. I then asked what she had done to show him that she liked him. Crickets. Her response was, "What am I supposed to do, jump in his arms?"

Again, women see in extremes instead of accepting that most things in life require you to read between the lines while using tact. It's not about being overt and saying you're interested; it's about flirting in a way where even Stevie Wonder could pick up on the "I want that dick" vibe. The way you hang on certain words. The sexy smirk you give, as opposed to the goofy laugh. Even body language can spell out interest.

It doesn't matter if you're talking about the weather or your boring weekend, a woman who knows the power of voice inflection, strong eye contact, and doesn't mind flashing a sly smile can make those topics sexier than discussing bedroom positions.

Hos aren't afraid to talk. Everything they do is built around their ability to speak to any man without that awkward feeling that she's not on his level financially, physically, or mentally. **Hos win out over most women because they aren't afraid to sell themselves.** Attractive, well read, yet shy women fail to realize is that no matter how great you are, you don't come with a billboard listing those traits. You don't have a cheerleader running behind you like, "Sara owns a business, doesn't have kids, has only slept with six guys and loves football!" All you have is what you step into the room with, your looks and your actions. Your looks are good, but your actions have you standing in the corner talking to the one person you know. How will any man know that you possess all those great qualities? Who else is there to inform a top shelf man that you are a top shelf woman? For him to uncover these things, he would have to walk over, interrupt your lame conversation, and see what you have to say. There are men who will do this, and it still doesn't solve the problem because an introverted woman who is afraid to rise to the occasion won't know how to interact with this man in a way that's flirty and engaging. A typical educated yet awkward woman will stumble through conversation, over laugh, have pockets of tense silence, and leave the man thinking she's weird. Let's delve into how to transform you from awkward to alluring.

The first observation to be aware of is that most men with money, status, or those things that will make him a perfect trick or sponsor, aren't going to stroll up to 90% of the women in his city. Not because they aren't pretty, but because they may not be worth the risk of rejection. Every man has his own taste when it comes to attraction, and just because he thinks you are cute doesn't mean he's willing to put his feelings on the line by approaching you.

I've had at least two girlfriends that I would have never approached in public. If it weren't for being a friend of a friend, I would have never gotten to know them well enough to form a relationship because they didn't fit that flawless "worth the risk" category which had become my cowardly way of protecting myself from rejection. Today's man is just as bad, on the internet it's a bit easier to shoot his shot, but in public, there has to be a reason for someone with all the trimmings listed above to put himself on the line. Single and looking normally means that you only speak when spoken to, or you wait for an introduction as the cultural brainwashing dictates that a woman shouldn't chase after a man. In the Ho game, you will have to speak first.

"I don't feel pretty enough to keep a man's attention..." Kill those weak bitch thoughts! If you know the mind of man then you understand looks change after a conversation, a connection, or flirting. That charm I spoke of earlier will win over that picky man who rated you a six from across the room. To walk over and compliment him, make him smile, share a story, etc... will endear you to him and raise your stock. You go from "she's alright," to "she's sexy," and you didn't even reapply any lipstick. That's the power of compliments built upon bonding. It's similar to not liking Miley Cyrus then seeing her in public and she's actually really nice and jokes around with you. The next time her song comes on your radio, she's not "that wack bitch that can't twerk." You know her and she knows you, so now you turn it up and say, "Ayyy, that's my girl." What changed? Hos understand that flirting and compliments lead to endearment. This is what gives them the confidence to walk over to any man regardless of how she looks because conversation will always upgrade appearance!

Tricks may still approach you, but that's not the point. I need you to accept that finding the right man to hustle will often require you to make the first move. There are women who men consider "next level" beautiful, and they will walk up to them in public… if the setting is right.

So yes, Mr. Heir to a coffee company can chase you down if you're what he's looking for that night, but why leave it up to his discretion. Why let this trick choose you when you can choose him and from the jump have him thinking you're infatuated? A man of means has a million excuses not to go after a woman, but the main thing at work is that the male ego doesn't want to be curved. To spark the conversation begins the process of making him want you. Guys get over eager with thoughts of, "She spoke first, that must mean she wants to fuck." Good! Inflate his ego. Let him wag his tail, meanwhile you're going to lead that dog by the leash and drain his pockets way before you drain his nut sack. Do not fear starting a conversation! I get it, you're Queen of the world, you hate the thought of getting out of your comfort zone and going after some random guy. You want to sit pretty and have them rush you. That's not going to happen! If this is going to work, you must get your hands dirty. You don't get rich outside of the mine, you must go into that mine to dig for gold.

Hoexample

Now that we know what most women do wrong let's look at what Hos do right in terms of approach. **Let's call our example Ho, Maria.** Maria isn't in a ratchet club scouting for a baller. Nor is she at her cousin's birthday party in the Bronx hunting for a come up. Maria isn't a weekend Ho or a basic Ho, she's about this life <u>every day</u> and doesn't feel the need to go to the typical places in order to find marks. Maria can pull her Ho Tactics out any and everywhere because it's not about the place or situation, it's about being prepared to sell yourself as life changing at the drop of a hat. She's armed with confidence, she's willing to speak first, she knows how to flirt, and her primary objective is to size up every man she meets as a money bag: Barely full bag. Midsize bag, Full bag, Bursting at the seams bag. Her aim is to get that bag by using her wits, not her vagina. Now, let's see how she does this step by step.

Maria & The Mark

Maria is at Best Buy, not looking for a man; she's just shopping for herself and understands that the Best Buy crowd is much different from the typically thrifty Wal-Mart shoppers. Again, Maria is always about that life even when she's not "on the clock." Opportunity can knock at any time if you place yourself in better environments, so why hit the flea market when you can go browse the Apple store? Maria doesn't have to be glammed up so long as she's not looking sloppy. Like I said earlier, all women should dress to impress themselves, so although she's toned down in a pair of high-waisted shorts and loose-fitting blouse, she's wearing bright yellow heels that draw attention to her bronzed legs. Maria is still accentuating her positives even though she wasn't thinking about hitting a lick when she walked into the store.

A few guys stare at Maria, she may make eye contact with the cute ones and grin, just to size them up, but she's not looking for easy prey. Maria is not going for the cutest or even the best dressed, if she's going to take a break from shopping and catch a mark, it has to be a guy that looks like a true winner in less obvious ways, like that business professional who wears polished shoes, not retro Jordan's. She spots a guy testing out a laptop. He's nice looking, well put together in terms of wardrobe, and he's testing out the expensive computer, not the $300 Dell that's still running Windows Vista. Maria knows the odds of him being a worthy trick is still 50/50, but she's going to trust her gut and go for it.

Maria puts on her game face and walks over to the computer next to the mark. She pretends to be reading the specs and then comments to herself, "What the hell is the difference between these things?" There are two types of men. Those who like to brag in order to impress women with knowledge, and those who like to wisecrack about things they don't understand to impress women with humor. The mark knows his shit and responds that it's the CPU. Maria doesn't give a fuck about CPU or RAM she's about DOLLARS. At this point, the guy may be afraid to keep talking, so Maria keeps the conversation flowing by asking which one he's going to buy. This opens it up to his shopping agenda; from there it's on to if he lives in the area or just happened to be near the store. The conversation continues as he tells her what part of town he's from, and Maria responds that she knows that area and has a girlfriend that used to live around there (not really, but it's something to talk about). From there, Maria shifts to work, smoothly asking if this is a computer he can use on the job because she's thinking about getting one just for home. The mark then answers that he does need it for work. Now it's organic to ask what he does for a living without seeming as if she's digging.

Maria will have just learned everything she needs to know in order to date this man in less than seven minutes. Did he live in an area that's known for being upscale or is it the hood? Did he name a job that affords him good pay or is he working some job any moron with a high school diploma could apply for and get? If he answers that he lives near the Trap and that he works as a lead associate at Lids, Maria will thank him for his help and keep browsing. If the mark tries to ask for her number, she'll let him off easy and say she has a boyfriend — sorry. Again, you're not here to waste time, you're here to win.

Let's say that this mark lives in a nice middle-class neighborhood and works as an account specialist for Charles Schwab. At this point Maria has done every Ho Tactic listed in previous chapters properly. She jobbed checked him and found out what type of area he lives in which allows her to go through her **Ho Estimate of Wealth**: His field of banking is usually lucrative — Check. Where he lives is middle to high class — Check. The initial Ho research is done. Maria doesn't know if he's lying or if he has money to spend, but he's a better prospect than most. With that information, Maria goes in for the kill. She tells him that she has to go check out, but would love to grab a drink with him sometime soon.

This is the moment where a Ho uses flirting to secure her date, unlike most women who just hand out a number and hope a man calls. The mark is most likely single, so he'll take Maria's number the moment she suggests drinks. Maria will give it to him and say, "I don't do texting… I like men who call." She just checked his ass with a smile and a wink. Hos can't game men via text message because verbal communication is a must for the seduction step. He'll promise to call and maybe diss texting to seem cool. Maria now has to exit in a way that has him on her clit, so she extends for a handshake and says, "I'll be talking to you, handsome." Maria doesn't just shake his hand; she holds his hand, remarks on either their hardness with a sexual connotation or their softness with a purr. She slowly lets go of his hand and switches away knowing that he's watching. That's what we call a Mind Fuck! This man is going to call in a day or two, and Maria is going to test him over the next three dates to see if he's a Treater, Trick, or Sponsor.

Alternatively, if the mark has a girlfriend and instead of giving Maria his number, he informs her, "I'm actually seeing someone," then it's still on. Maria's aim isn't to be side pussy or main pussy; she just wants a come up. Maria respects that this man is honest, but that doesn't get him off the hook. She fakes happy, asks how long they've been together, and his girlfriend's name... this puts him at ease. Maria then tells him to take down her email; surely, baby girl won't mind him having a new "friend."

Again, the sexual undertones in her voice are direct and tantalizing. If the mark hesitates, Maria checks his ego, "Don't tell me she has you on that tight of a leash," which is a phrase that stings any man with pride. The mark exchanges info with Maria, and like before she goes for the handshake, and flirty goodbye. **No matter his response, Maria wins.** It had nothing to do with her looks; she was in a random place, feeling as sexy as she always feels, and she used her aggressive actions and flirtatious behavior to get what she wanted. The way she came off will have a single man at home daydreaming about that meeting or a man who is in a relationship planning on ways to keep this going without his girl knowing.

This is how Hos pull men. No matter if it's a stuffy club, holiday party, bar, supermarket, coffee shop, or picking up their kid from school, flirting can be used to get the number of virtually any man that she chooses. If a man looks like a good candidate, she sizes him up then makes contact. Those simple steps are things that most women would rather die before doing or shy away from because they don't know what to say when it's time to speak first. There is no such thing as, "wait on him," in Ho culture because money is always worth the risk.

Hoing Up

You saw how easily Maria does it, now are you going to sit there and come up with a million, "but what if he doesn't respond the way I want," excuses or are you going to focus on the fact that this level of flirting will not fail? If you aren't confident in your approach, if you're awkward and scattered, then don't even bother going forward. You don't have to be the best talker, funny, or witty, all it takes is the ability to perform the following things with a smile on your face and twinkle in your eye.

♥ **Invade His Personal Space**
The closer you are to a man the more you arouse him. That's sexuality 101, and you should have noticed this back in elementary school when boys wanted to sit next to certain girls in class. The body heat, the smell of perfume, the scent of hair care products, those are the easiest sex triggers because they transport a man back to the various women he's experienced in life. To be inches away from a man disarms him in a way words can't, calming his nerves and igniting his libido at the same time. Maria the Ho stepped up next to her mark, shoulders inches away from him. That's the ideal position to be at first; side-by-side, or side angled towards a man. By not directing your body fully towards him gives the feeling that you're into him, but not too open or thirsty for him. Face to face is too close. He doesn't need to know you had Chipotle for lunch, so avoid breath-smelling range.

A man should be close enough to want to touch you, yet feel as if he can't touch you. Women usually stay at least a foot and a half away, and face men straight on; you don't play by those rules. It's taboo to touch a stranger, but you don't play by those rules either. Shoulder nudges, lint wipes, even light chest smacks, are weapons at your disposal, you can even brush him "by accident." Men love that shit.

♥ **Unrelenting Eye Contact**

Where do you look when you talk? You'll probably say, straight, but that's not true for most people. The eyes tend to wander when lost in thought. You're trying to think of the next thing to say, and depending on what type of thinker you are, that can take your eyes upwards, downwards, or left to right. This is the hardest part of flirting to master because eye contact is habitual. You have to break your bad habit, shake off the nerves you get when looking into someone's eyes, and master the art of staring through a man. When I was in New York for a seminar, there was an amazing woman who made the best eye contact I've ever seen. I told her this the moment I felt "that" feeling. The co-host, another woman, even said the same thing later that night like, "holy shit, that was sexy." Good eye contact isn't about how wide you open your eyes or squinting as if you can make your eyes sexy and almond shaped. Your eyes are your eyes; you can't change that, so stop working against what you were given by trying gimmicky tactics to look sexy. Instead, focus on the feeling behind that stare.

Models, real models, not IG models, know how to gaze intensely and get across the following emotions: *joy, sadness, anger, and desire.* You want desire, but most of you are stuck on joy. Someone must have taught women the way to show interest is to be happy, but happy isn't sexy. Don't sit there over-smiling with eyes wide open afraid to blink. Find your desire spirit animal—that feeling in the pit of your stomach that makes you want to fuck the shit out of your favorite R&B artist when he licks his lips; that's the feeling you want to channel. That's not a smile or a blank expression; that's thunder! The eyes don't lie, therefore, any man who you're looking at while channeling that desire will feel as if it's all for him.

You don't have to be that attracted to a mark to transmute sexual energy. The same way actresses think of past tragedy to bring themselves to real tears, think of your strongest sexual desire, and bring it out during that initial conversation. While you're looking at an okay guy, your mind should be fantasizing as if he's stallion that you can't wait to ride bareback. The way you look while lost in lust is a unique glare, but it's on you to isolate it and use it as a weapon. Get a mirror and practice this look, don't giggle and laugh, have confidence that you can epitomize sex, and you will every time a man makes the mistake of looking in your eyes.

♥ The Sexy Highlighter

Your voice can make a man hard just as quickly as stroking his dick with your hand will, maybe faster. The unheralded superstar, when it comes to flirting, is voice inflection. I meet women all the time that have given up on the sex appeal of their voice because they sound like MC Lyte with a cold. No matter if you were born with a cute baby doll voice, have a deeper tone than most women, or accent that people laugh at, you can still make it work for you. Maria would hang on certain words when she was reeling in her mark. Things like "hard," "look at you," "you're funny," "Let's chill sometime," can be said conversationally or they can be highlighted with sex. It's a little difficult to describe on paper, but take the sentence: *I hate shopping alone.* Say that as if you're mad and annoyed. Now say that as if you're Marilyn Monroe. It goes from being dry and bitchy to insinuating that you want somebody to go shopping with you... or that you're using "shopping" as a code for something filthy.

Marilyn trained herself to talk like a flighty bimbo because men are powerless against low, slightly whispering, yet pointed tones. Girls regularly use this trick, but mostly when they're trying to be sarcastic, such as, "oh did I hurt your feelings," you speak like a baby towards a man to be condescending, but if you take the bitchiness out of it and use it in a normal conversation on certain words, it's highly effective. Say the word, "hang," but hold on to it and spread it out. It's not a big word and to say it fast means nothing but to baby voice it or hold on to it for a half second longer tells a man, "damn she really wants to hang on this dick." Of all the flirty tactics, this one will benefit you the most going forward.

When we get into phone sex, defusing an argument, and even asking for money or favors, the ability to use sexy inflection will be the difference between him eating out of your ass or kicking you out on your ass.

♥ **Know The Script**

You're leading him he's not leading you, which means focus on your goal when you first start talking to a guy and don't get sidetracked by the things he's saying. You are trying to size up a man who can trick on you, not looking for a potential boyfriend that thinks you're cute, so don't let him sweet-talk you out of your mission. **Where does he live, what does he do, and what do you know about his world?** Those are at the core of your hustle, and you need to remember to hit all of them. An actor is allowed to improvise his lines, and you're going to be made to improvise in each conversation because no man is predictable down to a conversation. I gave you the example of *Maria the Ho in Best Buy*; I could give you another one of Maria the Ho at a party, but none of the details of what she says makes a difference, it's all about making contact and then flirting. Actors have the freedom to create, but they still have to get the important exposition out during their scene. Be free to do you, so long as you get those three things across in the process.

A man with just as much game as you will over talk you; he'll dodge questions, and use his own brand of Dick Tactics, such as compliments or random responses to get you off your square. Go back to the well if you feel as if he's being aloof. If that mark dodges a question about work, pretend not to hear and let him talk about what he wants to, but then stroke his neck as if he had something dangling from his collar and responds with,

"I'm sorry, what was it you said you did, those lips are distracting." What just happened? You got closer into his personal space pretending you were dusting him off, you used inflection on the word "lips" to get him open, and complimented him with something that makes him cheese internally, now he's back on track and will have to answer your question.

Remember, you have all the power! He thinks that you're a slut because you approached him first and that all he has to do is say the right thing to hit. You're not going to fuck him, you may not even date him; the only thing you're doing is using your feminine wiles to get this man to tell you about his life. Hit all three points of your script, or you may be wasting your time… and we all know time is money!

♥ **Leave Him Wanting More**
The worst thing a woman can do is hang around too long. Flirting is like a strip tease, not stripping, but the old school Gypsy Rose Lee[8] strip tease. What made Gypsy so different is that she knew that men want what they can't have. Any girl could take off her bra and flash her tits, but the buildup is what guys pay for. Flirting is all buildup, with an undertone of sex. You're close enough that he can taste your Chanel No.9, he's staring into your eyes, and he's hanging on every word you say because you're verbally stroking his penis with voice inflection and sexual innuendo. He's putty in your hands, but once you ask for his number, it's time to go.

---

[8] Gypsy Rose Lee was a Burlesque performer attributed with redefining the art of the strip tease and bringing it into the modern era.

If he wants to talk more, that'll cost him a phone call. It's always hard to walk away when someone wants to talk you to death, but don't be afraid to be rude. Make up an excuse about an appointment, a friend waiting in the car for you, anything to exit. If you're in a spot like a club or at a party where you're not leaving, be smooth when distancing yourself, "I don't want to be rude to my friends, we'll continue this when you call me," or "I should let you get back, sexy, I don't want to stop the other girls from trying to get some attention from you too." It's all ego stroking and a promise of continuing your connection later. You left an impression instead of overstaying your welcome, and because of that striptease, his interest will remain high.

You only get good at flirting by flirting. For the next week, practice these skills in public on unintimidating guys aka practice tricks. Even if you don't want their number, go through the motions of invading their personal space, eye fucking them and questioning them in a sexy way. You must be able to prove to yourself that you have the confidence to approach a man and stay focused. Don't merely remember these tactics and save it for the day you finally meet a guy that seems worthy or you'll struggle. Practice makes perfect, and repetition forms habits. Get into the habit of talking to men, looking at men, approaching men, and figuring out what works best for your personality type. Do this a few times before continuing on to the next level.

#7:
How to Seduce
the Ho Way

Spartans interview men intensely because the objective is to make sure he's honest and trustworthy enough to be a boyfriend or potential husband. Hos substitute the interview process with the seducing stage because they know the way to a man's wallet starts with his dick. His life story and past relationships don't matter when you're trying to hustle a man because you're not looking to bond on a real level. All a Ho needs to know is if he's paid, how paid, and how generous he is willing to be with that money. Once you establish that you have a guy who is willing to treat you to nice things, you dig the hooks in deeper by using what a man wants the most against him—sex. A Ho's job is to be a fantasy woman. A woman that listens, isn't judgmental, never stresses for time or attention, and most importantly knows how to be a filthy whore. **I remind you that these are the non-sex tactics**, so if the way you've been taught to seduce is by letting him stick the tip in, you're going to need to throw that game plan out. You're about to learn to become a master of making a man cum, without using your pussy.

Seducing is the progression of flirting, yet girls who are good flirts often freeze when it's time to really get down and dirty. Earlier, I spoke of the first date as being one where you hook him with a shot of your personality, which isn't about, "I went to this university, I'm starting this business, and I traveled to this city last summer." Personality has nothing to do with random facts about your life. To make a man see you as sexy, desirable, and indispensable, you have to show him that you are a good time. **What makes you funny? What makes you edgy? What makes you nasty? What makes you different?** Answer that in your head. Now, look back on the last time you were on a first date and think about how you brought out those <u>four</u> things. Most of you can't answer the question or aren't sure, but the truth is in the results. Men aren't impressed with you nor do they see you the same way you see yourself in your head. "My personality is dope!" No, it's dry! You don't project anything special, thus you don't separate yourself from the pack.

The last first date I went on was with a very corny woman. Here's what made her corny: during that dinner, she didn't say anything provocative or interesting. She just laughed at my jokes and played coy when I made a perverted comment. In the movie theater, I got my feels on, but she kept her hands to herself, not because she wasn't into me, but because she was afraid. After the date, I took her back to my apartment and proceeded to gas her up about how fun it was spending time with her (lie) how sexy she looked (she was pretty, but not that pretty), and how I didn't want her to leave (truth). After about forty minutes, I had her bra off and my hands down her pants. She stopped me and told me she had to go before she made a mistake. I tried to go back to sweet-talking her into staying, but to her credit, she didn't give in. Although I wasn't impressed by her personality, I was excited by the prospect of having sex after seeing her half naked.

The next weekend, I skipped the going out to eat stuff because why waste my time when all I was doing was talking to myself? I got her right back over where we left off. A week of talking on the phone, flirting, and gassing her up had won her over and she was willing to go all the way this time. I got head, had sex with her, and promptly got head one last time before telling her I was about to go to sleep (aka she had to go). Asshole move, but this is how most men operate when they come across a cute girl who isn't exactly intriguing. The average woman is unsure of herself when on a date with a guy she likes, which leads to awkward behavior and a corny vibe. Men don't want to hang with a cornball no matter how phat her ass is or how big her breasts are. Think if you do these things:

Counter Conversation: Wait for him to talk and you simply respond to his question with the answer and a dry follow-up about the same subject. Never sparking your own topic.

Over Laugh: You don't have anything to add on to what he's saying, but don't want to be quiet so you laugh harder than normal, or giggle when nothing's that funny.

Walk on Eggshells: You don't want to say anything to offend this man, so you keep the conversation safe and inoffensive. It's like putting someone whose best jokes are about homosexuals in a gay bar, they don't want to offend so they tone way down.

Don't Rape Me Body Language: You don't point your body towards him or inch close when walking. At dinner, you sit across, not next to him. Walking to the car with him, you keep your distance.

These things are understandable when you're not familiar with a person, but this isn't modesty tactics to get a man to see you as a sweet woman, this is Ho Tactics to eat these men alive. Hos get real comfortable real fast, and because it's such a different way for a woman to act on a date, men are taken off guard and easily impressed. "But, G.L., I can't help being nervous on dates. How can I Ho Up, when I'm shy and reserved?" You have the ability to get comfortable around ANY man because you've done this step before without knowing it.

Most women have agreed to a date with a guy they didn't really like, and I wager you're in that boat. Some dude gave chase, you saw him as "okay," but you were bored, so you agreed to go out because you had nothing to lose. You were accidentally Hoing! Selling your company for a date with no intention of ever doing anything else, it's something that all girls do. A free dinner or movie with a man that doesn't look like your type, act like your type, or has a shot at winning you over. That's a mini-Ho Tactic done out of boredom.

On a date with Mr. Not My Type, you didn't give a fuck so there was no counter conversation, you said whatever as if he were a girlfriend. There was no over laugh because you didn't want him to think you liked him by over laughing. You didn't walk on eggshells because this guy was more like the buddy than prince charming. As for body language, you probably kept your distance, but I'm sure you were relaxed, not bashful in regard to how close you got to him. That man wasn't a threat, so you didn't act awkward, you projected your true personality—Dope Chick. In response you weren't seen as corny, you were seen as the fun, slightly goofy, girl with good conversational skills. That clown is probably still trying to take you out again because you impressed him. Your mission is to be that comfortable with men who are winners.

Hoexample

Let's go visit our friend Maria the Ho on her series of dates in which she seduces a mark. The first date is one she allowed him to select, and it's the Cheesecake Factory, a nice inexpensive place that literally has food from every damn country on their menu. Maria doesn't usually do dinner here, like most smart Hos she comes to hang by the bar after the businessmen get off work, because sitting down with a girlfriend and splitting an order of buffalo blasts doesn't leave her room to flirt with a man like standing at a bar surrounded by stressed stockbrokers will. They get a booth in the back and Maria takes a seat across from the mark. She orders water, not liquor because she has to be in tune tonight, not turned up. Immediately Maria pouts, "You're going to leave me all alone over here?" The mark is taken aback, he doesn't know this girl like that, yet she wants him right next to her. Of course, he rushes over and rearranges his silverware on her side of the table. Maria now rewards him by squeezing his arm with a hug as if she's super excited to be next to him.

The waiter comes over and asks about food, Maria begins to joke with the waiter about how the mark couldn't stand not being close. The waiter, like anyone who wants a tip plays along and adds on his own compliment about Maria being pretty. Maria continues to sass the waiter in a non-bitchy or demeaning way, maybe saying that the mark doesn't think she's that pretty, she had to beg for a date, etc... self-deprecation leads to compliments, that's human psychology 101. Of course, this attention whoring technique puts the mark on the spot in front of another man and he must keep up with her wits by firing back his own teases and jokes. Less than 10 minutes into the date and the ice has been broken. The mark is now having fun and thinks Maria is a wild child.

When it's time to be serious and order. Maria lays her head on the mark's shoulder fake-flustered, "will you order for me, anything but red meat." The mark may not know how to react if he's not a decisive man, but Maria will urge him to order something "that taste as good as an orgasm." This shit is even making the waiter blush, and the mark sees that he's gotten a hold of something special.

Throughout the date, Maria keeps it playful and flirty, she touches him sporadically, makes inappropriate jokes about people that walk by, and delves into his business and talks about what she knows about that industry as a light test. When he makes a corny joke, she doesn't mind saying, "whomp whomp," but follows it up with one of her own corny jokes to show that she's on his side, but not a yes woman that giggles by default. The mark likes her and more importantly, he's having a good time. When the check comes, Maria grabs it first, "If I look, it means I have to pay it right?" The mark may play along but isn't serious about her paying. The mark pays, but Maria asks how much tip she should give their waiter friend. **If the mark tells her not to worry, it's a good sign, if he tells her the amount and makes her go in her purse, it could mean he's not a spender.** It's only the first date, so she can let something as petty as asking her to put up the tip slide, but all of his actions will be inventoried for later analysis.

After the date, Maria holds his hand as they exit and thanks him for taking her out and ordering the right type of meal. The mark is going to be enamored by this time and the night's still young. <u>Maria now tests him about where he lives</u>. She jokes that they're going to grab coffee back at "Casa de la Buckhead?" The mark will be excited that he may fuck the first night, but play it cool with, "If you feel like it…" Nevertheless, Maria was just checking for an excuse such as, "Oh damn, my cousin is staying over tonight." That response would tell her that he's full of shit about where he lives or that he has a wife or girlfriend staying there that he hasn't been honest enough to talk about yet.

In our example, the mark invites Maria back proving that he's not lying, but she plays it off as kidding. Adding that it takes a while before she has "coffee" with new men… striptease, bitches. After Maria is dropped off, she'll end the night with a kiss. No tongue, just a sweet kiss followed by a slight suck on his bottom lip as she pulls herself away with those piercing "I would fuck you like it was our last night on Titanic" eyes.

The mark is riding high and most likely Maria will get a text from him when he gets home. She's not his text buddy so she will respond with a brief follow-up. *It was a great, can't wait to see you again soon. Good night, baby.* Now this man is reacting as if he's just hit a homerun, "Damn, this bitch is calling me baby already, I'm in there!" He's not in anywhere, but Maria is all in that mark's head. Her shot of personality even had the waiter wanting to fuck her, and now it's time to unload on the second date with her true Ho test to make sure she's not wasting her time with a dude that can only afford Cheesecake Factory.

The Kill Shot

Maria now has the power. Further dating is not about when a mark is free; it's when she is free because a man who wants new pussy will rearrange his schedule to get it. Maria is a seasoned Ho Tactician so while she's spoken to the mark over the past week, it's been late at night, short and full of flirting. She hasn't given him phone sex, hasn't sent one nude or semi-nude picture and hasn't allowed herself to fit into his schedule. Guys will do things like call when they get off work, pop up wanting to grab dinner, or lure a girl to the house with a home cooked meal. Maria is educated in the ways of horny men and since she isn't thirsty for love, she plays it cool when he tries to be spontaneous and catch her off guard with bullshit dates or chill sessions.

Maria will only go on that next date when she decides to, which assures her that he will do what she wants to do once she finally "frees up" her imaginary schedule. The mark gets excuses for a few days and then finally gets an opportunity to see her again a week later. Maria wants to go hear a singer at the House of Blues on Saturday. The mark wants to take her to this Hookah lounge around his way. Maria isn't a Hookah Ho, and she doesn't need to be in a room full of locals who only go to the Hookah spot. She demands live entertainment and a chance to dress sexy. The mark agrees because if he doesn't play ball, Maria won't ask again and his window for new pussy will close. This fear that led to "do what she says" is a result of Maria using excuses to make her time seem valuable. The game isn't to chase men with money, it's to make them feel powerless.

Mariah and the mark show up at the House of Blues, she was hot on the last date, this time she's show stopping. Hair in an updo, face made up tastefully, her dress showing her curves, and heels fresh out of the box. She's impressive and she knows it, therefore, he knows it... more importantly, he will remember her luxury style and feed into it. This time Maria orders for them, she wants to drink tonight, and she only drinks vintage Chardonnay. She wants some food in her stomach, and she's going to get a sample of a few appetizers as opposed to a big meal. She's even touchier this time around; the conversation is more comfortable as well because they know more about each other. Maria can bring up things that happened during the week, how happy she is to finally see him again, and even say that she had a dream about him—*isn't that crazy*. This is all done to break the next level of ice and play into their chemistry.

Maria isn't his girlfriend, but it feels like it because she's easy to talk to and doesn't mind letting him touch her. The music starts and Maria sways in her seat, not looking at the singer, but looking at the mark, she's singing and directing her affection at him. As the night progresses Maria's dancing in front of the table, it's a public place, but it's a private dance for her "man." She's well aware that other men and women are watching her, but she's not shy, she's embracing her sexiness. If there's room for movement, maybe Maria pulls the mark up to dance with him and quickly rubs her ass against him, which is the ultimate physical seduction.

By the end of the night, Maria has run up a bill of two bottles of wine and food she didn't eat, just to test him. The mark happily pays because he thinks he's going to fuck in a few hours. Maria and the mark go back to the car, she initiates the kissing, and this time, it's all tongue. She even strokes the bulge in his pants, and moans, "You just do something to me, baby. I can't explain it." This guy is ready to drive her back to the spot and bust it all the way open. Maria tells him that she should go home; she's been drinking and doesn't want to bring out her inner Yoncé before he's ready. She shifts it on him not being ready, more so than her, because this offends a guy and challenges his manhood in a way that spells out that she's not afraid of dick or celibate. They joke about sex, and all Maria says is, "we're going to see how you take your coffee, soon enough, baby." However, she turns serious and says she should get home. The mark is worked up, but Maria has shown that she's not an easy lay. The mark is headed home to take a cold shower, full of disappointment... but there's also hope. He's spent money, but at each turn Maria has rewarded him by intensifying her seduction, which means he has no reason not to keep dating her. Their next time out will be D-Day, he can feel it in his bones!

Two dates down, Maria has touched him, kissed him, rubbed on him, and gave him an IOU on the pussy. No matter how smart this mark is, he knows that these actions lead to sex, it always does, all he has to do is stay on task and keep her happy. Entering the next week, between the 2nd and 3rd date, Maria rewards him with phone sex for the first time. **The day after phone sex, she drops the headphone test on him.** Phone sex would be a lot better if she had good earphones for her iPhone, using the thought of sex she then asks if he could grab a pair for her before they meet up on the next date. Of course he does, and when Maria sees that she got a pair of brand new Beat ear buds, not the generics or his old used ones, she recognizes that this dude isn't a waste of time. He doesn't mind tricking, so now begins her next step of becoming invaluable to this man, so she can dig in his pockets for what she actually needs.

***

Maria took all those basic flirting skills to the next level, from the personal space to the voice inflection; she upped the ante and used her sex appeal to excite him. At the same time, she used compliments like "baby" to endear herself to him. The most impressive thing was that Maria was able to be sassy and fun, in a way that put him at ease and made her seem cool, not corny. If Maria were a nervous chick or one who thought turning a man on was all about saying a bunch of nasty things, she would have failed. **Maria played by her rules but made him think it was his rules.** The first date set the pace as she submitted to him and let him be a man by picking the place and ordering her food. The second date she pouted and asked to be taken to a better place, then took it upon herself to get whatever she wanted right under his nose as if it's just how she rolls.

The mark sees Maria as new pussy, but he also sees her as interesting. That, above the potential feeling of a new nut, is what had him running to Target to grab a pair of $100 headphones. Understand that seducing a man isn't just about sex, it's about making him feel young and carefree. A mark with money can go pay for an escort, he can go jerk off to a cam girl, he can go butter up an ex—it's not about sex. Maria is making herself the best part of his week by being a good time girl! At the same time, she's still testing his pockets, at each step she's taking mental notes about his attitude and actions. There are men who would have complained about the cost of the show, the wine, and the food, which probably cost well over $200. If a man doesn't have that to spend on a second date with a girl that's impressed him, made out with him, and who walks out of the house dressed like her pussy is worth a million dollars, then he's a window shopper that must be dropped immediately after he complains about money or the price of something. Maria's mark went with the flow and had a good time because anything worth doing is worth paying for if you have it to spend.

Guys with money don't mind paying for a good time even if it doesn't end with them dipping their dick in something at the end of the night. If a man does start to keep track of what he's spending, consider that a sign that he may not be holding as much in his bank account as he acts. It's okay to choose wrong, men are good liars, and your intel may have been wrong. **This is why you research him with THREE dates to be sure that he has money and has it to spend.** Maria put in a good amount of work building up to the third date and it would suck to have to start over, but she's not lazy, she can do it again with a new mark the next week. If this mark would have reacted by not showing up with headphones or by pressing her for sex because he's tired of being patient, then she would have lost his number at the end of the date. Never feel as if your seduction skills must be rewarded, that's ego. If he doesn't respond it doesn't mean you're a bad seductress, he's probably a cheap bastard, so cut him off and go hunt for a new trick.

Hoing Up

Do you understand how to seduce now? I doubt it, Maria the Ho performed these things so subtly and precisely that it's like trying to learn a magic trick by watching David Copperfield YouTube clips. I'm going to slow it down and point out precisely how to seduce men during the three-date courting stage, and again all of these are things any woman can pull off no matter her looks or personality, as long as she's willing to erase fear from the equation and go full steam.

♥ **Compliments Kill**

Men are rarely complimented. Use this to your advantage! Understand that a male goes through life getting very few verbal compliments from the opposite sex. No matter if he's an athlete that looks like he's cut out of stone or just your average pretty boy, very few women will confess to his attractiveness. Older women may call him cute because they're old and don't have any reason to fear being curved. Maybe some random drunk girl at a party will remark on him being hot, but nothing to the extent where he becomes used to it. Women don't like to put themselves out there because it makes them seem thirsty or overly interested.

I've seen women on Twitter respond to a picture of Colin Kaepernick[9] with, "Damn, I'd suck his father's dick as a thank you," but in real life, those things are reserved for private thoughts. Women think sexual all the time, but it's usually held back. There remains a vanity inside all men that any woman can exploit if she's willing to get a little dirty with her compliments.

---

[9] Colin Kaepernick was the young 49ers quarterback who became an NFL sex symbol, before evolving into a political landmine.

To engage a man and flirt with him in a way where you stroke his ego, will always win him over. Men don't know for sure that they're the shit, they just think they are. To confirm his greatness under the pretense of flirting as if you like him, will put the biggest Kool-Aid smile you've ever seen on his face. When you're on a date with a man, drop these words at random, "baby," "handsome," "sexy," and it will put him in a different mind frame. Be sure to say these compliments casually, as if they aren't big things. Unlike words that need voice inflection, these adjectives are strong enough to live on their own. Men are constantly guessing "does she actually like me," the same way women do. The typical non-Ho is worried about if a guy thinks she's cute, funny, etc... regardless of being taken out on a date they don't know how a man really feels. A guy will have the same anxiety because he isn't sure if you are into him or just in it for a free meal because you're bored. You can flirt and sit close, but they still have doubt. **To seduce is to erase that doubt**. By using compliments in a normal nonchalant way, the sincerer this all feels, and the quicker it will break down his walls.

♥ **Submission Expert**
Do men like submissive women? Hell yes. Males like to be in control, take charge, and dominate. Should you be submissive? Hell no... but tease that role at first. Play possum and give him that power over you, then slowly start to take control and he won't know what hit him. When you're on a first date, let him order for you, let him pick the place, let him decide if you're driving together or meeting.

Don't do this in a way that makes you seem indecisive like, *"I don't know... where do you wanna go?"* Be decisive in your submission and put the ball firmly in his court. **Tell him to tell you.** Where do you want to go? *Somewhere good, pick for us, cutie.* Do you want to meet me there or should I come get you? *Do what's most convenient for you, daddy, I don't mind you planning our date.*

Even a half-stepping man will feel empowered by you literally putting everything in his hands. On the date Maria let her mark order for her, you can try that trick, or you can just wait until the server comes over and be even more submissive, "I'll let my boo decide for me." Now he must answer in front of another person. This builds up a position of power and confidence. You're seducing his ego and softening him up for the step where you begin to tell him in ways that make him think you're asking.

♥ **Inside Jokes**

What separates you from the pack? These tricks will be talking to various women that have their eyes on his prize and are giving up free pussy. How do you compete? Bonds destroy competition, and the fastest way to bond with a man is to relate on a personal level about tangible things. Give a man a nickname or let him give you one, it doesn't have to be something he calls you all the time, just something that relates back to a shared experience. For instance, if you two met at the supermarket, call him *Aisle 9* or something related to what he had in his cart that was funny or interesting. Reminding him of that first meeting connects you two.

Create your own jokes early and often. The first date will usually be out in a place where normal everyday weird people are. Be it waiting for a table and making fun of a song that keeps playing or clowning on a person with a weird walk who passes by you, take those moments and make them inside jokes that you can bring up later. There is always someone or something that you can laugh at, so be aware that these things aren't just funny, they are seducing his brain in a way where he has to call or text you when he sees something similar in his everyday life. Friendship is built on comfort, laughing further drops his guard, and being the only girl he can share certain things with makes you important.

♥ **Kissing As A Reward**

Doggy treats are still being used, and kissing is the easiest treat to give out. There are women who don't like kissing strangers, and that's understandable, but if you refuse to reward his actions with affection, it will make a man feel as if you're putting on a front. Remember, these men aren't robots doing nice things for you just because, so you have to give a little to get a lot. To go on a date and project a lack of attraction will leave you dead in the water. **Be willing to kiss, but ration it.** Some women kiss a man as soon as he goes in. Don't be that easy! Kissing should be used sparingly at first. The first date, if it goes well, should end with a kiss, no tongue, short and passionate, leaving him begging for more. That's just a taste of what's to come. The second date you should go French, and really kiss the fuck out of him. Don't get into a make out session like a drunk blonde during homecoming.

There should be a two to three-minute limit, then pull back. Before you say goodnight give him another kiss, but this time, you should initiate and pull him in. When it's time to stop kissing, pull back again, this time as if you don't want to stop, but you're a good girl, so you have to stop.

This seduces his body and makes him instantly hard. "That's gross," no, it's not gross, it's proof that your seduction is working! You need his dick to be hard; it's the final mission before you end the night, because if you're not going to have sex, you must at least inspire the thought in his head. Kissing, stroking his pants, it's all a seduction technique to get him associating you with desire. As you go forward beyond the second date, kiss him like that when he does something you approve of, and train him to only expect that level of kissing as a reward. He doesn't get to kiss you just because he wants to kiss. Pecks and cheek kisses, are all he gets when he's not going the extra mile. You're not a teenager in love; you're softening him up for the hustle, so keep your kisses on a tight lock until he realizes that he doesn't get sugar until he makes you smile.

♥ **C.L.I.T.T** (Call. Listen. Ignore. That. Text)
It could be two days between dates or an entire week, but this is where women normally lose a man's interest even after a good date. Waiting for him to call, being afraid to call him first, texting and not talking… these things are a product of fear. The most admirable thing about Hos is that they are just like Spartans when it comes to throwing caution to the wind and taking control of their fate. Spartans call when they want because they made a connection and don't need to play

games. Hos call because they can't get paid with a dry phone. Same confidence but they exist on different moral plains. After you wow him on the first date, call to check up on him the next night if you haven't heard anything during that day. Men usually have a rule that you call a girl a day or two later, but girls today overthink and get paranoid when they don't receive a call or text 12 hours later. "Oh my god, he didn't like me, maybe I should have done more to impress him," stop being basic! Overthinking will kill your hustle. Some guys wait a few days, while some guys contact the same night. Neither is right or wrong. Regardless of how he responds, fast or slow—he wants you!

Don't wait on him to hit you up like some scared little girl, initiate. Late at night is perfect because it catches him winding down and vulnerable. Call and thank him for taking you out, throw out some inside jokes, whisper about how you were daydreaming about kissing him earlier, and compliment his lips. If you do these things, his dick will be harder than fingerwave gel. He now wants to know what every man wants to know, "when can I see you again?"

Don't react and be submissive this time and let him plan the date. Now is when you play hard to get. Unless he has something interesting coming up like an awards dinner, show tickets, or some formal event, that you should go to, keep him in the dark. You're busy, you have a life, tell him the weekend might work, but you'll have to let him know. This keeps him hungry. You denied him the right to see you, but only after you rode his dick about fantasizing about this kiss. That's not a mixed signal, because the affection/reward of kissing is the proof that you do like him.

See how it's all coming together now? You're challenging a man where most women throw themselves, he knows(thinks) that you want his dick, but he just can't get to you. As a result, he will move heaven and earth to make Friday, Saturday, or even Sunday work as your next date night. This is all happening because you're always better at enticing a man over the phone than via text message.

♥ **The Power of Excuses**
Are you a woman that can say, "No, not tonight?" Can you stop yourself in the middle of kissing? Can you stand your ground when a man is begging to take you back to his place, begging to sleep at your place, or offering to rent a hotel so you won't have to drive in bad weather? This is the part where you will be tested so remember the earlier chapter on discipline and how to fight through impulsive thoughts that may put you in compromising positions. After the first date, a man will not want to go out again, but he does so he can get closer to sex. After the second date, a man will expect sex, so he will try to maneuver it to intimate places. A man will not complain directly about taking you out, he will simply go the alternate route and think of other ways to see you. Most likely, his ideas will be places where he doesn't have to spend money and where you two will be alone.

House dates, house parties, kickbacks, or pop up visits. In a man's world, this is the same as going on a date because technically dating is just spending time, and that's what women who are looking for love need to see, that he's going to spend time consistently. Ha! Of course it's a trap, and men end up isolating these thirsty women and having sex after a few weeks. This is the world that basic bitches have created, not Hos. Basic Bitches are afraid to turn a man down because they don't want to be seen as mean or uninterested. A Ho doesn't give a fuck about the way she is perceived, because she knows he wants her pussy, she's virtually put it in his face, and even if a man is annoyed with dating, he will continue to entertain the things she wants to do because she's not going to bend and fall for Come Over & Chill.

Forget all the basic love-sick moves you normally make when trying to find a boyfriend and think like a Ho trying to secure the gold. The more you make him wait and make him chase, the more valuable your vagina becomes. Be comfortable with the words, "not tonight." You are not going to lose his interest because he still wants to fuck you and just as importantly, he enjoys hanging out with you. If you were to have sex with a guy and then spend Monday-Friday, saying you don't want to come over and watch Netflix, he's going to call the next girl and put her over you on the pecking order because you're old news. **If he hasn't had sex, he may call the next girl, but you will remain at the top of the pecking order because you're a code he can't crack and that drives him crazy.** It's not about how you make excuses, don't get caught up in having good reasons, fuck the reasons, be able to get the point across that you do things on your time. Men hate when they can't have their way, but hate is only frustration mixed with passion. This will easily turn into desire if you aren't afraid to seduce him by making him chase after you.

♥ **Tell Don't Ask**

Um, they're having this wine tasting at this tavern uptown. Is that something you would be into? That's how the average woman asks to be taken out to a place that interests her. *Hey, they're having a wine tasting uptown, let's go.* That's how confident and decisive women ask to be taken out. No one likes to be told "no," or given an excuse, but women especially don't like to see their ideas or plans rejected so they humble themselves and ask permission like a kid with a slip to the zoo. By asking if he's "into it" or "free" you've already fucked yourself because you don't sound sure if you even want to go. If you act indecisive or position yourself as a timid asker, then a man won't feel bad about coming up with something that he wants to do instead such as Dave & Busters or going over to his friend's place to drink and smoke.

Don't fall into the trap of being afraid to scare him off by asking for your kind of date. Asking for a 2nd date is the initial step in learning how to get him to give without asking. If you can't finesse a man into going somewhere how are you going to finesse for money or gifts? Remember these three things: Conviction in your voice lets him know that it's not up for negotiation. A hint of excitement in your description of where you want to go will make him feel guilty for even thinking of saying, "no." Finally, the ability to say, "okay, I understand." As opposed to pouting like a brat will prove to him that he's not your only date option. That's how you train him to become your Yes-Man.

***

There is an elitist concept, not just resigned to millennials or spoiled brats, where some women think they don't have to give to get. These tactics are sex-free, and they are also ego-free. You must step out of your "I'm the princess of the world, men should give me money just to go out with me," nonsense. This is mental warfare, and you can't wage a war where you think you're too good to get dirty. Speak first. Seduce. Reward his behavior with kissing. Pull away and make him chase a bit. End by making him take you somewhere you want to go to exercise your power over him. These are easy things to do and they lay the ground work for all the mind-fucking to come. But you must do it the same way Maria did—with intelligence.

#8
Getting Nasty with It

Between the 2nd and 3rd date is where you take the seduction to the next level. All the ice has been broken and men are going to start to get a little bold with their line of conversation. "Stop being nasty… Boy, you crazy… You always make it into something dirty." Those are the corny things women say when they are trying to keep sex under wraps. So-called classy ladies don't want to shift the focus to sex because they don't want to get a man's hopes up nor get themselves worked up. They want to keep this image of themselves that screams, "Respect me!" Hos don't play in that league, they know that men claim to be disgusted by freaky behavior, but they all salivate over girls who talk openly about their sexual behavior. There is an art to it; no one wants a woman that's on social media telling the world her pussy taste like strawberry Fanta or sharing her last orgasm story on a double date. **Exclusive freakiness makes men think they are special.** Therefore, your nastiness has to be relayed subtly in order to give a man the impression that you're not a freak; he just has the power to bring the freak up out of you.

Tap Out Pussy

This Pussy'll drive you crazy, drive you crazy. Those are the lyrics to one of the most famously ratchet Baltimore Club songs from when I was growing up. I remember when I first heard it; I was amused and turned on at the same time. To talk about sex in a way that challenges manhood as if he won't be able to satisfy or hold his own is like throwing down the vagina gauntlet. As a man, you want to prove that no woman can make you tap out, but secretly it's the curiosity of, "Is her box really that bomb?" that makes a dick rock hard at the very thought of sampling that kind of magic pussy. Ho appeal isn't merely new pussy appeal. Every woman who a man hasn't had sex with has new pussy appeal, but that doesn't drive a man crazy. Hos can keep sexual interest where other women are just dismissed as cock teases because they don't say "no" to sex, they say, "You're not ready."

Women looking for relationships treat sex like the elephant in the room because they think sex lowers a man's opinion. Hos embrace sex talk because sex doesn't lower a man's opinion it keeps his interest. **What lowers a man's opinion is actual sex with little to no effort put forth.** Talk privately about how you want to ride his face, how good your pussy tastes, or how only one man has ever made you squirt, and it will have him all ears. Even when you pull away from that 2nd date kiss, he'll still stick around because he remains intrigued. Even when you go days without seeing him, he'll still reach out because his imagination is running wild at what lays between your legs. All you need to do is fan the flames between these next two dates, and he'll remain in lust. Other women break under pressure, they fall for tricks like, "let's be exclusive," and give it up, shattering that fantasy and losing all power. Hos, know that being nasty yet unattainable, puts a man on a string which she puppeteers.

Your pussy is Floyd Mayweather, it's humiliated all challengers, and you don't want to waste your championship coochie on a Manny Pacquiao. You're not just talking shit, you've asked him about his dick game, you've felt on his cock, and you've dirty danced against him and felt that poke, yet you're not convinced he's ready. That's the internal motivation you use when you talk about sex. You don't insult him, you simply tease him as if you will snatch his soul if you ever had sex. His response will be, "prove it," to which you will respond with a smirk, "In due time." He'll keep challenging you, and you'll keep being coy. Don't feel attacked, don't get an attitude as if he's pushing too hard, this is a game. Roll with the punches! Laugh it off. Moan a bit at the thought. Ask him questions about how long he'll last. Even make bets about it. This cat and mouse shit talking is important during the first few weeks because if he passes the <u>Headphone Test</u> of the 3rd date, then you'll turn the sex talk knob up, but for now, you're seducing him with the promise of the best pussy he's ever going to feel.

Talk about sex often, talk about the porn that you now study, make up stories about the "6" guys that you've been with and how they just couldn't lay it down. Make it sound organic and let him ask you first, don't just blurt out a bunch of nasty things. If you're on the phone and he talks nasty or says something on the subject, become an actress; laugh, hesitate, speak low as if you're telling him a deep secret, then you hit him with a nasty intel. *You don't need foreplay because you automatically get wet, you cum from giving head, you haven't met a man that can last longer than ten minutes hitting it from the back*, and the list goes on… make it up, pull it from your life, steal from stories you heard. It doesn't matter if it's true or not. Pussy propaganda is highly effective, so talk your vagina up as if it has all the answers!

The Secret of Phone Sex

An honest person knows how to have phone sex. If you're a woman that tells me she doesn't know what to say, how to initiate it, or how to get a man off verbally, then you're a liar. You are lying to me, and you're lying to yourself. I don't care how shy or introverted you are, you know what turns you on. You know what has made you moist in the past. You know what you want to hear a man say, feel a man do, and most importantly, what you want to do to a man to excite yourself. You know how to have phone sex, but you're afraid to say those things to a relative stranger. Phone sex is hard because it forces you to open up about the most secretive thing you can ever talk about—sexual desire. You may be into some nasty shit that will be judged. You may be into some boring shit that will be judged. The reason you struggle is that you're afraid to be judged on that level or to be thought of as impure. Hos have phone sex down to a science because they don't give a fuck about what comes out of their mouth, they have no reason to fake modesty, and they understand that to know what makes a man tick sexually is to control him mentally. Phone sex in a normal relationship should be beneficial for both parties, not all about a man trying to relieve his stress. However, when you're seducing a trick, you want to steal from the playbook of an old school prostitute and be his fantasy for those twenty minutes that he lasts.

Think back to the previous Hoexample and how Maria picked a time to talk to her mark. Carve out a spot and make him reserve it for you, don't get pushed into the role of the Basica that waits for a man to call at random times. You aren't his girlfriend, you're his fantasy, so he'll accommodate your schedule if you train him right. We'll talk about setting a call schedule more in depth later, but for the purpose of phone sex, be sure you have access to him at night when he's alone.

How do you initiate phone sex? You can't come out and say, "my pussy is so wet right now," while you're in the middle of talking about how bad the traffic was this morning. You have to ease into being nasty. Like everything a Ho does, you have to guide him to that point, not wait for an opening. Have your game plan already formed. You're going to small talk, then bring it to how you miss him, drop an inside joke about the last date you went on (remember, never have phone sex until after date #2, it's a reward for a great evening out) and bring up something sexual that happened. *That last kiss was everything;* now go into detail about how it felt. Bait him into using his low voice and then tell him another place he can kiss...

Now you're rolling, you made bullshit chitchat into a sexual fantasy by directing him exactly where you wanted him to go. From there, he's going to show you how he gets down. Some men are aggressive, other men like to be led. You have to test the waters and play it by ear to see which side he falls on. The last time I had phone sex I wasn't for the pleasantries, I told her to get her vibrator, and let's just go for it. There have been other times when I wasn't sure if that girl was going to be down, so I beat around the bush and kept seeing how far I could push it by asking about basic shit like what she's wearing, where her hands were, etc... Every man will vary, and some guys will not want to cross that line, so make it easy and be the initiator.

This is his fantasy, so start by asking what HE wants YOU to do to him. Of course, he's going to say something dumb like, "do whatever," So go for the dick. Talking about sucking dick is the golden goose that will always deliver. Even if you're not the type that enjoys head, immerse yourself in that role. You are going to describe that dick in your mouth, beg for his cum, and ask permission like a dirty little whore if you can lick his nuts. He will gobble it up, and be beating off with a fury by this point. From there, you can really get him open and ask if he can turn you out. This should make him want to get aggressive and start living out his fantasies such as girl on girl, choking, tit fucking, facials, eating ass, it will all come out because he's trying to get you to moan and cum just as much as you're trying to get him off. He'll demand that you call him Daddy or Master or want you to repeat the dirty things he's saying. Wherever he is trying to take you sexually, don't fight it, simply follow along as if these things are about to make you cum as well.

The fantasy of phone sex is double-barreled. You're maintaining a fantasy fuck session, and then you're in the real world feeling on yourself (or so he thinks) which makes him interested on two levels. He occasionally will want to stop the fantasy and know how you're reacting over in your bed. Maybe you have a toy, maybe you have your fingers; either way, he will want a play by play on that as well. Give it to him in a more honest way than the fantasy talk or he'll think you're bullshitting. Instead of exaggerating about having a fist in your pussy, treat it like a sidebar. It should be subtle and believable. You're rubbing your clit, and it's gotten super wet. Even chuckle as if you're amazed at what he's doing to you. From there lead him back to his fantasy world, and tell him how you want him to fuck you next. From the back is always the power position, but spice it up. Confess that your wish is to clone him, so you can have double the fun, one of him hitting you from the back and the other fucking your mouth. He can't believe how filthy you are, and he's falling in love with every sadistic word that comes out of your mouth.

If you keep this pace, he won't last long. You will know when a man is cumming because he can't hide that rush feeling of an orgasm. Take this as your cue to fake cum at the same time or a second later. You don't want to keep it going because fantasy talk after the dick goes soft, is just weird due to the lack of arousal. After he's finished, tell him how good it was and how it was the first time doing that since you broke up with your ex. **Remember, "I don't usually do this," may be phony, but dudes believe it.** Remark on how you can't wait for it to happen for real, and he's going to think he's all the way in there at this point. Tell him he wore you out and make sure to get off the phone within three minutes of the nut busting. You aren't here to talk him to death as if he's your boyfriend, he's a trick in training, and you must leave him wanting more.

Bait Set

These things are proven to seduce a man on a level where he doesn't even recognize what's going on. You're being personable, funny, and cool. You aren't blowing up his phone or begging to go out. You aren't easy when you are out, and he respects that he has to work to get to see you again. When he does see you, you're intensifying his thirst with kissing, touching, and complimenting him as if he's the only man on your radar. To top it off you've made your pussy seem like it belongs on Mt. Rushmore and you know how to have incredible phone sex. This man, even if he isn't looking for a relationship, is so impressed with you that he can't help thinking about you throughout his day. He's infatuated, and it's come without him touching your vagina. This is how you seduce a man early on and make a connection that most women are too uncomfortable to make. Two-Three weeks, that's all this section is covering, that's how quick you can imprint yourself on a man's brain, and just imagine all of the typicals that waste months and can't even get a guy's attention even after sex. Ho Power!

"Can I use this, not to work a mark, but to win over a man I want as a boyfriend?" Yes, you can do these things to a man you like and want to be with seriously, but the way Hos usually operate works flawlessly because they aren't emotionally connected to their marks as you would be connected to a potential boo. You care about what that man with good looks and a better job thinks, so by nature you'll hold back during this step. When you're dating normally, your mind is focused on "husband material," for the future, so are you going to present yourself as utterly nasty, wanting two dicks in you, being into girl on girl action? Most likely not, even if you are, because you want to be thought of as "wife material". You don't want to blow it by making the wrong move, but Hos don't give a fuck about wrong moves or having a few dates not work out. You want to be respected because you have hopes of him taking you seriously, but Hos don't want respect they want lust. Respect can get you a meeting with his mother and maybe the official title of girlfriend. Lust, if done the Ho Tactic way, will get you a meeting with his Amex and maybe the title to a car. If you have the discipline to use this on men you want a relationship from, you will turn him out, but you must go all in.

Let's recap. The seduction was in full force and he made it past the second date where you picked the place. He earned the reward of phone sex which has set him on fire. You asked him to bring you headphones on your third date, and he passed the test and proved he doesn't mind spending a little. Congratulations, you have him open. Now it's time to step up the pressure and see just how much you can get out of him.

#9:
How to Make Him Fall in Love the Ho Way

Sexual attraction is a shallow desire, which is why men lose interest so quickly after checking you off their bust it open bucket list. As a woman, you may be confused as to why men spend so much of their waking life trying to get something that isn't even that serious. The same reason restaurants can charge $90 for a steak and build their business around the fact that they have $90 steaks. It's the allure of something bigger and better. Wanting to have sex with various types of women is the itch that can't be scratched. He's never had a girl with D cups, has never had a girl with A cups, has never had a Spanish girl, has never had an Arab girl, has never had a girl with natural hair, has never had a girl with that Cassie side shaved shit going on—men are in awe of anything that appears different and can't wait to experience it!

Old pussy tastes just like new pussy, probably feels physically better than new pussy, but like the guy who eagerly makes reservations to try out that $90 steak, men have a burning desire to try out new women just because it's on such a high pedestal. **Your pussy is the bait, and the way you flirt and seduce will raise you to that high pedestal.** Nevertheless, those things don't guarantee shopping sprees or condominium down payments. The deep desire that makes you different from the average pussy is love. Men fall in lust quickly, and they fall in love even quicker if you know how to push the right buttons.

Take a man that has a little sister, he will do anything to make sure she's taken care of and that she's not being taken advantage of by men like him. It puts a smile on his face just to know that he's the one holding her down and sheltering her from this cold world. Men are protectors by nature, it's in the male's DNA to hold down the fort, but it's not property that makes him so caring, it's the love of being needed by someone special to him. Little sisters often don't want their big brothers to watch their backs, but they do it, and when that girl finally sees how he looked out, she embraces him with love. That's a special feeling that not even little brother or mother love can touch.

Take family out of the equation, men still take certain women under their wings. Every man that I've ever known has had a "sister" that wasn't related to him. That relationship was deep and other friends weren't allowed to talk to his play-sister. Outside dudes had to be approved and anytime she was in need, he did what he had to in order to make her happy. Bitter women who have never experienced this level of platonic male love often turn their nose up when their boyfriends inform them of little sis. These women only see a man/woman relationship that's not built on family, so it must be sexual. They are right and wrong. Not every man wants to fuck his play-sister, but the kernel of romantic love is at the root. It's not the same as "I want to marry you" love, it's more of this "I want to keep you in my pocket and protect you," selfish and conditional love.

Terms of Endearment

The same way men fall in love with their play sisters, they fall in love with Hos. They provide that sisterly love where they look up to him, they need him, and they appreciate him for helping. These women also represent that "Be My Daddy" sexual fantasy. Daddy's gone, so Big Brother is there to guard her heart and facilitate her wants, but at the core is the reality that unlike real family, he can have her sexually. **A Ho makes it clear that she is not his woman, but she also makes him feel as if she belongs to him.** No other man is as embedded in her soul as he has become, and that emotional ownership makes her special. The one Ho Tactic that will solidify your relationship goes beyond flirting and seducing, it's all about being dependent like a little girl, and making him feel as if he's your protector.

Hip Hop has promoted this, "You can't save a Ho," or the "Captain Save-A-Ho" rhetoric, but the truth is most of the guys rapping about not loving Hos are obsessed with them. A man with money or status treasures a girl that he can have fun with, who doesn't bring romantic stress, and who always makes him feel like the only man in the world when they are together. That's the emotional jackpot; he doesn't have to commit to something scary or grow up and take on a responsibility like marriage or a long-term relationship. This Ho is a friend, a confidant, a lover, and best of all she doesn't put any pressure on him. Women looking for marriage or a square relationship could never be happy with that self-centered role in a man's life, but Hos are built for a concubine lifestyle. Earlier in this book I went over the "good time girl" traits, this is how you get there.

When a woman like that needs help with a bill, wants to go on vacation with him, or needs a pair of eight hundred-dollar shoes to match the dress she just bought or it's going to ruin her night, that man will go into big brother mode. He takes care of that woman, not like it's his wife, but like she's his defenseless little sister. Men love Hos because unlike normal women, they don't scream, "I don't need a man," they squeeze him tight and say, "I wouldn't know what I would do without you." That feeling of genuine appreciation even if it is sparked by what he does for her, is a real feeling, it is real love, and it completes a man on the deepest level.

You can be his girlfriend, be there to hold him down through bad times and party with him during good times, but what you have with your boyfriend is a partnership. You aren't indebted to him, or owe him shit; you both do for each other in your own little ways. Ladies tend to fall into two categories: Independent woman who does for herself or a maternal lover that spoils a man because that's how you were raised to love. Men do appreciate those women, they wife them, they love them, but they rarely trick on them.

Many of you reading this have boyfriends or husbands that don't buy you shit, but you know they have it to spend. **Your man is more likely to trick on a Ho or his "sister" before he tricks on you, a loyal woman that gives him endless love.** This developed because you have established that you don't need him to take care of you. A man gets comfortable in your independence to the point where he forgets that you are still a woman that has a need to be spoiled like a princess every now and then. Trophy wives and Hos usually have one thing in common; they need that man, are dependent on that man, and they stroke his ego in a way that plays to his fraternal caring side as well as his savage sexual desire. Girlfriends can't compete with Hos because they are delivering two unique experiences. His girlfriend hopes that he will take care of her, but doesn't expect it whereas a Ho submits to a man and pleads for his help. The open mouth is the one that is feed. Read this over and over again until you understand this as the nature of every man. You were looking for the answer to why men take care of Hos when they can find women who will do what they want for free, well there it is.

Hoexample

Maria has sized up her mark perfectly. They've been on three dates, and he's proven that he doesn't mind treating or tricking a little, but how far will this man go? Maria calls at her regularly scheduled time, but she's not herself, she's feeling down and wants to see him right away. The mark says he can come over or she can come over to his place, so Maria takes the opportunity to finally see how he's living. Maria comes over, dressed down in jeans, yet still sexy. She immediately kisses him and holds him tight, a reward for being there to talk. She opens up about how much really likes him… *but*—there is always a *but*… she doesn't want things to get complicated. She's known guys who change when things get too serious, she wants him to promise that they'll keep it fun and not let bullshit like titles and lies to get in the way. The mark wasn't expecting a "let's have fun" conversation he's used to a "what are we," ultimatum.

Maria pushes him down on the sofa and straddles him, she's saying that she doesn't want to be his girlfriend officially, but she's showing him that she is his girl in a non-friend zone way. The mark is on his home turf and thinks that it's now or never. Maria smacks away his advances; she wants to talk about life. For the first time, Maria isn't just full of flirting or jokes, she talks about her situation as if she's finally being honest. She tells her mark what she wants to do, her goals, her dreams, all in more detail than she's done before.

After an hour of talking about life, the mark is feeling even more connected to Maria. He understands her story, her struggle, and she's hooking him even more by asking his opinion on things like her career or her relationship with her family. At this moment, he's the wise older brother who wants to help. This mark isn't looking at Maria as new pussy, he sees her as a good girl who isn't ready for anything serious because she's been through a lot and is still struggling.

Maria tells the mark how much she values their time together, and again she brings up sex, "I'm going to fuck the shit out of you regardless." She mentions this casually not jokingly and reminds him that she doesn't want that future event to change anything. This is music to any man's ears. It's getting late and Maria has to go. The mark wants her to stay the night, but she has to get up early tomorrow (power of excuses) but she will call him, and maybe they'll have a movie night this week… or make a movie all night. Maria kisses him again. She's now positioned herself as a non-emotional threat in terms of being a girlfriend, has promised that pussy to him, and has shown that she's just a little girl lost looking for a real friend who won't use her. Maria exits back to her car, leaving the mark feeling like a brother, guardian, and most importantly, a soon to be lover.

Did you catch what Maria did? She went in for the kill MTV unplugged style. No fancy date, no fancy clothes, and gave him a show that didn't even feel like a show because it was so intimate. Hos are people too; they are women with stories, scars, bad habits, and problems that they admit to. Unlike the average guarded women, Hos own up to their dark side in order to garner sympathy. They don't hide, they lean on a man, they want to be saved, they want to be healed, and they want a daddy. **Many women legitimately feel this way, but don't trust**

any man enough to reveal these things. Hos aren't worried about being hurt by exposing their daddy issues or abusive history. Some of these stories may not even be true or are exaggerated in order to sink those emotional fangs into a man.

Girls like Maria show their vulnerability knowing that men want to protect those they care about. If she had done this the first date or the first two weeks, he wouldn't have cared. This comes after three fun dates, epic phone sex, and a true bond that made him spend money he normally doesn't spend. Maria isn't a stranger, this is his baby, his homie, his fantasy, all wrapped in one pretty package. He wants to have sex, but it hasn't been that long where it feels as if she's gaming him, and now that he knows her backstory, he understands why she's hesitant about sex. The mark probably has other girls who fuck for free or a subscription to Pornhub, so he will be fine with phone sex. He knows he's going to hit that eventually, but for now he just wants to make sure this girl is okay and taken care of because she deserves a dude to look out for her for a change.

Hoing Up

You don't have to be an actress or have some tragic story that makes this man see you as a stray kitten, it helps if you can pull from things that are fucked up, but if not just stretch the boring truth. Most women go through bad breakups, childhood drama, and things that have defined who they are. **In order to make this man trust you, you have to give him something worth believing in.** It's like filling out a scholarship application, or trying to be admitted to a good college, there is always an essay that states why you deserve it on a personal level. This trick may fund your business, your lifestyle, or your next two cars, so it's important that you give him a reason to fall in love with your soul. Men love bad girls trying to be good or good girls who are one-step away from relapsing. All of you have a story to tell, but let's make sure it hits the right notes that will make even a heartless man want to invest in you emotionally.

♥ **Carve Out Your Territory**

Weak women never know when it's okay to call a guy, they text like crazy, and date as if they don't want to interrupt a man's regularly scheduled life. They do these things because they are afraid to come off as clingy, but by trying to get in where they fit in, they become slaves to a man's lifestyle and once a man knows that you are willing to be accommodating, he will exploit that at every turn. Hos don't get in where they fit in; they carve out their spot in his life and force a man to clear that area. I spoke before about a set phone schedule. This is extremely important because it makes your time valuable. A man who likes a woman will want to call her whenever, drop texts in the morning, and feel as if he's always a phone call away from her. Fuck that. If he wants to talk to you, he has to wait until you say so.

I don't care if you are unemployed and do nothing but wait for your favorite TV show to come on, or if you're busy working and going to school—you need to come off as busy, <u>but always have at least an hour for him each day</u>. That hour tells him that you care and that you are invested, but it also demands that he be available, or he'll miss out that day. People in Long Distance Relationships do similar things to keep the spark going, but they stay on the phone all night trying to compensate for not being able to see each other for large chunks of time. You don't need to overdo it because you will be seeing him regularly. Forty minutes to an hour is good enough to chitchat and joke, without him becoming tired of you. I suggest you pick a time at night, a few hours after he's off work and has had time to get settled. If that doesn't work, find a time where you know he has a hole where he's not doing anything and make it work for you as well. You don't have to say, "I'm going to call you at 9:45 every night." You just do it, and after a few days, he will be trained to expect that call. When he texts you during the day, text a little, but tell him you'll hit him that night. If he calls just to say hi, say hi, but be in the middle of something. Shower him with affection, and then rush away because you have to go, that's training.

It's important that he doesn't feel like you're ignoring him or being distant, so always call at that scheduled time and say things like, "I was smiling when I got your text this morning," or "I couldn't focus at work after hearing your voice, daddy." Remember you are building on the flirting and seduction techniques I spoke of early. Compliments are still killing him and keeping his interest as the only man in your world that matters. Don't be afraid to skip a day if you know he's going out of town, or his favorite team is playing that night. However, send him things like selfies or funny pictures to let him know you are going to call him the next day. Not only have you carved a space in his life, you've proven that you aren't annoying when it comes to letting him enjoy his time alone.

♥ **Secret Swap**
People share some of the most personal things with me in confidence, and I take that seriously. I don't even tell my wife things because there is a certain loyalty and honor that comes with being entrusted with

embarrassing or hard to talk about secrets. There are men who are motor mouths and can't hold water, but if you frame what you have to say as if it's exclusive and no one else knows it, then he can't speak on it. If it were to leak only you and he know about it, so he would fuck himself over, and he's not going to do that while he's still benefiting from you. Alternatively, women are well known for letting things slip. Men aren't willing to share because they've been burnt by women who crossed their fingers and dry snitched to the world.

Hos are superior secret keepers, which make them like therapists to many men. Of all the affairs that have broken in the media, few are the result of a woman snitching, it's circumstantial evidence or male sloppiness that uncovers what that woman would have never told. If a man is going to be tricking on you, spoiling you, or sponsoring you, he's not going to want the world to know. What he does for you stays between the two of you. In order to get to that level, you have to prove your trustworthiness early. When he asks what you tell your friends, don't respond like a happy bitch, "I told them we went out to a concert, that you order for me at restaurants, that you're so sweet..." Nope. You tell them nothing and inform him from the jump, "I'm not a bird that needs to brag, I like to keep to myself."

Add on to this confidentiality by sharing something with him that you haven't told anyone. Let's say you were almost molested when you were nine by a neighbor, but you got away. That really shook you from that day forth, and you've never been able to tell anyone. Tell him how that still makes you feel, how you can't really let your guard down, and that you feel like you need to get it out, but you haven't really felt this comfortable until now. He will be flattered and honored to find out that you trust him. Once again, you give to get. Your confession may eventually lead to his confession. Don't push him for his secrets; establish that if there is anything he wants to tell you, he doesn't have to worry about judgment or you ever bringing it up because you wouldn't want him to be that way with your secrets. He may never share his dirty laundry, but it doesn't matter because you've established that you are on a friendship level few people ever reach and that you trust him more than any other person in your life. Like in the headphone test, you don't have to use anything tragic at this point like molestation, that's just an example. Be creative and think of something that sounds personal.

♥ **Lift The Sanctions**
Up until this point, I've told you to beware of the house dates, nightcaps, or pop ups that men use to pressure women into sex. To prove that you're not a gigantic cock tease, start to bring the guard down. Do invite yourself over to his place. Don't stay the night. Do let him come visit. Don't let him hang around for longer than an hour chilling. Open your world up to him, but don't let him get comfortable to the point where he thinks you will be having movie nights or that he can come see you with a pizza in hand instead of taking you out. You have established this man as having trick potential, but he's not a fool. If he sees an opportunity to slack, he will kick his feet up and set his phone to your Wi-Fi network as if he plans to be over there often.

Take sex out of the house hangout. If you go over, it isn't to spend time, it's to talk about something that's bothering you or that you don't want to discuss on the phone. When you're alone and he's caressing you, let him get a little feel on, and vice versa, but bring it back to what you wanted out of the visit. Lounge with him, put your ass on his lap, give him a shoulder rub, but this isn't "boo time," it's putting in work to prove that you're slowly but surely letting him inside of your world. **The sanctions have been lifted but the boundaries remain the same.** Be disciplined and don't fall for him wanting to give you head, or him begging for a hand job, that's too close for comfort. Make these visits short, meaningful, and leave him wanting more. If you jerk his dick after a visit, he's going to want you to come back over and do that the next night. If he eats the box, he's going to expect that going forward. Don't go down that road. He should be hard and horny every time you leave him, which guarantees that he will continue to take you where you want to go and get you the things you want. In his mind, he's one good date away from having you, and you must keep that fire going.

♥ **Hate Titles**

If you aren't sleeping with a man, yet you're spending a lot of time with him, he's going to get nervous. Are you the type of girl that needs a relationship first? Do you expect this to go somewhere real? Men get just as nervous as women do when they begin to overthink and read between the wrong lines. There is always a catch with females in terms of what they hope to get out of a romantic situation. The catch is that you want to get in his pockets, not get a ring. He doesn't know this because your actions have shown him that you're super into him and extremely attracted to him physically. The male ego will distort the truth about Hos the same way the female ego will make a woman think that a man wants her for more than sex. You've shown interest in him for him, and anything he's gotten you has been an afterthought at first glance. He doesn't know you were testing him, and he's taken the bait thinking that you're falling for him.

Moving forward, you must ease his mind about relationships. Most women wait for a man to let them know what it's going to be, and they get impatient when a dude keeps down the "friend" path while showing lover signs. Hos don't wait; they confront a man's fear just as ferociously as they confront his desires and use it to their advantage. Have "The Talk," the same way Maria did, but make it about letting him off the hook, as opposed to putting pressure on that man to be with you. You don't want to be his girlfriend. You are a woman he has, but isn't cuffed to, so he can breathe easy. That's what makes you a turn on. Tell him how attracted you are, how much fun you're having, and demand that it stay on this level. Tell him that you aren't like those girls that need a title and expects shit to escalate just because they fuck and hang out all the time. Sell yourself as his best friend with a pussy that's always available… or so he thinks.

Some of these tricks will be so floored by your tactics that they will want to lock you down and throw away the key. You have been more impressive than most females, therefore it's common for a man three to four weeks in telling you that he loves you and wants to be with you. If a mark wants to be your man, the same rules apply. The only audible you have to call is, "Please don't think I'm dealing with any other men, I'm really not in the right place to do all of the girlfriend boyfriend stuff," then with his hand in your hand you eye fuck him with, "You don't need a title to be the most important guy in my life anyway." Then you seal it with a kiss!

♥ **Sex = Trauma**
Men are used to sex early on even in non-relationships these days. Although it's only been a matter of weeks, he will begin to worry that you are playing games. *She says she wants to fuck, yet she's shot me down twice... hmm.* Once again, you play the sister role and make him see how other guys have damaged you. If you really are a victim of sexual abuse, use it! How do actors cry on the spot? Not eye-drops. They dig into something real. That may sound fucked up to use your actual past, but how is it any different from someone hired for a reality show that has to spill intimate details to be cast or reveal it on camera to get the fans to like her on the show? **VH1, Bravo, and the like exploit trauma for millions. You would be a fool not to weaponize your past.** This isn't about being a saint, it's about getting Saint Laurent!

The most successful excuse that I've been emailed about over the past few years has been to create a bad sexual experience that you don't want to talk about. Be mysterious, maintain you're almost done healing, but it's something you still need to get over. As your protector, he will respect that. One reader noted that she had gone over a year without sex pressure from her trick because he didn't want to push, so I know for a fact this works! Another trauma you can go for is tied to the theory that, "men can't handle the aftermath." Create a story where you had a stalker or how some guy flipped and got jealous after sex. The trick will point out that he's not that dude and hasn't given you any indication that he would change up on you. Agree, and say that it's something you're trying to work on and not a reflection of him. Don't make it seem as if you don't trust him. He must believe that you're waiting for the right time as opposed to waiting for him to prove himself.

Trauma only lasts so long, so when you reach the point where he's been patient, keep biding your time with more reasons. <u>Here are several that actual readers have shared:</u> Set a date to have sex then came down with a stomach bug. Embarrassingly admitted to having a yeast infection. The good old "that time of the month" excuse. Had a best friend interrupt a sex date. The list goes on because a good Ho is creative and inventive. There is room for originality, and the women that have used these tactics on various marks utilize their brains and keep the hustle going. A man will walk away if he feels you're lying, so make him a believer in your excuse for waiting for sex.

♥ **The Girlfriend Experience**
There are women who men want to hide away and fuck, and then there are women they want to hang around with outside because she raises his stock and entertains his friends. Many of the best tricks will be men who are serial daters or long-term bachelors. They miss out on things that couples do like double dating, wedding dates, family cookouts because they don't want the attention or the question, "So when are you going to settle down?" Let him know that you're cool with going places with him and playing that role. Men like company in places where they aren't comfortable, so be his

sidekick. He has to go watch his cousin's basketball game but hates that side of his family; tell him you'll roll with him. He has a trip out of town for a seminar and they're always boring, tell him you'll roll with him. You aren't the girlfriend, but you deliver the girlfriend experience when needed. After a few times doing this, the lines will blur. At that moment, you've become the perfect woman, and he will do anything to keep this going.

***

Let's review the hustle so far. You went after a man and he passed your *Mr. Nice Watch* Vs. *Mr. Fake Watch* test. You flirted your ass off on the first date, seduced and destroyed on your second date, and made him buy you something small to bring to the third date. You keep him laughing, gas him with compliments, and the way you look at him with those eyes is an instant hard on. Now you've lowered your false guard and let him in on the scared little girl part of you that just can't seem to catch a break.

This all has taken place over the course to 4-5 weeks, and while he doesn't really know you, he loves what you bring to his life. You are his carefree good time girl, but also a trusting little princess that has shared her deepest secrets with him. Unlike the other women he's probably dating or even his girlfriend or wife, he sees value in you beyond your pussy. You are his baby, his homie, his sister, his bitch, and now he has to learn that it costs to keep you on his team.

#10:
How to Ask for
Gifts, Money, or Favors

You can't rush the come up. I've heard ratchets talk about how you have to ask a man early on for small shit like salon trips or phone bill payments in order to weed out the broke dudes from the ballers. The girls who tell you to sprint out the gate with your hand out are most likely broke bitches or dumb Hos who fuck for basic shit like a $22 full set of acrylic nails. Even stupid men aren't that stupid, and to come out of your mouth asking a man you barely know for things is an easy way to get played. A dude's favorite line to use on a stupid or young Ho is, "I got you on Friday." On Thursday, he lures you over to him, gets what he wants, and tells you he'll come by with what you asked for the next day. When Friday comes, he's nowhere to be found. That's how real men deal with rookie Hos and gold-diggers. I've personally had girls ask me for things after a few weeks and it immediately turned me off, and now that I can look back, it wasn't what they asked for it was the brazenness in which they asked. One girl, in particular, came at me with, "Can you get my hair done," but she said it in a way that was confrontational.

When I gave her the "I'll see" line she responded with, "I usually don't have to ask." That was a wrap. Not only did she come with an attitude as if she didn't want to ask, she tried to use some sort of ratchet guilt trip as if I should have bowed down and offered. I already had sex with her the week prior, but even if we hadn't, I would have made the same choice—snip snip. **Men don't like to seem as if they owe you something or that you're offering an exchange of services for a favor.** As I touched on earlier, endearment is the key. Asking must be done in a way where a man feels as if he is saving the day for a friend or taking care of a little sister. If that girl would have come to see me, made me play in her nappy ass hair, and complained about not having enough money to get it done while sitting between my legs, I might have fallen for that Ho Tactic.

You can't bully a man into giving, you can't beat around the bush about what you want, and you can't offer a favor for a favor. Know exactly what you want and don't front as if you have the means to pay him back. When it's time to communicate these things, you must take all pride out of asking, and play submissive like a cat rolling on the floor for Fancy Feast. That sentimental side is what you appeal to because men rarely say "no" to someone they care about and who has no other option.

"Please" is a criminally underrated word. Take a listen to those people around you who ask with a "please" in their request and you will notice that it's usually said begrudgingly. People say it under their breath or with a sigh because folks today hate to ask for things, they expect them. Women especially want to seem strong, and to drop a please at the end of a sentence is like being defeated so it's often said with a hint of frustration. Test this out the next time you listen to someone ask and you will automatically notice the vibe I'm describing. Saying please in that manner seems fake, and most likely it won't get you anywhere.

Alternatively, listen to a child say, "please," and watch as it uncovers the real power of the word. With no ego and zero pride, a 6-year-old will ask, "Can I take this toy home, pretty please," and it breaks your heart to even consider telling them, "no." Hos are aggressive and decisive, but they are also masters at submitting when it's time to ask "daddy" for a new toy. Now that you've mastered how to tunnel your way into the heart of a man, it's time to tug on those heartstrings.

Hoexample

Our girl Maria is ready to move in for the kill with her mark. It's been exactly a month since they met, and she's made the following observations about this man. He has a career, not a job, but he's still climbing up the corporate ladder. He rents, he doesn't own, so he's probably saving money. In addition to the obvious, Maria has done her research on her mark's field of banking and guesstimates that he makes 100-130k a year, which is solid, but doesn't put him in the range of a sponsor who typically makes 5-10x that amount annually. Maria's been to his place, she's seen his car, and she knows that he's not a big splurge. He does have style and class, so he appreciates luxury without being a slave to it. Maria has thought long and hard about what she wants from this man in terms of benefiting her lifestyle. The ultimate hustle for Maria is finding a sponsor who could pay her housing and car expenses while she takes the money from her job and invests it in her jewelry accessory line. This mark won't be able to grant her this financial freedom, but he can help her stack her money and get to that place in other ways. Maria writes down her goal: *Clothes & Car Note.*

Maria doesn't just ask, she plots! She's done with dates and headphones and is ready to test the limits of this relationship and get something she really wants and/or needs.

Maria needs to include this man in a way that makes him a player in her "I'm struggling" game. She finds an event coming up in the city, it's a charity gala hosted by one of those tacky women from some mindless reality show. She tells her mark that they have to go; it'll be so entertaining making fun of the elitist idiots who don't care about charity and just want to show off. This isn't the mark's scene, but Maria isn't asking, she's telling. They can go shopping together since it is a formal event. The mark doesn't mind because that means he gets to see her before that date night. Maria and the mark go shopping, and Maria finds a nice evening gown that will turn heads. The mark is waiting for Maria to ask if he could buy it, but Maria plays to this and buys her own dress; she even offers to pay half of his. "You know I'm not balling like that, but I don't mind looking out for you, baby." Of course, the mark turns it down and pays for his own tuxedo, but he now finds another reason to love Maria, she's thoughtful and will give her last for him.

Come the day before the event, Maria springs into action with her struggle story. She calls the mark up but isn't her upbeat sensual self. She doesn't want to say at first, but finally lets it out that she doesn't want to go to the gala anymore. The mark is floored; it's all they've talked about all week. Maria doesn't have any handbags, and the one she thought would work is missing. The mark, like any man, thinks that's silly and tells her to get a new one. Maria now lowers her voice and says she did see a Celine bag that would look nice, but she's already behind on a few bills. She then submits, "Could you get it for me, bae? Pretty please…" Her voice is sad and hopeless, and he doesn't like to see her depressed like this. He asks how much as if he's ready to take the bullet, and Maria responds with, "3." The mark thinks it's three hundred; she cutely adds that he needs another zero.

The mark doesn't want to spend three thousand dollars on something that doesn't benefit him, so he doesn't commit with an answer. Maria doesn't push or get angry, she stays on the phone and changes the subject, but her energy is weak. She's distracted and says she's online trying to find a better price… she loves that bag and really wanted to go out with him tomorrow.

The mark cracks; he'll get it for her and save the day. Maria gives him the exact response that he was looking for, she screams and confesses how much she loves him and how she can't wait to kiss him all night long. After the promise, Maria goes to the website and asks if he wants her to send the link or if she can use his card and save him the effort.

Maria just hit a lick and it didn't cost a backshot nor blowjob. Even though she promised to kiss him all night, they are still in a world where Maria has equated sex with trauma; he knows she's still in a waiting period, so sex won't be expected just because he spent three stacks on a bag. The mark did this out of love for his friend/Boo/Sister/Fantasy and feels zero remorse, only the joy of being appreciated. If this were a prostitute who he paid even half that money to in order to have sex, he would have felt guilty or like less of a man because he paid for pussy. **All men pay for pussy in the long run, but the male ego would rather be fooled into thinking the sex is free than exchanging currency**. In this mark's mind, Maria and him will have sex very soon, and it won't be because of the dates or the bag, it'll be love. That's the epitome of mindfucking a man!

If Maria's mark would have said "no" and let them miss that event, Maria would have been cold enough to cut him off that following week. Yeah, they've gotten to know each other, but she's a businesswoman, not his friend—snip snip and his stingy ass is gone. Maria can go for her goals because she's not tied down to fear or love, only what this man can do for her.

Maria's mark came out of pocket and now that she's established that she's dealing with a trick, she repeats this same desperation scenario in various ways. Maria needs shoes for a girl's night out, these are cheaper than that bag at only $900, so she gets them. She needs a new wardrobe for work, and she shows the mark her tattered blouse. He can't have his baby living like this, so he kicks out another $1200 on a few outfits. She wants the two of them to go out of town for the weekend, the mark is excited this is what he's been waiting for, but first it's to the jewelry store, she needs a nice watch and he should get one two. Another $5000 down and the mark doesn't even see a trend. Maria has managed to get in the pockets of a working-class man who doesn't even have it like that, but he doesn't mind because between the helping out, they are still dating, still having fun, still phone boning. Most importantly, Maria is confiding in this man about things that make him seem like her only real friend. This is where she tightens the noose. The biggest conversation begins to be Maria's bills and the stress they're causing. Maria has established that her job as a customer service rep has run its course and that she needs to get her own business off the ground. She has yet to ask the mark for any cash money or any favors that she has to pay back, which makes Maria independent in his eyes.

Maria has a $400 car note because part of her image is to drive a BMW, but that swallows up most of her money each month. She needs that note gone. Maria goes over to the mark's house and asks to stay the night? Maria and the mark stay up late, talking, teasing, playing, and enjoying each other. He keeps trying to slide the panties off, but all she has to do is say behave, and move in to cuddle. When a man respects a woman, he may try for sex but he won't push for sex even if she's in the same bed. Maria fakes asleep but suddenly begins to sob. The mark is confused, is it something he did? Maria doesn't want to tell him because it's embarrassing. They are friends, best friends, and the mark is mad that Maria is being secretive. With hesitation in her voice, she comes clean, It's her car, it's going to be repossessed. Maria is out of credit cards to borrow from and her paychecks barely cover her rent. Maria goes even further, it's not just a car, it's her life, it's a fucking mess, and she feels like a loser, she doesn't even know why the mark likes her.

This self-deprecating behavior is heartbreaking to hear. The mark is going to help her out with the car note until she can save enough money. Maria thanks him and falls in his arms crying tears of joy; he's not going to try to take advantage with sex, so he'll just spoon his baby until the morning. What the mark doesn't know is that Maria will always need help with that car note, that soon it will become his expense altogether. Meanwhile, Maria will be able to stack her own money with her current job or use this as a chance to go get a different job that's more conducive to her schedule. Maria shares her life plans with the mark, so he doesn't feel like he's being used, he feels like he's being charitable because $400 a month and a pair of shoes or purses here and there aren't going to break him. Meanwhile, Maria is using this new fashion and new disposable income smartly; she's trying to land more mice with the cheese.

Ho Ambition

Maria, like most smart Hos, multitasks and rarely works one man at a time. They get to the point where one trick is hooked, and then the dates become fewer and far between because she needs space to go out and find other men who can do the same thing, if not more. Maria's hustle goal was to get a new wardrobe so she could lure more men and to alleviate an expense. She's done both. Her ultimate goal isn't to be treated or tricked on; it's to secure a sponsor. With her fancy handbag clutched, her luxury car keys dangling, and her open toe heels click-clacking on the sidewalk, Maria is now scouting for a man that looks as rich as she feels.

Maybe Maria finds a fat cat that wants to take care of her, or maybe she keeps running into tricks that drop a few stacks and only last a few months, either way, Maria has become the type of woman that turns heads, that oozes sex appeal, and that knows how to make the type of man that you would do anything to be with, into her bitch. She's done this all without breaking a sweat or opening a condom wrapper. To look at Maria is to see a woman that obviously has sophistication, who talks with charm, and who appears to be just another woman standing next to you in line at the bank. The stereotype of the groupie or the gold-digger is an exaggeration. Maria is a Ho, but you she's not skanky, she's not loud, and she's not thirst trapping on the internet.

By the time the mark gets tired of helping out or after Maria stops spending as much time with him it will be too late. She will have dined like a queen and hit him up for over 10k dollars without him noticing it. That mark won't take to the streets and call her out, any man who admits to being suckered in this manner by someone he thought of as a friend will be joked by other men and looked down upon by other women. Marks rarely snitch on Hos because it hurts his image going forward in that city. Like most people who get played, marks keep it to themselves. In the end, who knows Maria is a Ho? No one, because she will never admit to it, and no man will ever dare expose her hustle if it also means exposing his naivety.

Unlike a celebrity that gets exposed for a shady past, there is no one willing to come forward and talk about an ordinary woman's history. "Hos be winning," because they are anonymous, and the more society swells with loose women who fuck for free because a man promises them a relationship, Hos will become more and more successful. They are one of the few groups of women that understand that it isn't the sex that keeps a man, it's the enticement.

Hoing Up

By now you should have seen all the tricks that Maria did, and on paper they may seem transparent, but remember she didn't ask like some ratchet with her tits in his face looking for some Malaysian hair, she asked as a good friend who had previously earned his love and maintained her place as the object of desire. Many women get played by men who just want sex because his game seemed sincere. Others can point out relationship red flags easily from a distance, but those women who have been caught up know how hard it is to see the manipulation when faced with a person who is in tears and telling you how much you mean to them. These tactics are stealth! Hos operate using real emotion, and it's always hard to tell real from fake when that person has a sob story or can cry on a dime.

We all have a need to be loved, we all want to trust in people's goodness, and help them as much as we can to get to where they are going. Hos, much like male players, take advantage of this humane behavior. The hustle Maria pulled off can be done by any woman who cultivates her charisma, builds her confidence, and believes that what they need to thrive is more important than the need to be truthful. Asking in a submissive, back against the wall type of way, is the easiest Ho tactic because you are giving a person who cares about you on a deeper level than sex, no choice but to save you from failure. By the time you're actually using the tools in this chapter, all of the real work will be complete. The first three dates told you that he has money to spend or he doesn't. You can't hustle someone who doesn't have it to give. You can't turn a trick that has nothing to trick on you or get sponsored by a person with barely enough money to live on their damn selves. No man will ever sacrifice his own lively hood for yours. The ultimate trick or sponsor is a person who has it, and you know they have it. Therefore, when you tell a person who loves you and who wants you on every level that your condominium HOA fee is going to lead to you not eating this month, it becomes a life or death situation. You are being dramatic, but it doesn't matter because you're selling your struggle like Kate Winslet on her best day.

Men who you hustle will become soft on you, so there will be no tough love like Mom and Dad would give. He will not leave you hanging, yell at you for not handling your money better, or say any of the judgmental things friends or family say. He can't tell you, "I got you next time," and then disappear or pretend as if he forgot. Why? At the root of this relationship, there remains two things that make you invaluable to a man—that Disneyland friendship that you may take away if told "no" and denial of that new pussy that he's so close to that he can taste. You have proven your value, and you have shown that you don't mind cutting him off if he acts contrary to your wants. After spending so much time talking to you he realizes that he can't go to the next girl to replicate what you do. **She's basic, you're a Unicorn!** In the end, that man will come to your rescue because vacation or shoe money can be made back in a week, you can't be gotten back. Remember, it's not tricking if he has it!

♥ **Work Within His Means**
Earlier I told you to know his world, not just to sound intelligent and knowledgeable in conversation, but so you can fill in the blanks of his bank account. So many women have no idea the difference between a rookie NFL player's salary and a player that's in his prime, so

they often are played like groupies because they think that a rookie fresh out of college is going to set them up for life. Additionally, when you're dealing with a guy who works at a good company but doesn't have a good job, you can fool yourself. A Product Manager at Coca-Cola doesn't mean he's managing every product, it could mean that he's one of twelve guys working on one flavor and making just as much as an assistant manager at Hot Topic. To know that man's industry is to be able to figure out roughly what he's making. Don't rely on the cars, the watch, or the shoes. After a month of dating, you see how he lives and how he spends. Now you go shopping for what you want as if his money is your money.

If you were to take your own paycheck and splurge, you would work under a budget because you still have bills and need food to eat. That man has the same dilemma as you, so don't ask for a five-thousand-dollar purse when you know that realistically he only brings home ten thousand a month before taxes. His car is paid off, but his rent is a certain amount. He has a gym membership, he eats out nearly every night since he doesn't cook and has two phones that come with two bills, all of these things should be taken into account. **Do the payroll math in your head and budget out the thing or things you want to get out of him because he's going to do that exact same math before answering your plea with a "yes" or "no."** If you ask for a pair of thousand-dollar heels, he can afford that, it won't hurt his pockets. He doesn't want to spend it, but because you need it, and it may hurt your friendship/lustship then he'll help you out. If you ask for a seven-hundred-dollar gift every other week, he can afford that too, but be careful not to get greedy and not to go over his guesstimated budget.

The moment his funds are low he'll have to tell you "no," and one "no" will turn into many once he knows that it's not life or death.

♥ **Be Specific**

You got dressed, drove all the way to the market, and as soon as you walked through the door you stop and think, "Fuck, what did I come here for?" From there you walk aimlessly trying to remember what you need, and end up picking up groceries that you want at the moment, forgetting all the items you need for the week. When you're hitting a lick, know what your goal is, or you'll end up getting things out of him that don't really benefit you in the long run. I talked to a woman that had a trick who would do anything for her, but she ended up asking for dumb shit because she didn't really know what she was doing. After the relationship ended she had nothing to show for it. Looking back now, she told me of all the stuff that she could have gotten from him that would have helped her make more money today. Could have, should have! Be focused *now*, and make a list no matter how big or small your aim happens to be.

If you can't afford to go to the Drake concert, get a man that treats you to tickets. If you have student loans, get a man that can pay them. If you want to enter into that socialite world in order to meet richer men, then get better clothes or a boob job. If you want a long-term investment, get jewelry that you can sell later. This isn't a game; it's your livelihood or your child's future. No matter what level the man you're dealing with is on, know what he can afford. Write down all the things that are within his price range and get that shit.

♥ **Give & Take**

Men have feelings too. It's great that you spend time, compliment him, make him nut with a phone moan, but what are you really giving him besides company? Be considerate and pick up cheap gifts with priceless meanings. If he's into a sports team, get a mug for him after a win. If you know he has to wear a tie to work, pick up a nice tie that isn't too expensive, but looks like it is. This man doesn't need these things, but they are an expression of your love and devotion and solidify that this isn't a one-way relationship. You are always thinking about him and want to show it in a way that you can afford. That little will go a long way in securing your reputation as his sweet princess who would do anything within her budget to show love.

♥ **Expand Slowly**

There is no rush to get everything on your list or to get the biggest payoff first. Have confidence that your hustle will not be exposed before you get what you really want. Pressuring yourself to hit a lick quickly tells me that you are being driven by the fear of not being able to replicate these actions. **Remember that every day that you go outside is a day you can get meet a bigger and better trick.** You've put work into softening this guy up, but this man isn't irreplaceable. If he gets turned off after he buys you the first thing, oh well! He closed the bank, but there are more banks down the street, so you go to the next one having gained a little something yet lost nothing. You are playing with house money! Relax and take your time. Get the smaller thing, then get the next thing, you're training him to take care of you, not on a timed shopping spree. Things like bill paying and big items may take some easing into at first. It's up to you to get a feel for this man's personality and how far you can push him and how fast.

♥ **Don't Go Soft & Don't Get Lazy**

You're only human. You will start to like this guy, enjoy your with him time, and possibly feel guilty about getting him to trick or sponsor you, and thus settle for being treated. You're still using these Ho Tactics, but you've lost your nerve and settle for dinner dates and vacations with him. If you want to be a kept woman who gets the bare minimum that's on you, but if you go this far, why not get what you actually want. This isn't about your friendship; he can be your friend for the rest of your life, but the window to get tricked on may disappear. A trick is still a man, and in the end, if this guy has shown you that he's an easy mark to hustle, do you think you're going to be able to keep him from the next Ho?

The moment you get lazy, stop going after your goal, or get into a sexual relationship, it exposes you. **Your mark loves you, but he will get bored, and he will always have eyes for other women.** Most tricks aren't monogamous to begin with, and while you didn't care about other women when you were digging for gold, they will become public enemy #1 after you decided to make a trick into your bae. Another Ho will get in his ear, offer him something new and different from you, and now he can't pay your Obamacare every month because he has to take care of his new Ho. That mark will start telling you "no" because he only has it to give to that new Ho and can't afford both of you. If you're going to go down this road, you must stay in shape emotionally or you've wasted your time.

#11:
Revenge Hoing

If a man breaks your heart and you want to get revenge on all males by toying with the next man that asks for your phone number, that's your prerogative. If your ex-boyfriend is playing games with you and you want to use the bond you've already established to run up his credit cards under the pretense of getting back together, that's your right. Most women aren't manipulative or money hungry, but a lot of them take on that role once they've been wronged. If you're one of these seasonal women who irrationally say shit like, "fuck men, I'm about to get all in their pockets," make sure you're cold enough to live with that decision because this isn't a game. **Angry women are messy, and when you get messy you get exposed.** A man who catches you red handed won't be as forgiving as one that was hypnotized into giving on his own.

Emotionally unstable girls who want to play in the big leagues don't last because revenge sex and attention whoring aren't Ho Tactics. Hos have issues like all people, but they have more in common with Stock Brokers. They aren't crying out for help, they're dedicated to getting paid and advancing in life by any means necessary.

If you are damaged and think using Ho Tactics will make you happy, or if you want to get revenge on the male species for all the pain they have put you through, then you are going to fail. Women are emotional creatures, most react with feelings as opposed to logic, and that's where relationship blunders happen. You can't afford to make blunders with Ho Tactics like you do with boyfriends. You are dealing with men that may resort to all kinds of craziness if they feel as if you've blatantly robbed them. Clear thoughts lead to clean getaways! You can Ho for revenge, but the revenge can't be the goal, the money or material is the goal. That sounds simple but it's hard to grasp when you're raging with anger.

You don't care about getting in his pockets; you care about letting him know that you got in his pockets by using devious methods. That line of thinking will doom you from the start. An angry female will not be content until the man that scorned her knows what happened. To get away with the proverbial crime will not bring her satisfaction, she has to let him know the full scope of her plan or there is no joy. No matter how good you may think it feels to go Angela Basset[10] and set his shit on fire after you've used him, it's juvenile. Regardless of how satisfied you may feel posting screenshots after you get away with hitting a lick that tried to play you, it's dangerous. Do not do a victory dance. Do not rub it in his face. Do not go back and inform people he knows about how you just hustled him. Don't gossip in group chat or at work in the lunch room. There is nothing to prove to anyone outside the situation, so while it may feel gratifying at first, know that it is better to walk away having won, then live watching your back.

---

[10] The classic empowerment scene from *Waiting to Exhale* showed Basset's character setting fire to her cheating husband's car, forever inspiring the "exhilaration of revenge" stereotype.

Ho Fail

One of the women who was instrumental in introducing me to some of the more successful Ho game practitioners was a girl I'll call Tanya because that's not even close to her real name. Tanya was on the treat level and was really trying to find a way to step her game up. One night, Tanya emailed me about an NFL player who was well known. She was excited to share the story of how she lured him into her web and was about to pull off a grand hustle. I was hoping that she would pull the hustle off so I could put it in the book, but that was the last I heard from her. Even when I sent her the original EBook, she didn't respond.

Recently I had a phone conversation with one of her associates who gave me the entire tragic run down. Tanya did, in fact, get involved with an elite NFL player, and she did manage to get him open to a point. Apparently, two months in Tanya was only getting treated, and knowing that this man had it to give she got impatient. As I said before, it is better to walk away than to get desperate, but I think Tanya's insecurity got the best of her. Keep in mind, I've met this woman in person and she is a solid ten, but she wasn't able to do what those other two women she introduced me to could do because she didn't have the mind or discipline for tricks or sponsors, only treaters. Again, it's a case of "I look better than them, why should I have to put in as much work." Tanya's ego made her concoct the stupidest idea you can think of if you're trying to get paid. She had sex with the NFL player in an attempt to get pregnant. After months of being friends with benefits and eventually getting him to have sex with no protection, Tanya gets pregnant, but in an even stupider move, she tries to use the pregnancy to blackmail him.

I'm not sure of the real amount, but for the sake of a reference number, let's say it was 10 thousand. In exchange for this money, she would have an abortion, and be out of his life forever. The NFL player agreed, and sent one of his goons to give her the hush money the day of the procedure, with orders to wait and make sure she went through with it. Tanya was driven home by the girl that was telling me this story. This woman wasn't her real friend, Tanya was paying her to drive because she was too ashamed to tell any of her real friends. Tanya kept playing with the money, saying how dumb the guy was, and how he shouldn't have tried to play her like some groupie, etc... As they pulled up to Tanya's home, the goon who had handed her the money earlier and a few other guys yanked Tanya from the car, took the money back, and waved a gun in her face daring her to make an issue of it. The funniest part of the story was this girl who was driving, a brilliant Ho in her own right, stops the guys and explains that she was owed some money by Tanya. These fools paid her! Tanya is still alive and kicking, but she's not talking to me or anyone else about the Ho life because she got burnt. It wasn't enough to get treated for months and move on, this girl was so money hungry that she tried to literally rob a man, and that shit came back to bite her.

No matter if it's a mark, an ex-boyfriend, or a co-worker who you want to Regina George[11], let it go. You can't force anyone to give you anything! You may laugh at Hoing being considered an art form, but it really is a skill that takes practice, focus, and discipline. Further proof of this, is that the Ho who told me this story, is currently milking that same NFL player and unlike Tanya, it took her less than a month to get him spending on the trick level. Intelligence, strategy, patience, foresight... those are the pillars of Ho Tactics, don't blow it by being emotional or undisciplined.

---

[11] Regina George is the lead antagonist from the film *Mean Girls*. A movie every Ho should own.

#12:
Exit Strategy

What if Maria falls in love with her mark, what if she finds a trick that proves to be her equal or falls for a sponsor that has just gotten divorced and is ready to have more than just a trophy that he spoils? You can't predict which way the heart will lead you, but you have to keep this strictly business. The moment you allow your mind to race to that fairytale land where Edward the emotionally detached millionaire drives up in the limo, faces his fear of heights, and sweeps Vivian the whore off her feet, you will start to focus on that more than your come up. If you want love, then you don't need Ho Tactics, you need to Spartan Up and find a real man who you build and prosper with—go read *Men Don't Love Women Like You*. This is the Ho world, you want money, you want to be pampered, you want to become successful using the finances or fame of someone else; therefore, you must always put money over dick, play your position, and commit to that way of thinking. This man isn't a potential boyfriend or husband, he's a trick, and even if he settles down with you, he'll always have trick blood in his veins, and that means you become a woman that can be replaced by a younger, prettier, and smarter Ho.

I'm sure the biggest follow-up question will still be, "People change, and I know I could keep him from wondering if we were to be in a real relationship," That's admirable and there are countless cases of tricks who settled for a woman that started off as a Ho working him. Hos do evolve into housewives like those I wrote about in *Solving Single* because they are real people that have skill sets that will always make them fun to be around regardless if they are on the clock or retired. You will find a husband, you will find a boyfriend, and you will find love, but I ask that you wait until you retire from Hoing or pick someone you didn't start out hustling. If NBA players can fall in love with groupies, then Hos, who are much smarter than those starfuckers, have the ability to capture a baller's heart for the long run as well. However, it should be a real love, not a long-term hustle because you got comfortable and didn't want to let go of your mark. Chapter 18: How to Go from Ho to Housewife covers this best-case scenario retirement, but let's focus on the normal Ho exit strategy for the following two scenarios...

Exit #1:
You got everything you need and want to move on.

Exit #2:
You hit a wall and he got cheap on you suddenly.

Your Ho hustle should last until you get those things you wrote down at the beginning of this journey, but in case of emergency, you must be ready to walk away with nothing. When you have milked this man for everything you wanted, begin to lay the seeds of discontent. Fake arguments where you make him out to have offended you or pressured you will put the "break up" on him and give you an out without having to be the bad guy. Reverse psychology continues to be your best friend when pushing a man away: He's been acting distant. All he does is pressure you for sex. He doesn't act the same as he did when you first met. It's all bullshit, but when you say it with conviction a man will think, "damn, am I doing those things?" There are all kinds of mindfucks you can pull off that make it seem as if you two are no good for each other, but remember that your Ho power can boomerang. This man is most likely so smitten that he will try to make it up to you no matter if your excuse is real or fantasy. A mark knows what you react to— gifts. He will keep trying to buy you back, which means you must be prepared to walk away without being overly greedy. You got what you came for; just because he's dangling a matching Rolex if you stay doesn't mean you circle back. If you circle back once, you will do it twice, and at that point, a man knows he has power over your exit.

The best way to end a relationship with a mark is to borrow a page out of a man's book and slow fade out of existence. **You've gotten busy with work; you're going through family troubles, or the classic excuse that you need space.** Excuses once again become your friend and doing things slowly will help you milk car payments or things he's already promised to give you. Eventually, he'll stop helping you out altogether, but sometimes it's better to let a relationship like this decay than to decapitate it. From an emotional standpoint the more you distance yourself the less in love he will be with that fun Ho side because he's not seeing it anymore. This frees this trick up to go find someone to replace you, and like all men, once he has a new hobby, you will be forgotten and free to go on to your next hustle without him annoying you with "I miss you" texts.

It could get tense once he sees the writing on the wall while still infatuated with you. He may take inventory of all the things he's done for you and realize he got gamed. Indian giving is legit, and a heartbroken man may look up past bills, feel dumb, and want to let you know that you aren't shit. I remind you that he can't take you to court for receiving gifts; the judge will laugh his dumb ass out of the courtroom. A mark won't want to tell the world that he got hustled either, so don't worry about him popping up at your job or blasting you on the internet, but he can yell at you one on one and try to break you down in order to get satisfaction. Don't argue with a trick that becomes bitter and don't be a Tanya and reveal your hustle out of anger or confrontation.

When a trick tries to throw all the stuff he's done for in your face, play offended. Remind him that he did those things willingly, that he was supposed to be your friend, and continue to make him feel guilty about insinuating that it was all a hustle. **This isn't to get back with him; it's to leave him doubting that you were indeed a Ho.** He may have come to his senses after seeing the receipts for the last four months, but so long as you maintain your humanity, he will always have doubt. After this man cools down, he'll most likely second guess his own anger and go back to thinking you were the best woman he ever had. Eventually, he will forget about the things he spent money on and become fixated on how much fun he had with you. The money is never important, the memory is what stays! If he has doubts that you were a Ho that means the doors to his heart and wallet are still cracked open, and maybe in a year you can come back in and re-up with this mark for something new.

Regardless of how you leave it, by making him seem like an asshole, by slow fading from his world, or by running out of his life the moment you get discovered, the point is to understand that all good hustles come to an end. This lifestyle is built on too many lies to keep it going forever. Don't get greedy and don't revert to a love-sick basica who wants to turn a mark into a long-term savior. Recognize when you've won or when you can't get anything from this man, and walk away.

Why Ho Serious

The key to the first part of this book is not to have sex, not even after you get what you want unless he's a man you would have sex with for free under normal circumstances. Literally, ask yourself, "Would I fuck him if he hadn't spoiled me?" If you even have to consider this for half a second, then you have no business having sex or giving him the pussy as the ultimate reward. Guilt prostituting is still prostituting. There are dozens of Gold-Digging 101 books or Sugar Baby manuals these days, nearly all written by women who sleep with men for money. That's not hustling, that's trafficking. I felt a duty to share this information in a way that promotes the intelligent clothes on method over the clothes off escorting that causes you to sell your soul instead of your company. Men will only give so much without getting what they want, but the genius of Hos (not an oxymoron) is that they move so stealthily that by the time a man realizes what's going on they've already won, and moved on. This part of the book is all you need to achieve your mission. No sex, no oral favors, no taking your clothes off, period.

As we move into the second part things become more sexual orientated because most women aren't dick disciplined or they reach a level where they no longer feel like making excuses about sex. Having sex can get you a lot more over a longer period, but it's a gamble dependent on how good you are in bed. There will be much to learn in terms of using sex as a weapon, and how to turn old pussy into new money, but again, this first part of the book is the safest! You can use these tactics to be a serial Ho or hit one lick up and be done with that lifestyle; it's your life to live. I only ask that you stay smart, keep your panties up, and never fall in love with your trick. For the rest of you who don't mind using sex, then continue reading because the hunt is about to get nasty…

Part Two:

The Power of Sex Magic

"Though men may be deep,

mentally they are slow."

-Camille Pagli

#13:

You Had Sex Too Fast...
Now What?

After reading the first part of *Ho Tactics*, women run into one of two problems. The first being the inability to muster up the confidence needed to approach a potential trick and begin their journey down the rabbit hole. As I wrote at the end of part one, this life isn't for everyone, and there have been numerous readers who enjoyed learning these tactics but have been honest enough to write in and tell me that they don't have the heart or the stomach to do half of what Maria did. That's fine; don't feel bad or pressured to Ho Up. The average person can watch a documentary on someone like Madonna and enjoy her rags to riches story, but in a moment of realness will admit, "I sing better and would love to rise to that level of greatness, but I would never have the courage to move to the big city with no income and hustle the way she did." Fear is a cage that few people completely break free of, but you can win small victories over self-limitation with these techniques. "How do I become more confident," by doing the things you're afraid or too shy to do naturally by substituting your persona for Maria's.

The best Non-Ho response I've received was from a woman in her 40's who says that she now pumps herself up to speak to a man first by thinking, "Act like a Ho for the first five minutes, and he won't be able to resist me." She isn't looking for marks, she wants love, but because she learned Ho Tactics she will never be afraid to flirt or pull a guy again. That power, above all, is the liberation I hope most of you received from reading the first half of this book. If you have to be an actress, fake true confidence, or put on a mask when talking to strangers, do so until the role playing becomes role living.

The second problem women have been running into is much more dangerous, and the reason I felt it necessary to expand these lessons. There are females who are great at talking, flirting, and seducing men. These ladies get into a man's head, are treated a little bit, but during a moment of weakness, they give into their hormones and have sex with their mark. Someone told me, "The flesh is weak, and it's impossible for me to hold out until I get even half the things I want to get from a man if I find him attractive." **The flesh is only as weak as your mind allows you to believe.** I won't revisit the topic of being disciplined around dick because reading isn't the same as being powerful enough to pull off the waiting game.

You had sex. Let's start right there. Does this mean all of these Ho Tactics are now unusable? Have you blown your chance at that condo on the North Side, the chance of getting those school loans paid off, or even an opportunity to be taken out on a nice date again? No! The only disadvantage to having sex is that you lose the mystique of how good your pussy is. A man will do virtually anything just to see what you're working with. As I discussed before it's not the actual tightness, wetness, or warmness of your vagina that he's after, it's that allure of the mystery that makes his heart race. The moment you have sex that question mark has been removed from the box, and like a little boy who rips open that gift on Christmas morning, he's either excited to keep playing with you the next day... or over it.

You can never get that mystery back, and unlike the pre-sex Ho hustle, you have zero leverage going forward. Stop sucking your teeth and feeling sad like you just broke the heel on your favorite pair of Aldos because I'm still going to show you how to upgrade to Jimmy Choo. I'm going to help you turn a fuck up into a victory by repackaging your pussy game, flirt game, and seduction techniques in a way you could have never done before you let him hit. Before we get into the sexual tricks, let's go back to the fundamentals. I will give two jumping on points. The first relates to those women who got caught up while trying to pull off Ho Tactics. The second revolves around those who are trying Ho Tactics for the first time with an ex-boyfriend or guy from the past that has already sampled.

The Girl Who Fucked Her Trick

Let's say you made it through the research dates, you got him to treat you, give a small gift, and just when you were about to sink your teeth in, you got too drunk and ended up bent over the ottoman. The morning after, you're thinking, "It's all good, I gave him a little bit of loving, but I didn't put it on him like I know I can or show any of my nasty tricks." Men don't give a fuck about what you have up your sleeves. To have fucked you once is to have won the championship. Guys don't need to score 40 points, be the MVP, or score at the buzzer to feel like they've won. Your pussy was the trophy, doesn't matter how it came about, the ultimate victory is now his. The first step to salvage your fuck up is to confront your mistake as if it was planned.

♥ He Didn't Catch You Slipping, You Were Rewarding

The worst thing a woman can do is play coy about the fact that she had sex as if she's an embarrassed 11th grader who did something wrong. There is something about giving it up that creates this feeling of guilt or shame in most women, no matter who the guy is or how comfortable she is with him. You must not give into the basic idea of, "Damn, maybe I shouldn't have done that!" The damage is done, so going forward you must rewire your brain into putting sex on the front page as opposed to holding it in as subtext that you two don't bring up. The day after sex, call him. Don't text, don't go meet up for a rematch, call him the same way you've been doing during your set bonding time. The first words after, "How was your day," should be about your pussy. Did he like how mommy put it on him, was he thinking about it, did he wait long to shower, or did he want to keep that smell on his dick? Be funny or go as nasty as you're comfortable going, but put it on Front Street within 24 hours or it becomes awkward.

Next up, distance yourself from any thoughts he has that you were trying to game him with Ho Tactics. Get into his head, "I haven't given it up that fast since college... You do something to me, baby... Don't think I'm going to start acting like a typical female now, we're still us..." Those points are crucial to get across, no matter how you verbalize it. The mindfucking of this man continues as you go from dangling your pussy to using the reverse psychology suggestion that he's turning you out. Men don't trust women, but they do trust Hos, because Hos know how to turn suspicion into trust quicker than Jesus turned water into wine.

If you were a Ho, you would have gotten more than a pair of headphones before you fucked. If you were thirsty for a relationship, you'd be acting different and asking about, "where's this going?" If you were a slut, you'd be acting like the sex was nothing and that's just how you get down. This is Psychology 101, know what a man thinks, and confront those thoughts to alleviate the paranoia. You're answering all his questions before he even thinks of them, and by doing this kind of damage control you make him comfortable and put his doubts to rest. Be a step ahead of his thoughts. This is how you outsmart a man you've accidentally fucked.

♥ **The Sex Was Okay, Not Good Or Great**
How you talk about his dick game is crucial to keeping him hovering around. I don't care if he made you cum three times or if he came after four pumps and disappointed you, play your position that his sex game was "okay". This goes back to being able to talk about sex instead of ignoring. Make a point to tease him about likes and dislikes. Men are controlled by ego. "Don't take this the wrong way, babe, but it felt like you were holding back, next time I want you to go all out." You must guarantee a rematch by challenging his manhood. Don't insult his penis size or how long he lasted, be aloof about what you did, or didn't like, i.e. "holding back." The positive is that you had fun; the negative is that you know he can go harder than that next time. Be a middle school teacher that rubs her student on the shoulder to instill confidence that his next science project will be better. If you praise a man too much, he becomes complacent. If you put him down, he becomes ashamed and may not want to risk another bad performance.

Find your balance somewhere in the middle, and this will create a new sense of want. His performance was a seven, better than your last (lie if you must) but not as good as your best dick… yet. There's room for improvement, and you know he can do it with the tool he has, so you desperately want him to show and prove.

♥ **It's Not His Pussy, But Pretend It Is**
The phone sex techniques we practiced before and all the nasty seduction skills that you only got to use a few times, you can now amp up. The biggest change is that you must pretend as if he has controlling shares of your pussy. It's not his, nor will it ever be his, but to keep him invested, he has to think he's the CEO of your coochie. **"*She* misses you," are three words that will have a man instantly hard.** Say it early and often. You're not his girlfriend, nor do you want to be, but allude that your pussy is reserved for him. When a man feels as if you are is his property, he has an incentive to stick around.

♥ **Talk About Last Time, Fantasize About Next Time**
We will get into sexual specifics in the following chapters, but one of the last things to remember is to get back to teasing him the same as you did before you two had sex. The first time was a demo, so when you speak about it, always add in what you can't wait to do the next time he, "gets to see HIS pussy again." If you only did missionary, joke about how you hope he can last as long hitting it from the back. If you did all three positions, fantasize about how one day you'd love to feel how that dick feels raw. The mission is to get him more excited for the second time than he was for the first session.

#14:
Using Ho Tactics
On Your Ex-Boyfriend

How do I turn my ex into a trick or sponsor when he's already had me?

I reconnected with a friend from high school that's now doing well, how can I seduce him when he's already sampled the goodies?

Men from the past will pop in and out of your life, and for most women, these men who they are already comfortable around will be the easiest to hustle. Unlike going to happy hour or perusing the local Best Buy, there are no nerves holding you back from speaking first if you see your high school sweetheart in public or from inboxing that guy you slept with twice in college. With an ex-boyfriend, co-worker, or random one-night stand from the past, you are already familiar enough to be confident. **If it has been several years since you were last intimate with this past guy, then everything in part one can be used without much change.** However, if it's been two years or less, the man you're sizing up will most likely be content with the fact that he conquered you, so it will take more effort to lure him back into the Ho Tactics web. Let's face it; it's probably a slim chance that your personality or vagina has gotten any better in such a short period. That's where you prove him wrong.

♥ **You're Not That Little Girl, You're A Woman Now**
Let's imagine that your ex-boyfriend Maurice bumps
into you at a mutual friend's cookout. It's been a year
and a half since you ended your three-month
relationship, and no one has a reason to harbor ill
feelings. Like most exes you see, you give him a hug,
pretend to be happy to see him, and make the
mandatory, "you're looking good" comment regardless
if you mean it or not. Who cares how his mother is
doing, you need to see if this dude can benefit your life.

Using your newfound Ho Powers, interrogate
him to find out where he's working these days and
where he's living. The Maurice you knew was working a
good job, but it wasn't great, so has his fortunes
changed? If he's still complaining about working at the
same dead-end job or still trying to make waves using
that same tired business plan that he's been trying to get
off the ground for years, then he's not worth more than
two minutes of your time. If he's still living at the same
apartment or still bunking with his mom or that
roommate he hates, again, he's not worth your time.
**What you want to hear is that he's at a new company,
invested in a new venture, or living in the good part of
the city.** Non-Hos who are looking for love have a weak
spot for ex-boyfriends because they are now lonely and
look back with rose-colored lenses at the good times. It's
in your best interest to separate the boyfriend thirst from
your mind so you don't end up catching feelings for
someone you once cared for. This man is a mark, not
your baby, not the one that got away, simply a mark.

Once you two have caught up and enough to see
that he's indeed winning at life, pretend to be open.
Unlike guys you haven't had sex with, men that have hit

need their egos stroked as opposed to challenged. Be impressed that he's doing it big; even make a comment such as, "Damn, I fucked up." This type of pandering will leave this fool with his chest poked out while grinning from ear to ear. Don't blow this opportunity by catching up for too long, remember, your job is to get this man in an intimate setting where you can seduce him properly and continue to research his funds.

Exchange numbers or emails without ever asking if he has a girlfriend or wife. If he wants you to know that, he'll say it. If he's hesitant to take your number because of a "Her" in his life, channel Maria the Ho and tease him about being afraid of you. Most likely, he will give you a way to contact him, and that's all you need. **Once you are back in his life, move fast!** Within two days, reach out and set a date, even offer to treat him. Remember, he has to see you as different, not just some ex trying to get a free meal.

It's only been a year and a few months since he last dealt with you, but you're a new woman, no longer that littler girl. You can't say this; you show this by going left where you used to go right. Do your research internally. All the conversations you used to have, the arguments, even the TV shows you used to watch, you must now upgrade it. You shouldn't even cross your legs and hold your fork the same. This man must see that you're the 2.0 version. Bring up your past relationship in a fun way. I don't care if he cheated on you, called you out your name, or simply vanished without explanation—forget it. You don't care about revenge; you care about advancing your life using his money or means, so don't get emotional or vengeful like some basic bitch amateur.

Reminisce on the good times you had, and keep him laughing and smiling as if you two had that Ross and Rachel[12] friendship. If you hit all the marks I listed during this first date, he won't see you as his ex-girlfriend; you're essentially a new woman by which he's extremely intrigued. At that point, you have done your job, which is hitting reset on your entire personality and allure.

♥ **Sudden Case of Sex Amnesia**
Another point that can be stressed on the reconnection date or soon thereafter is the history of sex. No matter if you had sex every weekend for months or only a few times, you can't remember it. You think about him, and maybe you've tried to fantasize about that sex, but nothing comes up. To prove this point, start to plant false memories about the time you did it in a hotel. He'll be quick to remind you that you have the wrong guy. Go further and really fuck with his head by giving him a trait you know he didn't have. For example, his curve penis stays in your mind… he doesn't have a curved dick, and he'll get pissed because you really don't remember. Offer up an apology and admit that you can't be wrong because you've only had sex with one (never go over two) other guy since you were last together.

With his feelings a little hurt, seduce him by letting him know you still have a weakness for him. "It'll always be kinda yours…" said with a smirk is better than stroking his dick under the table. Once again, men respond to control, and you're putting him back in

---

[12] Ross and Rachel were characters from the TV show *Friends*, that had a turbulent but loving on again off again relationship.

a throne he probably thought he would never get to return to. The key to this tease is to make him feel safe. Men who go back to exes want to reminisce not rekindle. Most of you have probably experienced that feeling for yourself, where you don't really like that old thing, but you sort of miss the sex part and even the conversations because it's a comfort food. Know that a man that had you is most likely trying to get the easy nostalgia sex and is afraid that you may want to work it out again as opposed to rolling around for old times' sake, which is why the next step after going *Eternal Sunshine of the Spotless Mind* in terms of sex is to make yourself off limits romantically.

Talk about how you don't really date much, and this outing is the first in about a month. Remark on the state of men and how they are just so corny. **Nothing endears a man to you by making him seem as if he's cut from a different cloth than the rival males in the world.** At the end of the date or talk, follow up by telling him how good a time you had, and that if he promises not to get all serious, you would love to be "friends." See what happened there? You are spelling it out for him that you don't want him as a boyfriend, just a fun friend… possibly with benefits. Like all Ho Tactics, going left when typical women go right, will impress this man and put you at the top of his list. His want is sex and his fear is being back with you. By taking that fear off the table you become desirable.

♥ **Hooking Him**

You can only tease a person you've already been with for so long before they get flustered. Unlike part one, you aren't risking anything by having sex with him, the damage is done. However, there are circumstances he must meet, he doesn't get to pick up where he left off. To go in there as if nothing changed is a quick way to get fucked and sent to voicemail. The most crucial part of any of these tactics is getting emotionally close and mixing it with a carefree good time. Your ex-boyfriend probably has a girlfriend or someone looking for that title. You have to be the opposite of her, all fun with no stress. We will get into the ins and outs of sexual manipulation in the next chapter, but before you get back to fucking him, you must show him this new Ho side to make him fall back in lust with you. This includes being down to go out whenever, talking nasty, listening to his complaints, and keeping secrets.

Two to three weeks of squeezing your way back into his life in this unique and exciting way will cause him drop his guard enough for you to gain his trust. Only at the height of his vulnerability, for example, him confessing new feelings for you or calling you more than once a day, should you agree to have sex. Be patient in your seduction and remember that talking about sex while being a casual friend will mind fuck him! Do not make a serious bedroom move until he sees you as someone he really needs in his life and can admit to it. If it's been two weeks and he's not really opening up or confiding in you about his life, then abort. A man that doesn't communicate doesn't trust you and isn't invested, so your chances of using him as a walking PayPal are slim. Once you hook him with the 2.0 version of you, move on to the next chapter and learn the power of reupholstered pussy.

#15:
Turning Old Pussy into New Money

Is sex all a woman is good for? Of course not. As a female, you can fill a Wikipedia page with all the qualities that make you more than a hole whose purpose is to supply a man with a good nut. However, you set yourself up for failure if you don't acknowledge how the opposite sex views you in their head. When a man first spots you, the want to have sex with you is the glue that makes him notice you in a room full of others, pay attention during conversation, and attempt to impress you. What does he want from you, why is he being nice to you, why is he joking around with you—sex is the magnet! The more you dangle this fantasy over his head, the more a man will salivate. Smart Hos dangle the *Coochie Carrot* so close that a man can smell it, literally, knowing that a man who gets worked up with lust will be putty in her hands. Lust driven men will do anything to seal the deal. Take you out, buy you things, promise their intentions are honest, be on their best behavior for months, even commit to a monogamous relationship.

Nevertheless, lust for sex is not the same as love for a woman, but a hard-pressed man will make you into a believer. Naïve women give in to lust courting because they feel wanted as if it were true love, but after a man has sex with a girl; she loses that initial New Pussy Power. **Men can be Hos too, and most of them apply Dick Tactics during the lust courting stage, stooping to all kinds of devious tricks just to get a few minutes of sexual pleasure.** *Why did he lie, I would have still had sex if he told the truth*. Maybe you would have, maybe not. Men don't have time to take chances, so they make up false lives, withhold relationship status, and create elaborate excuses to keep you in check. Men crossed the morality line centuries ago, and since then it has been in their best interest to play this pussy hustle game to keep women easy prey. Men are so good at this that even those women that have read the first part of Ho Tactics have fallen for Dick Tactics and given in to their sexual desires.

Some women take that to mean that they ruined their chances and that all the things they read are now worthless because of one horny mistake. False! You can still apply everything you learned, be it with an ex-boyfriend or a mark that outsmarted you in a moment of weakness. Let's go back to who you are as a person. Is your personality electrifying like Maria or are you dry as hell? If you're shy, demure, and boring then a man will shrug you off as soon as he wakes up from his post nut slumber. Your personality wasn't what was driving him to call and take you out; it was your unexplored pussy that had him blowing up your phone and dying to see you. Only after sex can he lay in bed the next night by himself and be honest about how he views you—"She's not all that." Hos are always "all that" because they operate on the mental plane more so than the physical. Some of you mistake these tactics for learning how to lie and be fake. False! It's strategy dependent on knowing how men think before and after sex.

Hos exploit lust courting because they recognize that it's all a male game. Even after sex, they can still regain their balance like Gabby Douglas teetering on that beam. The secret weapon isn't to have more sex or cross the line into fetish sex; it's the ability to go beyond the physical, and jerk a man off mentally to the point of no return. It's no longer about the mystery of your box; it's about the magic inside. Any smart person understands that real magic is nothing more than a well-executed illusion.

You All Fuck the Same

All women fuck the same way. Yes, even you Ms. "I made him cum in 13 seconds" and you Ms. "All I did was let him stick the tip in and zzzzz," your vaginas don't do anything new or innovative. The same way you ride dick, your grandmother rode dick. The same way you slurp on a penis head will be just as effective as the way your niece will slurp on one after prom in five years. Don't suck your teeth or search your phone for some guy to prove that I'm wrong because any man that has fucked you or wants to, will side with you having a magical pussy. Unlike men, there is no "bigger is better" or "motion in the ocean" debate with women. Tight vagina or loose vagina doesn't even matter because Kegels or six months of penis detox can get you back to 22-year-old pussy status. You can ride it from the back, front, sit on furniture, bend over backseats, or dig nails into his back, but what you are doing can be replicated by any woman that has seen porn. It's time to step up your sex game and show him something those other bitches can't do!

Every girl has made a man cum quick. Every girl has had a man call her "the best." It's common because men are easy to please and gross exaggerators when in the grip of ecstasy. Instead of tooting your horn about how fast you made some lame bust a nut, figure out how you can further separate yourself from the pack.

I'm not referring to gimmicks like toys or squirting, I'm talking about what you do before, during, and after sex to set this man on fire! In the kingdom of shy submissive, *lay me on my back and give it to me*, women—the verbalizer is Queen. Hos aren't afraid to talk. Not only does this help when it comes time to walk over and pull a mark or ask for favors from a trick, it sets her apart from the average boring lay. This isn't about talking dirty; that's only one aspect of Ho sex game. To conquer his mind and become the most memorable sex ever, you have to set him up then finish him with certain techniques. What are these before, during, and after techniques? I'm glad you asked.

- ♥ **Pre-Sex Promotion**
  What's the most important thing about a championship fight? It's not the fighters or the venue; it's the hype leading up to the fight that determines if a man travels to see that Mayweather fight versus streaming it for free. Life is built on the foundation of unique experiences, and fight promoters understand that "once in a lifetime" or the feeling that anything can happen, is a selling point that can't be beat. New Pussy IS hype; it's all buildup, and even if that girl is a corny lay, the man still feels like it was time well spent because it was a new conquest. Again, men aren't picky, ejaculating feels good—always. So even if it was too fast, awkward, or just vanilla, he's going to leave smiling. Now you're going to use his bias against him. Once you cross over

into the Old Pussy side of the field, you must sell the old not as if it's new, but as if it's going to be better than the first time. The next time this guy sees you is WrestleMania, and even though he's experienced The Rock Vs. Stone Cold once before, you must make him feel it in his soul that this time is going to blow the roof off!

We've already been over the "It wasn't that good, it could be better" rhetoric; this is much different. You can continue to tease a man before you meet, but that's not going to drive him crazy enough to start tricking as if he's never tasted you before. The true promotion begins the second time you decide to fuck him. Most women have sex spontaneously, they rarely plan to give it to a man; they just plan when they are not going to give to him. Sure, they shave their coochies in a loose preparation, but most girls play the bystander, simply waiting for a man to go for it. You can no longer play by the shy rules of "Maybe I'll give him some if the night goes well." Be in control! Your job is to set the time and place, then go about the promotion so by the time the night arrives he's worked up to the point of combustion.

Let's say this second sex session is going to go down on a Friday. That Tuesday you set the date and start to promote it as one where he should plan to stay out all night. Thursday, you confirm it and tell him you went shopping for underwear. That Friday morning you make the final push by teasing him in a way where it makes it seems like you're beyond excited. This could be sending a picture of you sucking a banana talking about, "Training for our date." It could be sending a screen grab from a porn movie or a ratchet sex meme. **Men are extremely easy to seduce via sexual visuals, so go for**

the kill as soon as you wake up, and he's going to be thirsting the rest of the day. That's 3 and a half days of ego stroking, sex teasing, and genuine mind-fucking. Doesn't matter if he's already started to feel as if you're not all that or if he's a busy man who plans on standing you up, he will be at that date with bells on because you've once again made your vagina a special attraction.

The last stage before the bedroom is to talk to him before he leaves the house, or you leave your home to meet, then threaten to pull out. A man doesn't know how bad he wants a woman until she's pulled from under him. Tease him that you're not going to meet up tonight, and make up a legit excuse. Don't joke, get into it as if you may not come… then reveal that you're punking him at the moment where he's about to say, "Man, fuck you!" He'll breathe a sigh of relief, and then you can work him back up. Escalate the build up by acting out a real-life fantasy. If you two are going to meet at your place, then you're already playing with yourself and asking, "Do you think you can make me cum before you get here?" If he's at his place and you're driving over, give him play by play about how you're fingering yourself in traffic. The point is to get in his head and make him reveal how much he wants what you are promising him. Once you know that he's really invested, get nasty and creative in order to push him to his limit before the date even begins.

♥ *Don't Just Jam It In There*
Men love to be worked up, but they hate foreplay. The only reason the majority of males even go through the motions of taking it slow is that society has forced it on us harder than an Iggy Azalea song. Cinemax after dark

movies showed little boys that they needed to suck and rub until a woman is in full blow moan… Silk sang slow jams about licking a girl up and down until she said, "Stop!" Growing up I thought you had to do those things to get a woman wet, this idea that a woman can walk into a room already soaking was foreign. So, if you don't need a man to build you up, why waste time? Your job is to create the illusion that you are the fantasy of all fantasies. Foreplay is good, but it's usually for the benefit of the female orgasm.

Again, your job is to be for his benefit, so you become invaluable going forward. Ice cubes, stomach licking, cock stroking… those are typical things women like to do to turn on a man. Nearly every man has had whipped cream sprayed on him because it's a movie cliché. Ever sit in a hair salon and hear that older woman tell freaky stories about the things she does to men? It's greeted with blushing because 90% of women are following the same turn-on playbook. That playbook is bullshit! For this sex date you must become that 10% of women that innovates.

I remember the only girl to suck my toes. I don't remember all the routine blowjobs I've had over the years, but I remember the girl that slapped her face with that spit-soaked dick while talking filthy. I also remember the girl that ran to her purse, got her vibrator, and told me to go harder while she played with her clit. They weren't Hos, but they made an impression because they did something different. When you're dealing with a well-off man who is most likely in his late 20's on up, he's not going to be impressed by giving him impassioned head. Fingering your vagina won't raise an eyebrow the same way as if you were to finger your ass then suck your fingers would. There are levels to nastiness, but all you need to do is pull ONE rabbit out of the hat for him to be like, "Damn, she's a freak." Remember this is a guy you've already had sex with, who has already judged you, who doesn't need your pussy. This date changes all of that. **Being overly filthy is important because it sets the limit at no limits.**

If you pull a dick out of the condom and rub the cum on your lips, next time you may tell him to remove the condom and cum in your mouth. If you're willing to accidentally lick near his ass while giving him a nut-to-shaft blowjob, the next time you may go full ass to mouth. This isn't about your sexual fantasy; it's about projecting his fantasy in order to cement the fact that if he keeps you around long enough, there is nothing your nasty ass won't do! What he doesn't know is that before you go to that next level of freakiness, you'll have gotten in his pockets.

♥ **Six Magic Words**

There is no blueprint for how to talk nasty during the act of sex. Each person reacts differently, and what a person does or doesn't react to is as personality driven as what they do or don't like on their pizza. I've listened to so-called sex experts mislead women by telling them to fake moan, not taking into account that some men are annoyed by over exaggerated moans or panting. The same goes for talking dirty, not all men are going to want to dominate you by calling you names like *bitch* or *whore*. Having sex is like playing an instrument; just because you've been playing piano since the age of sixteen doesn't mean you're going to make that guitar sing the first time you pick it up. **This is the second**

time having sex with this guy, which means it's time to do research on what he's into sexually. You must feel how his body reacts when you pull different sexual strings.

The bedroom is now your testing ground. If he's into the moan for the first five minutes, don't stay with it; yell out something nasty like, "Harder motherfucker!" If he gets excited, that was what he really wants. If he doesn't really respond to being dominating or you feel him turtle up with awkwardness, then go back to the moan. This is an exploration, test out the new then go back to the old if it's not working.

If the nasty yells don't move him, try the nasty whisper technique. In a low voice, similar to how you have phone sex, be submissive. If he speeds up or starts groaning, then that's his thing. Do you see what's going on? You're testing dominance, submission, and even the generic just lay there, corpse technique to see what he responds to the most. Do not be afraid to branch out and be creative. Sucking on your own nipples, rubbing your clit, squeezing his balls, those are all good things but don't forget to be verbal in some way.

What you want to get to are the six magic words that will make him happier than a Basic Bitch at a Gucci outlet. In your loud dominate voice, your whisper voice, or from the standard moan, you must say, *"You're about to make me cum!"* There is no man alive that won't upgrade his stroke or release the nut he's been holding back when he hears that. Predict when he's about to finish, and without overacting or sounding Jenna Jameson fake, hit him with, "You made me cum again." Contrary to popular belief, men don't just want a nut;

they want to make you nut because that's the ultimate pat on the back. I doubt that he makes you climax for real, but that isn't the point, it's the fantasy of satisfying you sexually that you want to get across. Make him finish up in a manner where he feels as if he owns your G-Spot. You don't do that with positions or toys, you do that with those six words.

♥ **Dick Appreciation**
Hos solidify their value after sex. Post-sex pillow talk finds a man at his most vulnerable if the sex was satisfying. Again, I'm not talking about whether or not he came, of course he came. What's satisfying is that he feels as if he turned you out by making you cum. The reason a man will get washed up and leave or give you a hint that he has to work in the morning and that you should leave is because he doesn't feel you're necessary anymore. **Pussy is worthless to a soft dick, so why would any man want to cuddle with Pussy once its job is done?** As a Smart Ho you built this man up, let him dominate your vagina, and now he's lying next to you with a smile, bathing in that glory. No man wants to leave when he feels like he's on top. This is where you get into his brain.

Tell him how you've never felt that kind of orgasm and that it must have been because your body was used to him this time around. All bullshit, but it makes this man think that he was the first to take you the top of Space Mountain. Once you pay homage to this imagined god sex, he will wind down and be as docile as a housewife on Quaaludes. It doesn't matter what you say specifically, the main point you need to get across is that you want the simplicity of what you just had. Make up a story about how your girlfriends always get attached after sex, they start tripping, and ruin a good thing. You want to assure this man that his sex and company is all you want: *Joke around, fuck like porn stars, and then chill.*

One Ho that I'm friends with told me that she plays video games with her trick because he loves that "one of the boys" feeling after fucking. That's what I mean by thinking outside of the box; sometimes just talking isn't good enough. Maybe you take something he's into and bring it up or do it afterward.

Don't try too hard because if you aren't into that it will seem fake. No matter if you want to grab that Xbox controller, build LEGOs or ask to turn on Sportscenter, you have to make sure that he's having a good time. A man won't remember your pussy twenty minutes later, but he will remember how much fun you were before, during, and after. Do not be afraid to stand out using the brainpower in your head as opposed to the flexibility in your legs.

Girl, He Got Money

Having sex is a gamble, unlike the tactics laid out in the first part of the book, this route is not guaranteed to make him trick. However, if you follow the sex promotion rule, get filthy in bed, and then lead this man to believe that he gave you the orgasm of your life, the odds are in your favor. The final step in getting back on track and making your old pussy even more desirable than before is to ration it out. No matter who else he's fucking or how busy he is, if you really put it on him the way I told you to put it on him, he will come running back for more.

The thought of you will make him hard, the sound of your voice will make him even harder... that's not from you touching him or saying anything perverted, it the result of his body becoming addicted to what you did to him during that second sex session. I've experienced this several times and couldn't understand what was going on. It wasn't love, and the lust shouldn't have been stronger than before since I already had her. What I failed to comprehend was that good sex isn't about the physical sex; it's about leaving a mental tattoo on the brain.

He can go have sex with another girl or watch porn, but his dick will not get as hard as it got with you. His blood will not race the same way it races when he looks at a picture of you. You are no longer a girl he had sex with; you are a Heroin fix that he needs an injection of to get back to normal. **What do you do with someone that's addicted to what you have to offer? You raise the price!** He got a few testers, now he has to spend. It's an unsaid rule that you don't barter like a prostitute, you ask with the underlying hint that if he doesn't look out for you, then you have nothing to talk about.

He will want to meet up with you within the next few days after you blew his mind. Be careful not to ask for things right after sex or even the day after. Post-sex favor asking only works once you establish in his mind that you're not Hoing. Asking for a couple hundred dollars for shoes right after he cums will raise suspicions. Suddenly needing money to get your car fixed the next day will make him delete your number. Do not rush this! He will push to have sex again, and when he does, establish the rules going forward.

If he wants to see you, say you want to see him too, but this time, you want to go out to a nicer place before going back to his place. <u>This is a test to see if the pussy was as good as you thought it was.</u> If he makes an excuse about just wanting to chill or being too tired to put in the effort to go out for real, decline his offer to chill and find an excuse to get off the phone. Remember, everything in this is about doing research before going for the kill! If your bedroom theatrics worked, he will fall in line and take you anywhere you want to go. If he gives you a "take it or leave it" attitude, then abort the mission. No matter how much sex you continue to have or how nasty you get, he's never going to spend on you because he's the type of man that is satisfied with having been inside you, not an addict that you can hook. As I said, it's a gamble, if you don't hook him, abort!

Let's assume that you did hook him. Once he agrees to treat you to a date, bring back the Dick Discipline. Do something nasty in public or in the car, to keep him worked up, but you must not have sex with him again that fast, or he'll think it will always come free. Over the course of the next few days is when you go for the smallest thing on your list and then build to the biggest. For example, if you ask for money for a spa day to prepare yourself for that date, and he gives you the run around, there will be no sex on that date. If he sends you the money or promises to give it to you when he sees you, and does, then that's as telling as the old Headphone test.

Sex is now a reward, never casual. Never shy away from punishing men. "He didn't give me spa money, but he may not like me if I don't have sex again on the next date." No Basica, that's not how it works. If he tells you "no" then you deny him. That way when you ask for something else, he will have to say "yes" because he just witnessed you turning him down on that date. Think don't just react like a rookie!

After he passes that first test you will know if he's a Trick, Treat, or Sponsor, so ask accordingly for what you want and don't shortchange yourself. Let's say he's a Trick, and you want a plane ticket to go spend the weekend with your girls in Miami. Plant a seed about this throughout your date or phone conversations. After the non-sex date, call him in trouble. You had to spend your paycheck getting your mother's water heater fixed, and now you can't go to Miami. Put on a Golden Globe worthy performance where you are so heartbroken about Miami that you don't want to talk, flirt, or have fun with him. Good time girl is now sad time girl. How can he get you back to the point where you're being fun and ready to have sex again? He must solve your problem!

Recap

Are you following? Hook him with epic sex. Test him out with a small favor to see if your sex worked. Reward him for giving, or punish him for not giving. Create a needy situation that requires him to save you, and then wait for him to offer. If he doesn't offer on his own, ask directly for that favor in the little sister way we went over earlier in the book. This is the first challenge to see if this man is going to be a benefactor or remain some treat who thinks he can hit for Red Lobster. If he says, "Sorry, I don't have plane ticket money." Then it's over. If he agrees to give you the money or any other favor you ask for, then he's worth keeping. His reward for "looking out" will be another dip in your pool, but this time, it's a tiny bit nastier. This is how Smart Hos use sex as a weapon. It's not the vagina, it's the experience that hooks him and makes him your junkie.

Now that you know how to use sex in a way that nets you things, I'll introduce you to the world of the biggest tricks and sponsors of all—men that are already in relationships...

#16:
On the Side- Making Her Man Your ATM

Not all the good men are taken, but they are preoccupied. Men break up, get divorced, or call off engagements every day. If you're looking for love, you can afford to wait around for Mr. Right to be single at the right time, but if you're looking for a come up, then you don't have time to waste with single men exclusively. Hos understand that successful men are rarely between women. We're not talking about looks; we're talking about winning, and men who have power, wealth, and exude the confidence that comes with that lifestyle are rarely alone for long. You're deep enough into this world to understand that Hos don't want to be the girlfriend; they want to be the good time that he can't live without and use that to their benefit. **What's the difference between a sidechick and a mistress? One gets fucked while the other gets paid**. To be the true "other woman" comes equipped with an emotional investment in addition to the lust for the New Pussy. Combine sexual desire with zero relationship pressure, and then sprinkle in the loyalty you earn after keeping a secret, and there is nothing this man will deny you.

You aren't Pussy; you're his "Girl," and making sure you're happy becomes even more important than keeping the woman he's with satisfied. What a man will do to keep the woman he has pales in comparison to what he will do to acquire a woman he's never had. Lust blinds in ways love can't because love, which is the most powerful feeling in the universe, can be taken for granted after time. No matter if he's in a monogamous relationship with his woman for 10 weeks or 10 months, lust is the key that will transform a content man into a craver. We all know that the attraction alone is useless. All men look at other woman, flirt when given the opportunity, and fantasize about that forbidden fruit. No man is above having a basic sexual desire for you, but to tip his affection from fantasy into reality, it will take more than a wink and a smile. <u>Men are only as loyal as their options</u>, so you can't just look good and talk sexy, you must give that mark an option unlike any he's ever seen.

- ♥ **Be Comfortable With His Situation As An Exception**
  Men have zero respect for women that would cheat with them without much effort… but they fall in love with women who are won over after serious effort. You don't want to be an easy side dish; you want to be dessert, and dessert always taste better after you work up an appetite, so challenge him! If a man wanted a generic pussy, he would get a prostitute or pretend to be single and pick up some freak at the club for one night. To separate yourself from "just pussy" and become his "baby" means that you can't be thought of as the type of girl that fucks committed men. The role you take on is that you're respectful of commitment but you're not so morally judgmental that you hiss things like "Does your girl know you act like this?" to make him feel bad for lusting. Show cracks of interest, so he feels he has a chance.

If he flirts with you, you entertain, but you don't go at him as hard as you would if he were single. If he tries to touch you, let him grab a little, and then smack his hands off. Now you may think, "He'll get turned off, and I won't even have a chance to get his pockets because he won't think I like him." Wrong! It's in how you deny a man, not the actual denial. The goal is to show him that you like him, but you have standards. You can hug, but you're not kissing. He can rub your ass, but you're not sitting on his lap. He can talk dirty, but you won't fire back anything more than a curious smile.

The next step is to make his relationship seem unfortunate, not a cause for jealousy or guilt. A man will promise you things, butter you up, and try hard to get you to crack early on. Your response shouldn't be, "Don't you have a girl for that?" To throw her in his face will make him feel guilty and you seem jealous. Your stance is, "I would, but you have a situation." After that, you make him feel at ease by adding that you don't mind being friends, even admit to enjoying his company, but maintain that you aren't that kind of woman.

This is all manipulation; you don't give a fuck about his situation, his woman, or his views on your morality. The only reason you're playing this game is so he respects you going forward. It may sound like an oxymoron to respect a mistress, but this is the way the male brain works. *She's not a bad woman; he's just a good guy that she really likes, and JUST FOR HIM, she is willing to blur that line.* What man wouldn't respect a woman that's willing to go against her moral compass to be his friend? That kind of exception is yet another ego boost that endears a man to a woman.

What does it take for a man to risk his relationship? That woman can't be just another Pussy; that temptation is not worth the risk. The perfect mistress has to be a non-platonic, highly personable, trustworthy goddess with standards. She would have the qualities of an actual girlfriend, one that wasn't easy to fuck, but who he worked to win over romantically, the same as his main chick. Men don't go out to meet, date, and court girlfriends when they have girlfriends, so finding that perfect mistress that fits that description would be like catching lightning in a bottle. That's where you come in.

You can become that lighting by learning exactly what it takes to make a man step out. He doesn't want a girl that's going to be rolling around with other men. He doesn't want a girl that's going to remind him that he has another girl. He doesn't want a girl that's going to become a crazy stalker. **Above all else, he wants confidentiality and loyalty.** Girls who are searching for true love want sole control of his heart. No matter how cool she plays it off, it's only a matter of time before jealousy changes the dynamic of their friendship, and she becomes irritated and even resentful of the arrangement. This bi-polar, "so are you going to leave her" boiling point is why most men will never ever cheat.

It's nearly impossible to find a girl that's not slutty, and who genuinely won't become envious enough to rock the boat of what he has with his main chick. By being okay with the fact that he has a girlfriend but flirts with you, lays the foundation for him to open up bit by bit. The more he trusts that you won't tell, the more he will give chase. You will wait for the right moment to finally give in, and he won't know what hit his pockets.

♥ **Find Out What She Doesn't Do**
When you're dealing with a single man, you must play the part of therapist, confidant, and fantasy during the time you carve out with him. Talking bonds and builds trust. You don't want to replace this woman; so never bring her up in a negative way. It's in your best interest that his girl stays around, so you need to swing any of his frustrated, "Man, she gets on my nerves," conversation back to positive reinforcement that his relationship will work out. By doing this you further prove that you are not a side Ho, nor a jealous girl that wants him all to herself.

Where your Ho Tactics come into play is in the way you bring up his sex life. Since you aren't flirting traditionally, flirt by asking filthy questions. How good is she at giving head? Can she take dick or nah? How often do they switch up the positions? Is she a moaner? Did you two do it last night? Whatever you can think of, be bold enough to ask. This should be done under the cover of a privacy. Texting is okay, but it leaves evidence. In person or on the phone is better. This guy has a girlfriend, and maybe he is with her most evenings, or she even lives with him, but you must find a time where you both can talk without fear of anyone hearing. **There are three points you must hit early on:** Gather intel on his sex life. Drop hints about how great you are in bed. Begin to act as if he's breaking down pieces of your honorable "we can't do this" wall. After two weeks, you should have this guy fantasying about sex with you every time he has sex with her. Stroke his ego with thoughts that he's opening you up to a point where you may be a bad girl, and you will shatter his defenses to the point where he will now see you as worth the risk.

♥ **Take Him To The Edge, Then Pull Him Back**
If this were a case of a Spartan woman trying to take another woman's man as her own, then sex would be off the table. As I wrote about in *Solving Single,* there are very definite rules to winning over a man who has a woman. Proving that you are superior to his girl and then pushing her out of his life in a public way like Ann Boleyn is the only way not to be played by a man that just wants to sample new pussy then run back to his girlfriend. However, the goal here is not to replace, it's to get treated, tricked on, or sponsored. New rules apply.

Remind yourself that this man is getting ass on a regular basis, even though he'd rather be in you, this lust is not all consuming. Thus, you have to give a little to get a lot. In addition to secret phone calls, schedule meet ups. At first, keep these meetups public, lunch dates on the other side of town, drinks at night, etc… You can't do all of this from a phone and texting back and forth. Even if you are out of state, you must either travel to see him or get him to travel to see you, so you can talk face to face. Seeing him is a must.

Once you establish a friendship, take him into deep waters by meeting up privately. Make sure it's just you and him, and then let the night unfold. If you've worked your magic the way I laid out, this man will be on fire and unable to keep his hands off you. Give in; let him touch more than before but know your limit! To have sex straight up is a gamble, so use your own intuition. Maybe you give him a hand job to calm him down. Maybe you keep it at kissing and breast sucking. I don't want you doing anything you are uncomfortable with, because it's not about giving in, it's about him feeling as though you are his or at least on your way to being his.

This is a roller coaster, and over the course of let's say, three weeks, he should feel that each time he's getting closer and closer to breaking you. In reality, you're the one that's pulling him into these closed quarters and making him crazy. He's now drunk in lust, while you're sober with dollar signs in your eyes.

♥ **Prove Your Trust, Not Your Ability To Blackmail**
The next step sounds simple but is extremely important. The days following your hot and steamy meeting, you must act exactly the same. Throughout this guide, I've talked about the importance of confronting things that most people keep beneath the surface. The women I've talked to, for the most part, are big believers in being casually open with men because most women are scared to talk about sex. That night, the kissing, the touching, or even the intercourse, should be brought up in a fun and playful way. At the same time, you're not trying to force yourself into his life. You don't mention the woman he's committed to; you don't call more than normal, you act like a woman that is having a fun time.

The basic bitch mindset, in terms of landing a paid man that's in a relationship, is to make him do something he shouldn't then hold it over his head. Let me lay one thing out clearly: **A woman with a man that's winning won't leave because of he said/ she said.** These men are prepared to face the music if you try something scandalous. These marks don't want to lose their girls, but they know that their girls don't want to lose them even more. Blackmailing may get you a few dollars or one gift, but the method I'm laying out will ensure that you stay in his pockets for months even years, if you gain his trust.

What about if he gets sloppy and she finds out about you? "I'm coming to you woman to woman, leave my man alone," is what a broken hearted basica will hit you with in an attempt to appeal to your "sisterly" bond. More unhinged girlfriends or wives may even hunt you down and threaten to get physical. When presented with this dilemma, don't get rattled see it as another chance to cement your loyalty.

Play dumb! You don't know what she's talking about and remove yourself from the situation by blocking her number or walking away from any confrontation. I don't care how bad your attitude is, be a professional! Don't let your pride push you into something that can get you injured nor stoop to her level arguing. Inform the mark about what happened, ask him exactly how she found out, and help him clean up his mess by either lying on his behalf or showing him the proper way to sneak around. Trust that these guys aren't as good as living double lives as you would think, so if you use this opportunity to show him how valuable you can be even as a side. Plus, now that you have so much dirt on him, it'll make it extra hard to tell you "no" when you hit him up as a reward for your discretion.

♥ **Become His Expensive Hobby**

Pop Quiz: *What's the core of getting a man to give you what you want*? Love! We needed lust to hook him, but as I wrote earlier, you have to make a trick fall in love in order to turn him into Aladdin's Genie. We already delved into that Tony Montana "I want to fuck/take care of my sister" love and how that level of dependency leads to a man giving up his free will to make a woman happy and content. Now let's focus on the other type of love that will make you irreplaceable.

What are men obsessed with more than sex? Toys! Men love electronic gadgets, exotic automobiles, boats, sports memorabilia, etc... Boys grow into men, but the need to have something beautiful, exciting, and inspiring to work on never goes out of style. As the other woman, you must become his toy. Not the Richard Pryor version of *The Toy* where someone throws cash and makes you do what they say, but the Smart Ho Version.

You earned respect by showing him that you're not "that" type of girl; he was just special enough to be the exception. You found out his fantasy and showed him that you fit that description. You finally let him break down your walls and be physical. Finally, you played your position as his loyal friend who will never blackmail or tell. At this point, you are his woman just as much as the one with the title. The gloves now come off. Begin to call him pet names, begin to miss him, and begin to drop the limitations on what you two do. If you haven't had sex, now would be the time. Don't be afraid that he'll be done with you because two things are at play: 1) You're his outlet. 2) He won't risk the possibility that you may expose him if he's a jerk to you after sex.

The squeaky wheel gets oiled often. Once you have his nose open, you must become needy. The same rules apply here as it did in the earlier chapters, meaning that at first you have to ask for things that also benefit him. Lingerie, dresses, shoes, or any accessory that makes you sexier should be the first things you get him to spend on. You're his expensive hobby! In the same way Jay Leno spends countless hours and hundreds of thousands of dollars working on his vintage car collection; this man needs to see you as a gift to himself.

Once again, I will invoke the name of my favorite rom-com, *Pretty Woman*. When Edward gives Vivian money to go shopping on Rodeo, it isn't about her it's about him. Men don't grow up playing with Barbie dolls; we adopt that habit as we get older. We want to see you at your best, at your sexiest, and make other men jealous. Unlike the woman he's in a relationship with, whom he most likely wants to hide away due to jealousy, there is a fantasy element with the other woman. He wants other men to want what he has to the point of shoving that beauty in their faces. These men do not care about spending money if they are getting something out of this arrangement. Be his toy, be his trophy, ask for things that make you shine, and you will always get it.

***

<u>This chapter has become the most used over the years</u>, as men with girlfriends or wives are often the most bored facet of our society. Men grow older, they need to feel like they still have it, like they're still wanted, and the woman he has becomes too normal to him to feel that spark. It's not about "he doesn't love her," it's about the male thirst for more more more! One reader wrote me of how blown away she was by the fact that the three men she targeted with this chapter, all caved in. Of course they did. As men the only thing that keeps us in check from venturing off is fear of being found out. If put in the same room with a woman that seems trustworthy, most men will not pull away if she kissed him first. Which means if you are aggressive, you will always win.

Remember that you still have to do your research dates. Some men may not have much money to spend on hobbies, so all you will get are dinner dates, maybe an occasional gift. If you're looking for a Donald Sterling[13] type sponsor that will buy cars and cribs for you then abort your mission if this man is only willing to trick Beyoncé tour tickets and handbags. As always you can't squeeze a dime out of a nickel, so don't waste these techniques on someone with limited means.

The final advice is to not let his infatuation with you upgrade you to his actual woman. Men fall in love with their mistresses, but you see this as a hustle, so keep focused on the prize. The moment he moves you into the last woman's position, you lose the fantasy aspect that allowed you to be treated like a princess.

---

[13] Sterling was the notorious Los Angeles Clippers owner who was exposed by his young mistress's phone recordings.

Instead, you will find yourself in charge of taking care of the home and being his pacifier instead of his toy. You must keep that other woman in her place! Play marriage counselor, relationship expert, or even threaten that if he leaves her, you'll leave him. It's a thin line between craving and being content. So long as his actual girlfriend is around, you have power over him. The moment she is pushed out, you become old and some other Ho becomes the new fantasy. You need him to crave you as his special treat until you get everything on your wish list.

#17:
How to Online Date...
the Ho Way

Take the best picture you can possibly stuff into 73 x 73 pixels. If your boobs are your golden ticket, expose that cleavage. If your ass is what gets you the most attention, perfect that side view shot so the world knows what you're working with. If you're built like Keira Knightley, then go with the traditional face shot, complete with "come fuck me" eyes and duck lips. Once you have your picture, go sign up for a paid dating site, not a freebie, because those are rest heavens for broke dudes that love to window shop as if they can afford you. Once you sign up it doesn't matter what you write in your bio, these things are for male picture browsing not waxing philosophical. Now it's time to go find a rich man. Ignore anyone that inboxes you, and go straight for the profiles that list income at 100k or more. Message him something flirty and then... **prepare to be disappointed** like the other thousands of women that think landing a rich man on the internet is as easy as that bullshit I just wrote.

Online dating sites and apps have become extremely popular, every year more and more people meet and get married on these sites because everyone lives on their phones. You can browse the internet and find all kinds of discreet "gold digger" dating sites where men search for "sugar babies" to spoil. You can get on Bumble and match with older men looking for a trophy. But these methods rarely work. I don't doubt that a few men on these apps and websites are sponsor material, the majority are most likely disgusting jerks using these sites as an alternative to escort services. To spell it out for you, men with money who use these sites are looking to buy pussy or looking to bait naive women by flashing money.

For example, you meet an investment banker on Hinge. You google him and see that he is wealthy. Now you're doing the dance of joy as if you hit the lotto. Mr. Banker takes you out to an expensive dinner, brags about the property he owns, then tells you how different you are from the women he meets on these dating apps. You get open off the potential bag you're about to secure, but you also get nervous because if you don't give Mr. Banker what he wants, he won't like you... you let your guard down, he fucks you, and you never get anything he bragged about. That's how men with money get free pussy on dating sites, they dangle the "I'm rich" carrot and you play yourself. Alternatively, you may meet a guy who just offers you cash to fuck. That idea may disgust you, but if your bank account has less than a thousand dollars, rents due, and he's offering 10k, your desperation may override your morals, especially when it's a guy who you won't ever have to see again.

Some of you are looking for easy money from sex. Many women say they want to learn *Ho Tactics*, but actually want an escort service that does the work for them. Maybe you're on the fence about being a sex worker and don't mind "pay for play." **This isn't Escort Education; this is Ho Tactics!**

The point is to get what you want without selling your body. I support sex workers in all forms, but the purpose of this book is to get the most value without spreading your legs. You can use dating apps to vet men, and date them like I wrote about earlier in this book. However, if we're talking about truly using the internet to level up, then there is a much more powerful tool than just swiping and being swiped on.

The Internet Is A Goldmine

If I'm anti-dating site, how can I show you how to land a Treat, Trick, or Sponsor online? Let me introduce the greatest Ho thirst trap invention since the wonder bra—social networking. Facebook is a world where you can connect with old boos or new baes, and see where they work, where they live, and research nearly every aspect of their lives if you can get a friend request accepted. Twitter gives you 280 characters to show off facets of your wit and even post pictures, but the best part is that everyone from platinum rappers to championship-winning athletes are only a follow away from you gaining direct access.

Instagram is unquestionably the king of the hill when it comes to attracting thirst. You don't need to be a part of some exclusive community, and you don't need to display your personality, all you need is the ability to take a pretty picture, and if you struggle with that, there are a dozen filters that can help you go from *Nah* to *Nia Long*.

I imagine that everyone reading this has at least one of these social networking applications. Nevertheless, how many of you use it to make money, gain status, or connect with a man that will fly you anywhere you want to go? Most women on social networking sites are more concerned with showing up rival females by getting likes, gaining followers, or having their opinions agreed upon by random broke men that are somewhere jerking off in their mother's basement. That's fine if your aim is to have fun and get basic attention while on your lunch break. Smart Hos aren't online looking to reconnect with old High School sweethearts for the sake of nostalgia or chime in on celebrity gossip. If you're not rich, then why are you playing on the internet? Why are you trying to get likes or comments or argue with people online when your pockets are empty? The Internet is a marketplace to find MARKS!

Every day you log onto any social media site the object should be to get wealthy men to take notice of you. Are you doing that or are you just wasting time on your phone? In the past year I've had a girl hook a married man by using Snapchat to send private videos back and forth. I know an Indian woman that used voice messages on WeChat to sex bait a busy and extremely rich businessman a thousand miles away. Smart Hos know how to use each site, Twitter, Instagram, Snapchat, Facebook, even TikTok in a specific way to promote the brand.

When I say promote, I'm not talking about some ratchet booking email to prove you model or host parties, nor am I referring to a link to some jewelry collection or T-shirt website that you run. Hos promote themselves! If you're nicely built, your body is your resume. If you have the face of a goddess, that mug is your spider web. If you're aggressive and witty, your words become the quicksand that will trap your trick. Regardless of what category you are in, know where you are the strongest. I don't want to hear, "I'm quick witted and a dime," I doubt that, because if that were true, you would be out in the streets turning the Ho Tactics from the previous chapters into a condo. Be honest about your best assets.

The first rule of thumb is that you can't believe what you read on the internet. That guy that is on Instagram posting pictures of bottles and leaning on a BMW could be stunting. Either he's playing sidekick to a friend that has money or waiting for the right moment to take a picture that makes him seem bigger than what he is. I once saw someone ask a valet if he could sit in the passenger side of someone's Maserati and take a picture. I imagine that flick ended up on "the gram" and got him dozens if not hundreds of likes. To a man like me who is watching this transpire, that guy is a clown, but to the rest of the world, he's a Hollywood baller. It would be so easy for a girl that's following him to bless his Instagram with a heart-eyed emoji, get a direct message, and end up on a date with him a day later. That man doesn't have to pull up in that car, he can say it was in the shop after getting rammed after the club, take her back to the hotel, and make her think she's about to lay next to a man that can change her life. That's how frauds exploit dumb Hos and naïve women.

The second rule of thumb is to aim for men on the level you can handle. Some of you may be cute enough for Drake to follow you, but Drake's not going to let you get in his pockets the same way he would let Bria from Hooters[14] get in his pockets. To these big-name celebrities, you are one of many internet THOTS[15], and unless you're in their city for the weekend and willing to come get tossed up at the Four Seasons, they probably won't entertain you the same way they would entertain someone with status like R&B starlet Christina Milian or even a girl they met in public. Go after men who aren't necessarily in the spotlight. Nelly's real estate agent that got a shout out on Instagram, that guy who directed that Coors Light commercial and posted it on twitter, the one that lists his employer as Google on Facebook. Those are the non-celebrity types that may have enough money to scratch your expensive

---

[14] Rapper Drake is known to name drop random women who he's met in ordinary spots, as a way to promote his love for the "everywoman".
[15] Those Hos Over There or THOT has become the go to label used by millennials to point out Hos or Hoish behavior.

itches. If you only focus on the Dallas Cowboy or Persian Prince, then you're going to get lost in the Ho shuffle and miss out.

Know what men on the internet respond to—beauty first, personality second. If you were to follow a guy on Twitter or Instagram, what would make him follow you back? Your avatar. If he doesn't follow back, that doesn't mean he thinks you're ugly, it could be that he didn't notice you, or he's not totally sold on your looks enough to make what I call, "The shallow follow." To get his attention, you follow up with personality. Some girls just retweet in hopes that will get a guy's attention or like a picture in hopes he will be appreciative enough to follow back. Fuck that, you can't be so egotistical to think that your silent *like* or *retweet* will be noticed. **Men with money or power are not monitoring every online interaction in the same way bored bums do, so you must be aggressive to get a man's attention.** Don't just retweet, be forward enough to comment on his picture or @ him directly in a way that catches his attention. This can be pulled off by making him laugh or by sassing him into a game of back and forth banter. Be prepared to really go for a guy if you think he's a golden ticket, don't assume that because you're pretty in your profile pic that every man will think the same.

Hoexample

Maria is too busy Hoing up in the flesh to play on the internet, but she puts her shy bestie onto the internet tactics game. Let's call our online thirst trapper *Imani the Ho*. Imani has an unlimited data plan and a desire to move out of her parent's home by the New Year. Imani is what we can refer to as cute, not necessarily a bombshell, but pretty enough to get attention when she feels like dressing up. The problem is Imani isn't outgoing, she's soft-spoken and reserved, and usually gets lost in the shuffle when she's around alpha females like Maria. However, when Imani is behind a keyboard she's fearless. Imani sees the life that Maria is living, and could use the money for moving and to get bills paid until she graduates from university.

For the first time in her life, Imani takes to her social networking account with a money goal. As I explained earlier, you must know what you want from these men first and then put in the work to get that without settling for distractions like sex or a boyfriend. To blow in the wind with no clear Ho intention, will net you bullshit results. Imani's goal is to find a man that can provide enough money for her to move out by January 1st. It's currently October, so that puts pressure on her to act now instead of putting it off like some indecisive Basica. Imani starts by investing in her online appearance. She's going to create new avatars for Facebook, Instagram, and Twitter respectively that show different aspects of her personality. Makeup, hair, and lighting are the most important tools at this stage of the game. Hair can be tricky, no matter if you have long flowing blonde hair, natural curls, or are weaved up; you have to go with the look that you love the most. My preference has always been toward longer hair, so I'm going to use this as my example, but I am not the male standard. Whatever hairstyle makes you feel good is what you go to the hairdresser and get.

Imani gets 18 inches of the best Brazilian hair she can afford on her budget and then gets her cousin who boosts from Lancôme to come over and beat her face[16]. Next, she chooses the perfect outfit, a corset that slims her waist and promotes her B cups to C cups. The last step is proper room lighting, you have to glow, be it in a selfie or a picture made to look as if it were taking in the moment aka the "caught me slipping" staged photo. I highly recommend face shots for Instagram and Twitter, and save the full body for Facebook. Internet stalkers will be blown away by your face and the epic way your bangs are layed, but they will also seek out alternative looks to be sure you're not Catfishing[17] or only good from the neck up. Have a full body lying in wait to prove that you are the total package. If you aren't comfortable with a full body, then go face shots with all three, it's not make or break.

Now that Imani has used the selection skill of Anna Wintour to handpick the best pictures for her various profiles, she has to test out the waters with a blatant thirst trap. With her face light on makeup, but still blemish free, she posts a picture looking upset. Instead of going with the passé #NoFilter tag, she blasts out "Just woke up, #BadHairDay," or if it's a nighttime shot, "Just got out of class looking like #TheStruggle." These are clearly staged photos, but they catch Imani in the moment minus a smile, which in turn will make the males on social networking feel a need to kiss her ass by assuring her that she's still a bad bitch. This isn't about thirst trapping undesirables; it's about testing your new default look out. Remember this is still the way you look in your avatar, minus a little makeup, so this is going to be your brand going forward. No matter if it's you dolled up or semi-natural it has to promote you as a dime.

---

[16] Beating one's face refers to the process of applying makeup.
[17] The act of deceiving someone online using false photos.

Going back to #TheStruggle thirst trap picture, Imani will know how successful her new look is by the response from the public. Imani has about 1700 Instagram followers, which means on average she probably gets 30-60 likes while the stalkers lurk waiting for a reason to show themselves. This struggle picture nets Imani 120 likes, the most she's had for a non-tight dress picture, which proves it's a win. On the linked Twitter account, it gets her a few retweets and a couple of "look at bae" comments. Those kudos proved that men like her new look, and with that foundation, she now has the confidence to go after the big fish knowing that she has the what the typical male is after.

What type of men are getting money but still have time to be constantly on the internet? Pro athletes! Unlike CEO's who are most likely working 16-hour days or musicians that do more promoting than thirsting, athletes have a lot of downtime between seasons, and because their careers require constant ESPN updates, they normally have their phones in hand. So where does a woman with zero sports knowledge start? With Google. It's October, and the World Series is going on, which means that all but two Major League Baseball teams are at home watching. Imani would ideally want a tall Basketball player, but that season is just starting, and she's unlikely to get the full attention of a player that's on the road every few days being chased by hotel groupies. Baseball it is, so she Twitter searches for a few baseball tags, and looks for that verified sign.

It takes a few hours, but Imani finds a potential mark whose very twitter active. He's attractive enough and plays for the Pittsburg Pirates. Imani lives down south, but that doesn't deter her because being long distance with an off-season athlete shouldn't be a factor if he's making "I'll fly out" money. Imani knows there is a thin line between thirsting and flirting when it comes to athletes. There are women in his mentions with the same intentions, but Imani, like any good Ho, understands that what she brings to the table can't be touched by the average groupie. Imani doesn't add the mark right away; a blind follow will most likely be ignored. Instead, Imani responds to a tweet of the mark criticizing one of the World Series teams. The groupie move would be to agree with what he said. The bitchy move would be to try to counter his point and argue. Neither one will really impress him. Imani instead piggybacks on his point to show that she's on the same wavelength as him. She then waits for his response, right? Wrong! She immediately follows up with a question that any casual sports fan can ask, "Do you see this going 7 games or nah?" It's basic, but unlike retweeting his comment, it does require him to take notice of her. He does respond back with his opinion, and at that moment, she follows him. **Being pretty enough to get a response usually means pretty enough to follow.** Now that he's taken the bait, the real game begins.

Shy women beat around the bush; Hos go to the source of the money as soon as they are given the green light. Imani takes the conversation private within 24 hours of the follow. The best Ho invention is the Direct Message. She has direct access to this man, which means that even a introverted woman can unleash the full power of her personality in a way that she couldn't do in person. Imani doesn't rush to give up her phone number or even ask for his. To follow a guy and then jump in his DM asking for the digits reeks of being a jumpoff. She isn't a baseball fan and has no interest in Googling random shit to talk about. Instead, she scours his timeline and notices a topic she can expand upon. <u>Always do research once you zero in on a mark!</u> In this case, it's a debate about J Cole versus Wale. She DMs him in favor of J Cole, and begins to bait him with a music discussion. For the next two days, Imani will continue to bring up random conversation points to build a rapport with him.

Meanwhile, her Instagram and twitpics get sexier and sexier knowing that this man's thirst is what she's trying to trap.

It's been less than a week, and this Major League mark asks Imani for her number, she teases him a bit, because to just give it out could paint her as easy. Imani lays the rules down in a flirty way, "I only give my number to men who use it, not sit on it." Of course, the mark affirms that he will use it. To hook him even harder, she gives it out with the warning of, "Let's see how fast you keep your word." Ho Tactic 101, Imani has challenged this man's ego and it won't be more than 20 minutes before he calls in order to accept that challenge.

Once Imani has him on the phone one on one, traditional Ho Tactics apply. Research his life and see how generous he has the potential to be. **Since he's hundreds of miles away, Imani can't do the date test, but she can do a "mail me something" test.** Let's go back to the traditional headphone example we used before. Imani complains to her new friend that her headphones broke, and she won't be able to buy any since she's a poor student. This man will either rush to send her a pair or tell her to go ask her mother for a loan. Imani's guy is smitten, so he does mail her a pair of new headphones, proving he's not tight with his money. Imani has established trick potential and now sinks her fangs in deeper.

When doing Ho Tactics long distance, the first visit is key. Imani refuses to come to him and asks that he fly to her city. Not only is it safer to be on your home turf, it ensures he won't have any hometown distractions. Hos think like men, they know that the only reason for a fly out is pussy. Imani doesn't run from this like the typical nervous woman; she acts as if her legs are open and waiting for him to come conquer. In the weeks leading up to their first meet up, she's done her phone seduction work and has all but promised the pussy to him upon arrival. However, when he arrives Imani digs into her

Ho manipulation bag and makes an excuse so she won't have to fuck him.

The story Imani creates is a good one; The night before she was at a club and stepped out to get some air. Suddenly a drunk guy cornered her, began touching her, and he might have even assaulted her if the bouncer hadn't walked out and put hands on the guy. This is all bullshit, but as I wrote previously, trauma is a line that even the horniest man will respect and not cross. The weekend was supposed to be a nasty affair, but it would be insensitive for this mark to pressure a woman that was just shaken up by a potential sexual assault. Instead of falling into the trap of being "fly out pussy" Imani turned the tables. The weekend is now spent bonding with him emotionally, insuring that he will return to visit for more than the sex he missed. The emotional glue has now been formed.

The next step in this online Ho hustle is to stop being active on social media. A trick cannot think Online Hoing is what you do, so you have to remove yourself from that world once you get this guy hooked. The mark is becoming obsessed with Imani, so he will be checking her page daily, looking for hints that she has someone else or to see if she lets her feelings for him slip out. **Men think every meme or personal comment is aimed at them; it's the male ego placing itself at the center of a woman's universe.** Imani plays this up. She doesn't flirt with other men, continues to show off her beauty, and makes sly hints about what she really wants. Imani doesn't want to be his girlfriend, so she lays out her mission statement in the form of a subtweet, "Too busy for a boyfriend, but never too busy for love. Can't wait to see him again."

Any mark reading this will think he hit the jackpot. A girl that doesn't want the title, but is wide open and down for a good time is priceless. By the end of November and their second meeting, the mark is beyond lust and now has love for Imani.

Imani is out of reasons not to fuck him, and she's already trick checked him, so she has sex with this guy and throws it on him Ho style. New Pussy Lust + Endearing Love + Nasty Sex = this mark is sprung.

Going forward Imani begins to go for what she wants, she shares her dreams of moving out, even making up some dramatic story about her mother being a bitch who is now demanding rent. In addition to that, Imani uses Maria's old tricks of mailing him small gifts, in order to get expensive gifts sent in return. By the first of December, Imani has found a new apartment and asks her lover if he can help with the deposit. This is the coup de grâce, either he makes an excuse, or he puts his money up and gives his trophy what she needs to be happy. In the end, Imani gets the deposit, and the promise of help, which guarantees that she won't be paying rent so long as this man gets to call and pop in from time to time. It's now the first of the year, and Imani's three-month goal has been completed all from the comfort of her smartphone. That's how to online date!

Hoing Up

Let's slow down Imani's hustle and bring it back to the basics because I know more than one of you will be unsure of your ability to hook a man off social networking this easily…

REBRAND: Make yourself over in a way where anyone from a random admirer to a celebrity stalker would pause there scrolling and say, "damn." **Regardless of what your looks are, you can make yourself over into a thirst trap.** I've seen new avatars on Facebook of girls I've known for years, and because they switched it up, I felt the need to go look at their pictures for the first time ever. I've seen girls on Twitter that only show from the chin down, but because their body was banging I felt the need to go see what they were tweeting about. Highlight your best physical assets! Men are controlled by their dicks, so your only job is to project an image that inspires want. I remind you, that this can be accomplished without being trashy, ratchet, or revealing… a little goes a long way.

RESEARCH: You don't have to go after anyone that's famous or even substantially rich. Most of you will want to find someone in your city, and maybe you think the only guys in your city that are paid are the dope boys. You're wrong, in every medium to large city there are industries that afford top workers large wages. Understand your environment, understand who is getting money, and take aim at someone who has the credentials to back up their internet claim. The best thing about dating in your city is that like the typical Ho game, you can expose frauds after one or two dates. You don't have to hunt for verified twitter signs or measure how many Instagram followers a guy has, simply look at how he's living in those pictures, what he's talking about, and once again listen to your gut. If you're following last chapter's hustle, then men with girlfriends or wives will be posting places he takes his lady or things he buys her—all signs of his will to spend.

Let's imagine that you found a guy who lives in Atlanta and works for a credit score agency. This guy could be low level, or he could be high up the corporate ladder at this Fortune 500 Company. It would be in your best interest to thirst him into following you, get his information, and see what he really does before agreeing to a date. **The most important step in any online dating or social networking scenario is to bring it into real life as soon as possible.** There are so many idiots that keep typing and typing, and they end up falling in love with the persona or getting hooked on a scripted fantasy. By the time they meet up or talk to that person, they have invested much more than they should have, and it turns out to be lies. Find a potential mark, but don't keep it all online. You must find a way to get him on the phone or face to face on a date, so you can research his funds properly.

TYPE LIKE A HO: Many of you who want to incorporate Ho Tactics are deathly shy, overly nervous around men, or simply lack the courage to go for what you want verbally. The internet makes the quiet nerd into the most interesting person in the world. All those nasty and flirty things you would turn red trying to say face to face, now must flow easily from your fingers because you're operating from your comfort zone. Use sexual innuendos, challenge his sexual skills, and don't be afraid that he won't respect you if you're being too forward about sex. It's a video game at this point, the mission is to get him excited before you exchange phone numbers or if this is already happening in text, to get him primed for that first date. Males hear so many catfish stories or girls that stood guys up, so alleviate that worry by giving him a little taste of what he thinks is to come. Don't keep it all online, before you agree to that first date, talk to him on the phone, get a feel for him so it won't be awkward when you do meet. I've heard several stories of DM chemistry turning into boring dates. It's not that Ho Tactics didn't work, it's because you forget the rule that you will always have to take it offline eventually and use your verbal skills!

For those of you that are gangsters behind the keyboard, you may not want to transfer that to that phone call or first date right away. Follow your strengths. If you think two weeks of hooking him via messaging is better than you on a phone or a date, then do that. However, don't go more than three weeks before meeting up with him in person if he's local or a month if he's long distance or you risk becoming "just another girl he texts". **A woman typing, "Can you buy me a new pair of shoes?" doesn't reverberate like a woman whispering that same thing in a low voice after getting that trick's dick hard.** Talking will always be the ultimate tool for getting a man to give you what you want. Verbal seduction will always trump sexting or sending nudes, so don't get caught up in new technology as the sole method of seduction.

MAKE HIM FEEL SPECIAL: I've met a number of Webcam girls that make a good profit off nudity, but they miss out on the big bucks of converting "slaves" that pay for a peep show into tricks that actually break the bank. They become too comfortable just playing up the role of the *Cam Girl* that's pay for play, strip teasing or masturbating, and don't know how to hook men when they have to be a real person. You can always find guys willing to jerk off to you, but the big money is in taking it offline. Become their friend, seduce his mind… not with the act that you already used online, but by being a real woman that's actually into him. Men want to feel special! These guys buying you stuff off your Amazon Wishlist to see your boobs or get a chat conversation know you're faking it, but they're hoping that you will see something deeper in him and give him exclusive access. To let him know your real name, to tell him he's different from the rest, and to talk about normal everyday life as if he's now your confidant will lead to hitting him up for bigger gifts.

Many of you aren't in adult entertainment, but you are very popular online. No matter if you model, sell flat tummy tea, are famous in your own right, or just a normal woman that's found herself a following—the same rules apply. These men who want you will be afraid because they figure you can have any guy you want or you're the type that's only fucking with other popular people. The same way that a Cam Girl can seduce her paying customer, you can seduce your admirers. Pinpoint a guy that's willing to spend and make him out to be different than all the other guys showering you with attention online.

One of my favorite students recently became very popular on one of the social media sites because something she did went viral. She parlayed that into a GoFundMe and cash app donations for various things. Every time she asked, she followed up with sexy pictures of herself. Why? Because men are hoping that you notice. That's an easy hustle, but let's say you want more than a few hundred here and there, you want to reel in a big fish? You start having private conversations with those admirers. He likes all of your pictures, watches all of our Snaps, or always @'s you, send him a DM thanking him and ask where he lives and what he does for a living. If he doesn't seem to be working with much, that's as far as it goes. If he does have a good job, then cha-ching! make him feel special, set up at date and follow the steps laid out above.

No matter if you're social media savvy, on the cams, or just like to have text buddies, understand that you can't be lazy even in the 21st century. Men want a personal experience, give it to them, by stroking their egos, but don't be limited by your love of technology. It's okay to pull him online, but in the end, you will have to go offline to get in his pockets. This week's homework is to test it out by building your DM confidence. Pick a practice man, doesn't have to be a guy with trick potential, just someone you notice noticing you a lot. Be bold enough to message him and start a conversation in an exercise to sharpen your flirting skills behind a keyboard. Once you get good at this and feel confident in your online persona, then nothing will stop you from hooking a man online and off.

#18:
How to Go From Ho to Housewife

You can't turn a Ho into a housewife, but a Ho can turn herself into whatever she wants to be, Lawyer, Doctor, Sports Analyst, Reality TV Star, Fashion Designer, Chef, and, of course, an international Pop Superstar. I debated on if I should include this chapter since the intention is to pull off hustles with a beginning, middle, and end, then go about your normal life or on to another mark. However, it would be imbalanced if I didn't, at least, touch on the proper way to transition from a life of Ho Tactics to a life of picket fences and baby strollers with a man that is fundamentally a sponsor but has gained the title of husband.

The classic Martin Scorsese movie *Casino*[18] popped on TV as I was debating this chapter, right on the part where Ace, the powerful mob-backed casino manager, decides to pursue Vegas working girl Ginger. For those unfamiliar with *Casino*, Ginger is essentially a Ho who has the charisma to pull tricks at the highest level, yet who isn't mentally stable enough to come away with anything substantial.

---

[18] *Casino* tells the true story of the mafia in Las Vegas. Hip Hop fans remember the Nas video for "Street Dreams" which retells the film.

Ace falls for Ginger's Ho appeal and marries her, knowing what kind of woman she is, but convinced that he can change her—that's his first mistake. In one of the great scenes, Ginger tells her now husband and the father of her child, that he's never been anything more than a trick to her since they first met. That solidified my decision to include this chapter because as I wrote in *Solving Single*, saying that Hos can't become housewives is a purely ignorant statement spewed by bitter women who resent fast women and dishonest men who fear falling victim. Hoing is an act, not part of your DNA, at any time a male Ho or female Ho can retire, and no one will be aware of that past life. However, the beauty of Ho Tactics is that it's an education that will always benefit those that take time to understand how to apply them. You can sit there and stand by your man's side for five years and not even get a friendship ring, but Hos, they not only get married, they get married within a year of meeting an overzealous mark, because they know how to play the game at the highest level.

The Benzino Effect

For those unfamiliar with ratchet reality TV, Benzino is a former rapper known for being Co-owner of The Source magazine, now he's best known for giving out engagement rings to women of questionable agendas on the reality show *Love & Hip Hop Atlanta*. Numerous men have a crucial flaw that allows even the not so Smart Hos to transition into the life of a married woman. Benzino isn't an idiot or a pushover; he just happens to have a penis. **The defining traits that sum up Ho Tactics is supreme confidence mixed with a seductive personality.** Hos shine because they don't flirt like normal women. Older men with money have run through sweet girls, freaky girls, intellectuals, and hood rats, and those women bore the hell out of them.

When a man reaches his later 30's or enters his 40's it takes more than pretty and sweet to impress, it takes the kind of exuberance and lack of filter that Hos epitomize. He never knows when she's going to flash a boob, grab his dick in public, or calm down enough to say something strangely poetic. These girls are all over the place, and for a bored man entering a mid-life crisis, he doesn't want that for one night, he wants to feed off that energy in order to stay forever young.

Men believe they are special enough to change a girl with a past into a Queen with a future. No matter what her history, or how many guys have allegedly slept with her, a man hypnotized by Ho Power will believe that he is the one man that can make her turn a new leaf and commit. Hos move in silence, but after spending enough money, any man will eventually see the writing on the wall that this girl has been working him. Most Ho hustles only last six months to a year, but when presented with an electrifying woman, even one that he realizes is hustling him, there are men that will still give into their ego and try to housetrain that good time girl. No bringing up the past, no prenup going forward, the right mark will take care of you for life because your personality is his fountain of youth.

For marks, marriage is the best way to turn a loss into a win. Sponsoring a young girl is an investment, he isn't a Sugar Daddy just for the fuck of it, as I wrote earlier, no matter if sex is happening or not, he's getting something out of the deal. What happens when that Sugar Daddy can no longer stand his wife or has a mental breakdown where he realizes that he's only happy when you're around, he stops renting and buys. Yes, he knows you used him, now he's going to make that pay off by using you back for the rest of your life as you make him feel young and loved. It's an arrangement not some foolish romantic reaction, and before the invention of the Disney Princess, it's the sole reason people got married.

For Hos looking for one last sponsor, it can be just as beneficial. He gets to have you for real for the rest of his life or until the money runs out. You get either a security blanket or a lifelong investor to back your ambitious plans. None of the girls that I interviewed for this book were married, but one had a close friend that married her trick. In a strange twist of fate, this mark turned husband ended up giving her access to his bank accounts, and with her mind for business, she took his money and tripled it within three years after opening her own business. That man now works for his former Ho turned wife and lives like a domestic. This isn't about being some kept woman; going from Ho to someone's wife can be a business partnership if you are savvy enough to choose the right spouse. As a woman looking to gracefully bow out of the game, there are two things you need to look for in a retirement plan aka a husband:

<u>**Long term Sponsorship Ability**</u>: If you're going to go all in it must be worth it. You don't leave your job at the Clinique Makeup counter to go work at the Mac Makeup counter that's a lateral move; you need to be climbing that ladder. Therefore, you don't retire for a treat or a cheap trick; he must be a sponsor with a deep portfolio. In the time you spent getting him to invest in you, a big part of your hustle was to learn more and more about what this mark does. If your mark was a 9-5er, with a hefty base salary, that's good enough to get your normal goal. However, if you plan to cut off your short-term hustles for long-term stability, you have to know if his job has security or if he's one bad quarter from being demoted or laid off from the company. Alternatively, if this man is a business owner, know how volatile his company is because if he is the boss that cuts the check or has the bank loans in his name, a bad fiscal year could lead to him having to file for bankruptcy, and you having to trade in that wedding ring and shoe collection to stay afloat.

Eventually, you will fall in love, have children, and it will be a real marriage, but from the inception, this is a business deal. **Much like the Ladies of the royal society that were presented to the Dukes and Princes of the time, you aren't marrying for romance, you are marrying for finance.** This is not only your livelihood; the man you choose will be responsible for your children and their children, and the last thing you want is your granddaughter to be left with nothing and having to read *Ho Tactics* in 2054, to get back on her feet.

Acceptance of the Big Reveal: The thing that really irritates the so-called good girls is when a girl is a Ho, gets found out, only to be forgiven for her past by a man that could easily have a "good girl." It's as if Hos get away with murder! If this were that good girl who did something sketchy, a man would most likely break up and make her beg for a second chance. Hos never beg to be taken back, and I'll prove it.

I once corresponded with a woman that was in a rage because she exposed a Ho to her male friend/crush. She was so sure that her friend would cut this girl off emotionally and financially, and then he would finally see that a powerful man such as himself should be with an independent and strong woman like her. The exposing worked; the friend was upset, cursed the girl out, but in true Ho fashion, she manipulated the situation back to her favor. This Ho was caught with her hand in the cookie jar, but put her hands up like, "You got me, but this doesn't mean I never loved you or will ever stop loving you." That's all that mark needed to hear to forgive. He tracked the Ho down and apologized for yelling! The woman who told me this story was blown away. This man was successful and highly educated, but that shit means nothing when you're facing infatuation. Hos make themselves invaluable through the steps listed in this book, and that story is proof.

Few men can separate themselves from a woman with superior Ho skills. This male didn't want to be in a relationship with his female friend that exposed his Ho because she wasn't fun or wild; she was just like the rest of the women around his age who had grown old and now obsessed with love, marriage and reproducing. Of course, the Ho won, she had the type of personality that doesn't grow on trees. **For all the women that claim to be different, Spartans and Hos are the few that prove it with actions.** While you may find a J. Howard Marshall, Benzino, or Orlando Scandrick that will embrace your past and allow you to *reset your Honess*, you want to be ahead of the curve. You don't want to be exposed by an outside force; you want to expose yourself in a way that will bring you closer together. If he's religious, tell him you were a sinner now you've seen the light. If he's a compassionate dude, appeal to his paternal side, and tell him how your childhood was horrible, and you didn't have a way out except men taking care of you. Be as genuine as you can be without doing damage to your chances. Get in front of the secret; don't let the secret get in front of you.

The Kardashian Effect

Throughout your Ho tenure, you will get marriage proposals; some legit some bullshit, and it's because you learned what men want and how to position yourself as that ultimate fantasy. A common misconception is that men look for wives like a woman would look for a wife for her son. In theory, if I were to ask my wife to pick her replacement on her deathbed she would list essentials like cooking, cleaning, and dependability. In short, someone that can come in the home and hold it down.

Ask a man what he looks for in a wife, and he won't list cooking spaghetti, he'll ask for a pen and pad, so he can sketch the physical. The male brain thinks fun first, what's for dinner last. Guys pretend to want all that domestic stuff and even wax poetic about it, but it's lip service. Men with real money are most likely to marry the trophy that stays at home, yet despite that free time still hires a maid to come clean or take care of her kids over the woman that spends her 20s saying "I have to bring something to the table if I'm ever to become wife material." It may not seem fair or progressive, but it's the truth. Men love Hos that bring fun into their lives and are willing to pay to keep her happy. Women hate Hos that don't have to do much to get a lifestyle they only fantasize about, and no one epitomizes this societal truth more than Kimberly Noel Kardashian.

Kim Kardashian received a lot of bitter hate during both of her publicized weddings. The consensus I gathered from those that were Anti-Kim was that she was not a woman that you share your home with; she's a woman you share a bed with and that's it. To be fair, no successful man will take a woman seriously if she is only good for sex. **Every woman has a pussy and more and more "grow" huge asses these days, yet they can't replicate what Kim has done, so it is not about the physical.** I've never had a conversation with Kim Kardashian nor was I impressed with her sex tape skills, but she oozes the kind of charisma that trumps book smart intelligence. I'm sure Kim can lay in bed at night and be a great listener and a master at lightening the mood when her husband's life gets stressful. Those traits and several others listed in this book become invaluable because they are conversation and personality skills that will be used on a day-to-day basis to keep notoriously bored men interested and engaged. Too independent, too focused on your own world, too busy to have fun like you used to have. Most career women fall under that umbrella, and they end up with a husband that starts cheating or get a divorced, because they can't tap into that Maria type persona every now and again to appease their man.

Your master's degree can get you a career, but for a man that already has money, that isn't a make or break quality. I applaud educated women who have their own money and make their own way in life without a man. This is not to say, "Drop out and Ho." This is not about the right way or wrong way, it is about the Ho Way. In a traditional marriage it should be a balance, but in a Ho marriage, you will have to play that role of submissive from time to time and revert to being that little girl that needs Daddy's help. The average man with money is not intimidated by successful women, he's bored by them. Say what you want about Kim K, but even without the looks, business, or fame, she would still win because she's a walking party. Will the good times last, who cares? **It's not about the end game, it's about mastering the current game**. Ho Tactics force you to become an engaging personality, not a phenomenal homemaker or great cook because the way to a man's heart isn't through his stomach, it's through his penis by way of his brain. Go back, study these chapters, and master the conversation skills, and I promise you these lessons will help you land a husband quicker than the ability to make southern style chicken wings.

The Aging Ho

As you enter the twilight of your Ho career, it may not be a man's pursuit that makes you want to retire, but the general need to cash out while you still can compete with the young Hos on the come up. When the average woman hits her late 20s she panics because despite where her professional life is, it's the romantic one that has to be satisfied before the age of 30 or she will feel like a loser. In response, these type of women force the issue. They go out on dates with men that don't meet their standards, pay for dating sites, and accept any blind date a friend sets up. That's an idiotic knee-jerk reaction based on fear. Hos have no fear; they were about money, not marriage, but looks only last so long, so most become open to the possibility. Even at this point, a Smart Ho will not chase. Don't get me wrong, she will continue to approach winners and entertain those that have trick potential, but she will never be hard up for marriage. The hustle used to be a car, now it evolves to half of his possessions or a place in his will, but the mentality remains.

What if you aren't someone that grew with your mark/husband, you two are strangers, and he may or may not know about your past? Doesn't matter! Cardi B was a stripper who recorded funny, yet telling, videos about her exploits as a Ho—didn't stop a man from getting down on bended knee after knowing her a short while. Karrine Steffans wrote a series of books detailing her history as "Superhead" the queen of the blow job—didn't stop multiple men from proposing to her. Even when you look to suburbia, you'll find women who had reputations in college or on the bar scene, yet there she is happily married. Even when men know the history, they run towards these women because he's not judging her statistics, he's judging the persona she brings presently.

You can use your old Ho reputation to entice men, so long as you lay your past on the table as if you're done playing games. Men no longer care about the old stories if you come off reset and reborn. They are turned on by the fact that you were once a savage. I call this *Dirty Sophistication*. You were once wild, and you can still turn up for him, but as far as living that life, you're retired. Not only do you express this with words, you show it with your presentation. You get wild to a point, but then you scale back. You reminisce on what you would have done to his dick ten years ago, but you do it in a teasing way where you act as if that was a completely different woman. Men love rehabilitated Hos that toe the line as if they may relapse at any moment, but only for him.

Most women don't know how to ask for a relationship, because they fear a man rejecting her with a "let's keep growing" or a flat out, "I'm not ready." In this book you were taught the power of speaking up, and when it comes to relationships the key will always be to state what you want, not ask. **When you ask, you make it a man's choice. When you state, you make it a take it or leave it ultimatum.** As a veteran Ho on her way out, all you need to do is work him like you would any mark, and then when his nose is open with the smell of how great you are, tell him you are done with the games. If you're going to have fun, be wild, be nasty, and provide a fountain of youth, then you need it to be legitimate at this point in life. "I'm ready for us to get serious." That's a statement. There is no wiggle room for bullshit. At that point, the mark will jump to give a real relationship a shot just as quickly as the old marks jumped to buy you those headphones or he will make excuses as to why he can't settle down.

If he doesn't give you what you want, walk away just like in every one of these tactics. Typical women chase, they pout, they negotiate—and they end up fucked and lose all value going forward. Hos do not care about rejection because they understand that their options will never be limited. There will be another investment banker who tries to court her, another NFL player that asks for her number, another attorney that promises to give her the world, so why get caught up trying to hold on to a man that isn't trying to give her what she wants? At the same time, a Smart Ho is aware that she is indeed a limited edition. Who else will this aging trick or sponsor come across that can make a marriage feel like an arrangement and not a prison?

All men reach a point where they want to settle down and have someone to come home to. Either he chooses one of these nags that are desperate and rundown, or he chooses a girl that won't mind bringing home another girl for his birthday or turning a blind eye when he takes a weekend out of town with a friend she's never heard of before. Not to say that this is a sham relationship where you allow cheating, he will understand by the way you two date that you are to be respected like a true lady or you'll divorce him and take all of his shit, because Hos don't believe in prenups. Any man who marries a woman with your personality and ambition will recognize that you are the type of woman that's not going to put him in jealousy handcuffs… so long as he keeps that bank account swollen and two cars in the garage. As I said before, men fear commitment because it signals an end of fun and the death of excitement, but you are not typical, you are the type of woman that makes marriage seem like a party instead of a jail sentence.

#19:
How to Win the Ho Way

Hos win because they live an enviable lifestyle that many women wish they could emulate. Each person's definition of winning is different, and the area where many women wish they could win isn't financially. They want the three A's: *Attention, Affection, and Appreciation*. When I say, "Hos win", it's about those three A's, because at the heart of female insecurity is the fact that Girl A managed to get a man to chase her with passionate desire and treat her like a Queen without doing much but providing him with verbal stimulation and mental cock-stroking. Whereas Girl B has worked hard to show that man that she's honest, nurturing, and his equal, yet can't get anything but promises and penis. While I am sure this book will have plenty of critics who misconstrue the theme of this book as something sneaky and underhanded; it is more empowering than any of these, *"Wait For God To Show You Mr. Right Blah Blah Blah This Too Shall Pass"* teachings that would have you place your destiny in the hands of men rather than use your brain in the same way males have been doing for centuries.

The Three A's are real, and most of you reading this have probably experienced frustration over your inability to attain that manner of treatment from men you find attractive. I talk to women every day of my life and I hear the war stories that they go through. I see how the younger generation of men are coming of age with little to no respect for women because the message of kitchen bitch submission has made many females docile and complacent. Millennial men don't see most women as smart, they see them as holes, and it's not just guys born in the late 80's or early 90's, the older generation of men are seeing how easy it is to manipulate and swindle women out of pussy and following the lead of younger men. Dating is the Wild West, and women are being wiped out like Native Americans because they refuse to advance with the times and use modern warfare.

What's happened is there is a "Us versus Them" line drawn in the sand where women have become so turned off by male behavior that they give into bitterness and defensive arguments about the role of a man in their lives. I always hear, "Maybe if men knew how to appreciate a good woman instead of a bad bitch, kids would be raised right" or "Tell these men how they should act because we're doing our part." Those attitudes are born from frustration. Women are disgusted that men don't behave the way they are supposed to behave. Meaning, if she treats him nice and respectful he should treat her the same. **That will never happen because men will always have ulterior motives when choosing mates that have nothing to do with what woman holds him down or is most loyal!** Instead of sitting back and watching beautiful women crumble because asshole after asshole rejects or discards them, I needed to show in the most blatant way possible, how any woman can win. It may require white lies, it may require you to forgo your Sunday School morality for a few weekends, but it unlocks real power in terms of confidence building and knowing your worth.

This book isn't about getting anything from men, it's about getting everything from life. Yes, you and your best friend are independent women who don't need to mindfuck a man because you are self-sufficient. I'll toast to that. You don't need to get spoiled or sponsored because you can treat yourself to a spa day or a handbag. I'll toast to that. Cheers all around because I love that "I'm both King and Queen" power. However, it would be foolish to ignore the truth. The truth is, there are many levels of female power and you shouldn't stop learning them because you are a content career woman or married.

I don't care what you believe in morally because your morals don't dictate what does or doesn't happen in real life. Someone told me early on in this process that she doesn't like the thought of women lying to men, and that Ho Tactics are dangerous. I don't like the thought of men lying to women, but guess what, all my male friends do it on a daily basis. It's not about stooping to a male's level, it's about understanding that level in order to tap into this Ho power whenever you need it. Why should any woman want to tap into this power when she can stay on the straight and narrow and be a phenomenal woman? The straight and narrow is failing! The most honest and loving women out there are being strung along because they are taught to pray on it instead of understanding why they are being hustled. I'm sick and tired of seeing single mothers who do everything right, then end up falling for players. I'm sick of reading letters from women in their 30s who are still chasing the commitment carrot from the same bum that's been popping in and out of their lives for years because they don't think another man would want them at their age. There is so much power to be regained in relationships and marriages, even if you dip a little bit into the so-called dark side of Girl Power.

No matter the case I state for the necessity of Ho Power, there will be detractors who will feel I've gone too far because these tactics don't mesh with their weak bitch programming.

Some of you reading this may feel confused as to if you should or shouldn't apply these techniques. As I said earlier, this isn't about following Maria, it's about understanding how you can be just as powerful as Maria in other aspects of your life. **Those of you who read this book and grasp the lessons will change fundamentally even if you never pull a mark in your life.** You will find a new level of confidence that will surprise you and even want to share it with friends who are immediately turned off by the mere title of "Ho Tactics" the same way the ignorant sucked their teeth when they saw the title *Black Girls Are Easy*. This is your journey, regardless of who shares it with you or criticizes you for it, you came to these pages to learn something new, and you have. It doesn't stop here; you must keep reinforcing the lessons until your confidence is untouchable. I don't care if you're too soft to be a Spartan or too honest to be a Ho. This book is proof that you are not at the mercy of men, they are at the mercy of you if you take charge!

Ho Conclusion

I want to dedicate this final section to those judgmental women that hide behind shallow Instagram quotes. Those critical females behind keyboards that have so much shade to throw at their sisters, but do little to progress womankind. Those women that believe in playing the victim because they don't have the heart to be the conqueror… I want you to look into the mirror. You sit around talking about Hos but secretly admire their power. You look for any occasion to party and lose yourself so you can be less of a prude and have fun like *The Hos*. You go shopping for a Thot-fit that hugs your body in order to emulate the sexiness and attention received by *The Hos*. The high of saying, "I'm dressing like such a Ho tonight," is the only way you can feel powerful and sexy. You drink too much, flirt too hard, and end up having sex under the cover of, "I felt like being a Ho for tonight." Only to wake up the next morning, back to talking shit about the women who did the same things you did the night before, but with better results. It's time to be honest about what you lack in life, and stop hiding behind this wall of elitism. Look at Ms. Educated and thirsty… your life is so boring, so predictable, and so by the book that every weekend, summer, birthday, or special occasion you have to go act out like the type of woman you hate just so you can feel alive inside. In the end you won't find love, you'll find dick and excuses.

The moment you let these men brainwash you with fast talk and handsome grins, you become the mark! **Men invented the art of manipulation because pussy is highly coveted**. Lie, steal, cheat, lie some more… guys are willing to break all rules in pursuit of women. Men you swear are down for you are using Dick Tactics on you right now, and you're too prideful to see it. Read and re-read the previous chapters until you understand how to win the way I laid out, or you will continue in the struggle cycle until you end up settling like so many before you.

This book is not a call for you to go out and get money, it's a call for everyone reading to think outside the box and understand how this world works. I love women, and it breaks my heart when I see them compete and tear each other down because they think finding a man to love is the most important thing in the world. You are the most important thing in the world, and love will come easily once you realize that you control your destiny! I didn't write Ho Tactics to corrupt you morally, but I did write it to enlighten you mentally. Now that you're awake, what are you going to do with all this knowledge?

Bonus Section:
Be Savage…

"Never look back unless you're throwing that ass."
-Ancient Ho Proverb

#20

What's Your Ho IQ

I f I were to introduce you to a trick who I knew for a fact was an easy mark, would you know what to do? You've just finished reading chapters loaded with psychology, insight, and strategy which has been pulled off by women just like you. With the perfect mark in your sights, again I ask, can you pull the right strings to make his pockets sing? Ho IQ, the ability to not only comprehend this book but the psychology behind it, was a missing piece that I never accounted for when I wrote the first edition of this book. It took until recently for me to put my finger on the concept of why certain women freeze up and revert to their old ways instead of doing these steps. Hos understand men, they read them and then connect their behavior to a database full of like-minded men to predict their behavior. Women with low Ho IQ see males as this big mystery. They aren't sure how to act or what to say, let alone how to take charge because they're in this basic mind frame of trying to impress not finesse.

In college football there are tons of incredibly athletic quarterbacks that not only pass the ball half the distance of the field, they run and catch as if no position is off limits. Each year these quarterbacks leave college, try to make it in the NFL, only to find themselves undrafted. The ultimate athlete is now asking what size shoe you wear at the local mall. What happened? He didn't have football IQ. He knew the mechanics, but he didn't know the "why" "how" or "when" of the game. It's a reason why Peyton Manning was able to win a Super Bowl with a failing body and suspect arm—he was smarter than everyone else on the field. **Are you a person that can do what someone else tells you and succeed or are you someone that can take learned knowledge and tell yourself how to succeed without having someone hold your hand?** If you're going to do this, you must be confident in your progressions. You can't simply look to replicate Maria line for line, because the moment a man doesn't react as written in this book, you'll fumble and cost yourself an easy win. To truly bring out your inner savage let's go over some perception techniques that will expand your intelligence.

Personality Types

Know personality types as well as traits. I recommend taking time to read Carl Jung's *Psychological Types* to get a basic handle. I'm not talking about internet personality tests. Those things are about as worthless as horoscopes because even in their specificity they remain generic and over-reaching. Saying that someone's a narcissist doesn't tell you how to manipulate them, it's most likely a blanket statement. Saying that someone is a INJF according to some test, doesn't really get you anywhere as you're not pinpointing specifics. It's like pointing out that someone is a Taurus, you're boxing them into imaginary labels, not real science. Keep it simple in the same way Jung did:

- **Extraversion Vs. Introversion** – A person's sense of energy either comes from the external world (extraversion) or their own internal world (introversion).

- **Sensing Vs. Intuition** – How a person perceives information. Either they're influenced by the external world (sensing), or they mainly believe information from their internal feelings (intuition).

- **Thinking Vs. Feeling** – How a person processes information. Either they use logic (thinking), or they use emotions (feeling).

I won't delve too deep into this as I don't want to overload you with the science of thought. I merely need you to connect the dots. Think about these traits under the umbrella of everyday life. You know someone that is always making gut decisions as well as someone that's always needing the advice or opinion of others before acting. Furthermore, you've seen how two people can get hit with the same bad news and react in totally different manners, one restrained and the other over-emotional. These are the small, yet telling signs you must be aware of no matter if you're working a trick for breast implant money, or looking to get in the good graces of your employer. Knowing how they process and perceive allows you to cherry pick your conversation and mold your seduction strategy with ease.

    The major observation that will help you tomorrow if you were to go out and use the tactics written in this book is to always know your introverts and your extroverts and what makes them tick. An extrovert craves attention, they like to be the center of other people's universes, and feed off others taking notice of them. An extrovert loves befriending introverts because they will always be allowed to take over the conversation, get their point across, or persuade them to do or go where they want without much argument. You often see this in high school clicks, where one Queen Bee is the glue that keeps the more introverted girls together and manipulates that squad into doing her bidding. An extrovert hates other extroverts because they will undoubtedly bump heads when it's time to talk or plan. You will notice this when you bring two groups of friends together, and the two loudest go from being super-friendly to debating each other over every little thing. Both must be heard, so neither is heard. When you approach a man, your initial conversation will let you in on if he's an introvert or an extrovert. Some men are naturally extroverted, but freeze up around female attention they weren't expecting. Still, to ask questions the same way Maria did during this initial scouting, will put him at ease and his natural personality will shine through. For example,

Introvert: *I work in human resources.*

Extrovert: *I deal with the evaluation of new hires for a major Telecom company; it's a cool because each day is something different, and I'm one of those people that gets bored easily.*

Do you see how the extrovert oversold and overexposed? This happens anytime you push them towards a topic that makes them feel comfortable, I call this a "personality reveal," and you should make it a habit of taking mental notes when it happens so you can use it later on when you hit the dating stage. Please don't think that one mark is easier than the other. Of course, there are personalities that are more susceptible to giving and trusting, but Ho Tactics works on any personality type because it's about feeding into their personal desires. You shouldn't pass up on introverts because you feel that extroverts will be easier to figure out and test, both can be worked if you take your time to pinpoint their wants and needs.

I know a young woman in Seattle that passed on this introverted Asian guy. She didn't think he was into her because of his short and blunt responses. She felt it wasn't worth the trouble to pull conversation out of him and doubted that he was interested because he didn't act excited. This Asian guy ended up with a girlfriend who traveled in her same extended circle. Vacations, jewelry, dinners, her Facebook became a flex session because this guy was not just rich he was wealthy. To add insult to injury when this new girlfriend ended up at a party with that would-be Ho, she drunkenly teased her, "You know he had the biggest crush on you." The other girl went full tilt and got him open, whereas the would-be Ho was a victim of laziness and low Ho intelligence. Know your mark, listen to your mark, and be patient enough to figure out a true game plan that plays off his personality and these tactics are damn near automatic.

Connecting

"I don't know what to talk about," go ahead and nod because you've had this thought cross your mind no matter if it's attaining a traditional relationship or trying to work a trick. Women tend to overthink what men want to hear as if the conversation is a Rubik Cube. You don't have to say all the right things to make a guy like you, you only have to say a few of them, and you're in his good graces. In the previous chapters, I went over flirting, invading personal space, using your wit, all aspects of charm. Charm is necessary for comfort. Comfort is necessary for trust. Trust is necessary for control. The glue of your Ho IQ is the ability to connect with a person so that they allow you to imprint yourself on them in a real way. Once you figure out their basic personality type, it will be easy to charm them by exploiting what their personality feeds off.

Storytime! A young woman who was Insta-famous reached out to me for help. She had a pro athlete in her DMs trying to game her, and she was offended. She told me she wasn't out for money normally, she was a romantic, but she hated how these men thought that because a woman dressed a certain way on Instagram, they were all sluts that would respond to the promise of, "let me fly you out and take you shopping." I gave her a mission that would ensure that she would connect with him within two weeks, and make it easy for her to get in his pockets. A week later she had failed her mission. Instead of connecting with him, she just sexted him and flirted. After reading through the screen grabs she sent me, it was obvious that this woman who talked to me with intelligence and poise devolved into a stereotype when talking to men. She didn't separate herself from the pack because she gave him exactly what he was expecting from a pretty girl on IG. Get her open off the money, get her to engage in sex talk, get her to agree to be flown out, spread her legs. Ego makes women feel that they're not acting in the same manner as every other chick, but the proof is in the conversation, and hers was weak!

"What do I say to him, I don't watch sports," was her reasoning for coming off basic. Ladies, men don't want to talk about their profession 24-7. I don't care if he's a carpenter or a power forward, your way to win him over has nothing to do with your knowledge of his day to day because you're not going to be discussing game strategy or housing schematics. This is romance! **Men with money and success tend to be nerds.** Those freaks and geeks from high school that were super-focused aren't the same as the Joe Cool's that girls used to chase after. High school athletes are sports nerds. Tech CEO's were computer nerds. Now that they have money and power they still don't have true swag. Hence, why these guys use Instagram to pull women and are horrible at conversation—they're nerds. You think because they have money, are famous, or look good that they're larger than life. No. Being smooth with women is a skill that most men with real money don't possess.

I personally know an actor on a network show who still has to beg for pussy. I've seen text messages from a famous musician that are corny as hell. Prostitution via escort services is a billion dollar industry because men you see as gods don't know the first thing about how to get women to give it up for free. Male players, who we'll discuss later, can talk a virgin out of her panties and be dirt poor because he has GAME, but these men worth 100x more don't have an ounce of game. Therefore, they do what this athlete did on Instagram, shoot a "hey, I'd like to get you better," and allow women to play themselves.

What do you talk about exactly? What he likes to talk about! The pre-date conversation is all about research. If you know the year he was born in, you know the shows he grew up watching. If he quotes a movie or tells a pop culture related joke, you know what genre of entertainment he's into. Remember *Rugrats*? No, he missed that but was *a Hey Arnold* guy as a kid. Did he see the last *Star Wars*? No, but he loves *Better Call Saul*. You've never seen it, make him tell you about it, then sound excited to go watch it. The same thing applies to talking about music and concert going, religion and spirituality, etc...

I told a girl to bring up the Nintendo 64 game "GoldenEye" to a potential mark. She wrote back that he talked more than he ever talked in the two weeks she had known him. It didn't matter if she played it, the fact that she bought it up brought out his inner nerd. Do the research, find out what he's into, google those things, and come ready to mention subjects you now know excite him. For Ho Tactics to work, you must become more than some pretty girl. Connecting via conversation is the only way to achieve that.

Agenda

A man who is taking time out to text or talk to you wants to fuck you. That's obvious. Let's take your vagina out of the picture. What does he want from women in general? A man that is getting out of a long-term relationship may say he doesn't want another relationship, but he's so used to having a girlfriend that he can't help but miss that. This means that while he may not want to put a title on what you two are doing, he does want to treat you like his girl and have you treat him like your man, it's a habit.

A man that's married and lusting after you isn't looking to make you his wife, he doesn't have a need for another one. He's looking for fun, excitement, and the spontaneity of his life pre-marriage. Finally, a man that's older or one that's been single for a long time will be looking to escape his life of man-whoring. He has enough notches in his belt, and he wants a woman to bond with not bone. On your first date with a mark, get to know his agenda by being able to read the subtext of a conversation or a life story. Your Ho IQ works in the same way a Spartan's vetting does. By the end of the date you will know what his heart longs for other than pussy because your questions won't be, "so tell me about your last girlfriend," they are meant to be, "tell me a story about your life."

Use your Ho IQ to break down the "why" of every man's actions towards you. Some girls are used to hard, emotionally distant men, so they call guys that are sweet, "corny." Go deeper! **What makes a guy act hard and uninterested when he really is?** He's been hurt-duh. A hurt man's agenda is to protect himself at all cost, so to get in his pockets, you must implant the idea during your initial date that you're loyal, that you're transparent, that you're different from the girl that hurt him. You don't do this by saying, "I'm not like other chicks," you show him by not letting your eyes wander to men that are more handsome, by offering to pay half of that bill on the first date, and by sharing some story real or fictional about how you were loyal to a fault. By the end of that date, he's mindfucked into thinking you're sweet, his agenda of protecting himself from Hos like you crumbles because you're no longer seen as a Ho, you're one of the good ones. This frees you up to get in his pockets despite his hard exterior.

What makes a man who barely knows you be overly sappy and trick on you before you even use any real tactics? He's lonely—duh. A man that's acting corny or overly-romantic doesn't need you to play along, he needs you to make him chase because through the chase he feels that his actions are working. The best strippers tease, they don't just take off their top and shake their tits. Why? Because there are personality types that need to feel as if they have to earn it. The so-called cornball wants to buy you dinner, he wants to send you flowers, but needs you to remain only mildly impressed. He needs to go to bed wondering what else he can do for you that will finally lead to the reaction he wants or even a kiss at the end of the date. Typical women who aren't up on Ho game will push a man like this away in favor of guys who wouldn't buy her a cup of ice in a heat wave. "I need a manly man boyfriend that tells me 'no'!" She's an idiot that's most likely battling daddy issues.

Guys that trick fast are testing you. A rookie would get a makeup set as her version of the headphone test and then ask for a purse because she figures this guy is a simp. The guy would see that the woman wasn't really into him and just using him and pull back, because even simps have eyes that can spot obvious hustles. An educated Ho won't be impressed by that makeup set, she'll thank him, kiss his cheek, and continue to bond with him. This would make him rack his brain on, "did I do a good enough job?" Thus, he will give again without asking. By the time you do get around to going in for what you want, he will be primed to say, "yes" because you haven't tried to take advantage. He trusts you, because you are playing into his agenda of needing a challenge. That's a smart hustle.

Playing Dumb

Make people feel they're smarter than you and you will always have a leg up on them. How can you be a threat when you're not bright enough to hustle him out of money? **You're just a simple sweet girl that's sexy and fun to hang around with, no way you could ever mastermind a plan to get him to pay your rent. Or so he will think.** Playing dumb isn't literal of course, it doesn't mean you go Ben Stiller playing Happy Jack. It's subtle. You ask him what things mean during conversations instead of saying, "I know," or you own up to the occasional brain-fart by saying, "I'm such an airhead," as to slyly plant the seed that you're not the sharpest knife in the draw. Women tend to lead with know-it-all conversation and a list of things they've done academically. While that's impressive, it creates this resentment of, "This bitch thinks she's smarter than me." As many of you in unhealthy relationships have seen, this causes a man to be paranoid or jealous. They see you as being smart enough to cheat or undermine them in secret. Your intelligence makes you sneaky and keeps their guard up. Ho IQ does away with that because the dumber he thinks you are, the lower his guard drops.

My wife watches this show called *Black Ink,* a horrible overly-scripted reality show about a Harlem tattoo shop. The shop owner, while good-hearted and caring, is an easy mark. During the later seasons the love interest, a slow-talking woman from down south who doesn't seem too bright at first glance, ended up usurping power through her relationship with him. She took control of his shop, ended up opening her own shop, and was later exposed for having multiple affairs. I wasn't surprised because that's what smart Hos do. They lay and wait, charm a mark, get their needs met, and then the rest of the world is left with, "I can't believe she would do that, she didn't seem like the type." That's what playing dumb is, it's misdirection.

A Step Ahead

A smart Quarterback knows when a linebacker is going to blitz versus fall back into pass coverage. Not because that linebacker motions in one direction or the other, but because he's studied film and has seen his tell signs for when he's bluffing versus committing to that act. That's the homework that separates good from great. A smart Ho doesn't just go out on dates with confidence that her flirting is impeccable, she studies a man, compares him to others, and uses his words and actions to predict how he's going to act going forward. Even if you don't have much experience with dating men, this book has already laid out several types of men and the things they do. Anyone can stumble their way into a few gifts, but the true art of Ho Tactics is being able to attain anything you need to make your life better by exercising your will over a man's brain. Know his personality, connect with him, figure out his agenda and play to it while pretending to be oblivious and that will put you a step ahead of him for the duration of your mission.

Ho Tactics: Mark Analysis Form

Interview Details

Mark Name: :   Age: Job:
_____   _____   _____

Personality
Type:
_____

General
Interests: Music Interest:
_____   _____

Movie/TV   Political/Religious
Interest: Interest:
_____   _____

Trick, Treat,
Sponsor:
_____

Your Ho Goal: _____

Pre-Date Questions

Question
#1:
_____

His
Answer:
_____

Question
#2:
_____

His
Answer:
_____

First-Date Questions

Question
#1:
_____

His Answer:
_____

Question
#2:
_____

His Answer:
_____

Breakdown Your Marks Wants, Needs, & Flaws

My Mark Wants:

My Mark Needs:

My Mark Is Weak In:

My Plan of Attack Is:

#21

How to Turn the Tables on Male Hos

You can spot a player a mile away, or so you have led yourself to believe. Men can't spot Smart Hos because, as you just learned, they move in silence and make themselves invaluable before ever asking for anything materialistic. Male Hos aka Macks or Players, don't have to move in silence or endear themselves. They use the Kryptonite of attention and interests. What do Typical Tina's want out of life? Love. Daddy wasn't around or didn't care. Mommy was too busy competing or judging you. Ex-Boyfriends loved conditionally. Knowing these women are desperate for validation, a male ho doubles down on the complements, on promises, and works hard those first few weeks or even months to be consistent until a woman loses herself in the potential that he may be different. Even when a woman is cautious the hope of true love can blind her. Male players don't win because of looks or rely on persistence; most utilize charm, confidence, and wit to lore a woman into his lap.

What is Game? It's not a series of pick-up lines and jokes, nor is it acting cool and unbothered. Game is the ability to read a woman's vibe, put her into a category of like-minded women he's known or experienced, and then muster the courage to invade her personal space until her attitude is defused and the guard is lowered. When you see the cliché image of the smooth talker walking up and whispering in a girl's ear or making some Bill Bellamy inspired sexual innuendo, you only see a small part of what a male's Game truly is. Not every woman reacts to dirty talk or sensual conversation. Players know the Game, be they white, black, or green, it doesn't matter the race or culture, these men make knowing women their business. He can look at the woman in the business suit and know that she isn't going to react to jokes the same way the younger woman in converse would. He can tell from her response to "hey how are you," if she's defensive, yet interested or if she truly doesn't want to be bothered. Women pretend to be different, but they have many tell signs that give away how they really feel. An average man gets intimidated, he gets annoyed, he only has one gear to shift into unless a girl is receptive to generic "what's your name, beautiful" game. Players have several gears, which makes him a chameleon when cruising for ass. He can quickly adapt his verbiage to make himself into whatever he feels this woman is looking for in a man. In the end, all he needs to do is get one smile, or one flirty comment returned, and he knows that the hunt is all but over.

You have experienced the corny stereotypes of guys asking for your number or the tired lines from men that direct message you online, and feel that's as deep as it goes. Macks slip through your defenses because they know how to inspire excitement. In a world full of "hey" texts and "I'd love to get to know you," come on lines, you're looking for someone that can make you grin.

No matter if you've sworn off love, think you're too busy, or are still healing, a guy who comes correct will make you think twice because 90% of women who claim they don't want anything serious still imagines finding prince charming. Therefore, you will see a man like this, who knows how to talk to women, as a breath of fresh air. I routinely get messages about how a man stood out as different, and the women who send these emails are often coming off a bad relationship or a long stretch where they couldn't get a man to look their way if they were standing naked in a hardware store. These girls are what I call "open" because females tend to judge their appeal by the last man that tried to talk to them. **Most of the women reading this understand that coming off a bad drought or a shitty relationship makes you vulnerable.** Your confidence is lowered, and you desperately need someone to chase you in a way that isn't lame or overly sexual. Male Hos understand this and look for that kind of opening because a woman on the rebound or sick of dating is ripe for the picking.

In the previous chapters you learned all the Ho Tactics there are to learn, you've seen how Maria manipulated the fuck out of her mark and got in his pockets by using her in-depth knowledge of lust against men. Put that in perspective with these male players because so-called "Hos" are nothing more than female Macks. It's only when men feel threatened do these women get labeled derogatorily. Maria and women like her are after money, status, or material goods. Macks are after sex, money, or material goods. Men will always be driven by pussy, even those that are smart enough to see their own savage urges for what they are. Society toasts the male players. While we openly tell little boys to respect women as if they all where Mom, we secretly pat them on the back and tell them to go out there and be a heartbreaker.

Men love to see younger males exploit women because it's a victory for all of mankind. "He got the pussy," means we all got the pussy! There is and will always be a brotherhood where females are seen as the enemy that is hunted for sport. **There are more male Hos than female ones; they just don't have the stigma attached to them because this is a man's world.** There's nothing wrong with Macking or Hoing or whatever you want to call the ability to use what's in your head to get what they got. The same way that a mark gives a Ho what she wants freely, women give these men what they want without a gun being put to their head because they chose to. It's not a crime; it's not wrong, it's on that person for being a sucker. Now that you understand what a smart Ho is, it's time to protect yourself from the male version. Some of you won't ever use Ho Tactics in a real way, you will chose to go after an authentic relationship with someone who can at least pass the headphone test. <u>I want you to use this chapter to sniff out any man you date, no matter if you're looking for love, a come up, or just bored and entertaining him</u>. At least one out of the next ten guys you meet will be trying to play you using the same tactics we've discussed but in a male-centric way.

Exposing Him On The First Date

Too many women think the best way to protect their heart is to live closed off and assume every man is full of shit. That's just as closed minded as men who believe all women are Hos looking to play them. You can't win if you don't play the game, so instead of rolling your eyes, hear him out let him pull you. All you need is one date to expose a male Ho, so play along and test him. This trial by dating won't cost you anything but a night out, and let's face it; you most likely want an excuse to wear one of those outfits in your closet that you never get to wear.

Step 1: Let Him Sell You

You must have an appreciation for good Game. It's an honor to be approached with something more original than "Excuse me, Miss." You've been courted by guys who probably say, "Ay, what's your name? I'm trying to get to know you." That is horrible game, but some of you entertain that. To hear a man speak eloquently or intrigue you with a challenging line of conversation is like night and day. Go on that ride and wait for that feeling… the feeling I'm referring to is that tingle in your shoulders or chest when he says something so cold that you can't even muster the brain power to fire back in your normal way. A man like that deserves your number, but after you give it up, test him to be sure if he's legit or one of these guys who gets his confidence from Reddit forums and Pick-Up Artist websites.

The first step is to let him think he's winning. It's okay to play the role of the helpless damsel that's impressed and gives out her number, but remember you are PLAYING a role. I've talked to women who are extremely shy around boys, and they describe this freezing effect a cute guy has on them that reduces them to this groupie like state where they can't think of anything interesting to say. I want you to channel that energy, let him believe he's blowing you away and that the war is already won. What this does is lull him into a false sense of victory, boost his confidence, and give him incentive to move on to Step 2.

Step 2: Let Him Set The Date

When you're Hoing you let a man set the date to see what he's working with, in this instance of Ho hunting, you still let him choose where he wants to take you. The purpose of this is that you still don't know if he's trying to play you, so you don't want to punish a genuine man by making the first date all about eating on his dime. A player won't pay too much for pussy, but he understands that he needs to invest in a place where he can further unleash his conversation in order to exploit you. In his mind, the first date is all about sizing you up because you are the mark. He wants to be able to tell if you're going to be first night sex, first-week sex, or a woman who has money that he can siphon for months to come.

Let's set a scenario where Ricardo the Mack tries to work you with his Dick Tactics. Imagine that you met Ricardo at a normal place—gas station, elevator, he held the door at a store. Doesn't matter, the point is you popped up on his radar, was a perfect gentleman but also funny and engaging to the point where you said, "why not" and exchanged information. How do you get in a person's good graces? By being different. What do men do when they get a girl's number? They text a reminder of "hey, this is such and such," and then they begin to bore the fuck out of you through text. The reason this works is that if a guy's handsome, you see those dry texts as amazing— lust blinders. If he's not that cute, you put up with it because it's something to do. The point is, men under the age of 40 will generally text first, and you accept that as just how the world works or expect it because you've grown accustomed to using your fingers more than your mouth. Males Hos, use their mouths not because they can't text, but because it's the best way to mindfuck a person.

Ricardo calls you the day after you meet and continues where he left off. What sets him apart from the average man you know besides actually calling, is that he doesn't press for some "When can we hang out," lazy date. Ricardo knows his fellow man, and he knows that they want to get you to the level of *Come Over & Chill*. You're expecting laziness, and he gives you real courting, most women are already head over heels off that tiny bit of effort. "Where do you want to go, beautiful, I don't care if I got to put you on my back, we'll go." Chivalry mixed with humor feels genuinely like he wants to make you happy. This PUA does want to make you happy, happy enough to drop your guard and spread those legs after the dessert course. Again, you must tell Silver Tongue Ricardo to surprise you by picking the date himself. He will already be prepared for this because most women in real life are indecisive when it comes to answering the question "what do you want to do." Shoot down his first suggestion to throw him off balance. He will reach for a place that's comfortable, and where he works his women often.

You don't want to be on his home turf, so reject his first idea as if you don't like their food or don't feel like doing that activity. Pick-Up Artist, like Hos, are taught to go where they can be free to touch. Restaurant tables block hands and separate, so he'll most likely try to steer clear of dinner. Steer him back to dinner, but do this in a way that doesn't seem picky or bitchy, make him understand that it would normally be a good idea, but you have a serious hang-up with the place. He'll probably struggle to think of a backup because you threw him off his square, but when he does find a new place, accept it with open arms and be excited. Ricardo now feels as if it's only a matter of time, but then Step 3 happens.

Step 3: Hijack The Date

Ricardo has taken you out for a dinner date at a medium price restaurant where he can sit next to you, order drinks, get you loose, and mindfuck you into falling in-like with him in three hours. This is the part that takes real effort because unlike most girls who get scavenged by players, you will go left where they would have gone right. He's going to focus on, You You You. What do you like to do for fun, your family history, your last relationship, your girlfriends and co-workers, your dreams and aspirations, etc... What men do is read you like a textbook, take mental notes, and then based on all the information you just gave away, rebuild their lives as if it's compatible to your own. **By the end of the night he'll be referencing things you mentioned as if you two have so much in common, in actuality it's Game.** Do not give this man the rundown of your entire life as if he's a therapist, he hasn't earned that, no one you've only known for a few days has earned the right to know you.

Hijack the date by turning the tables back on Him Him Him. You want to know his story, because unlike the average desperate woman, you didn't come on this date to vent and get all of your, "Life's so unfair" relationship stress off your chest. A player will tell you that he works a good job then give you an idea of what he does but not the specifics, because he's lying. Next he will talk about his expanded plan to be his own boss or tell you that he already has a side hustle. Basic bitches are his side hustle, getting loans, getting them to invest in his ideas, using their credit cards; it's so easy for a man to live like a baller and impress new pussy when spending another chick's money. Don't pay any attention to the moves he says he's making, the people he knows, or the pictures that prove that it may be true. It's a smokescreen.

Next, he will talk about his mother or grandmother depending who is in his life more. A man knows that women see respect and love for mothers as a good sign that he was raised properly and cherishes women. Again, blow past that stuff and dig deeper. Do not accept the information he volunteers because players are like politicians. They have their talking points and they will go Sarah Palin on that ass and redirect the question the moment you ask about something that's off limit. Know this strategy, feel him out by listening to his clean-cut answers, and get him off his Game during the first half of the date by not talking about your past and present life in ways other than simple statements. Instead, always be asking to know more about something he shared. Now you go in for the kill.

Step 4: 3 Questions He Must Answer

Ricardo is not having much fun if he's a player. If he's a normal guy who has genuine interest in you then opening up about his life in a real way is new and interesting. Remember that girls usually do most of the talking, so it will come as a shock when you come off as interested in what he has to say about his life. Guys love to talk and throw opinions out, it's a part of the male ego. The difference is some regular guy will talk about his love of Star Wars versus a player that's not talking about personal loves, just his big moves so he can come off as impressive enough for you to think you hit the jack pot. Players brag about what they can do for you, how they're living, bring up the issue of money or luxury things they own every fifteen minutes. Make a mental note of this as a conversation about pets will randomly go back to his income or his business moves. Pay attention to what's coming out of his mouth, don't just rush to talk about the things you do, it's not your interview or your time to vent, it's about exposing him. Let's assume for our experiment that Ricardo is on his heels trying to get the conversation back to a point where he's winning you over and flirting. Now it's time to unleash the "Squirm Motherfucker" questions that will test his true honesty.

-How long does it usually take you to fuck women on average? No man is prepared for this question because ladies don't ask about sex—ever! You've just taken it to Maria the Ho status by being this forward about fucking. Ricardo will try to play it off and either turn it into a joke or try to make those women he's dealt with in the past not as special as you. Mind you, this is a serious question that you want an answer to, not some wisecrack about jumpoffs. Second, he doesn't know if you're a freak or a saint, so any question that makes you out to be "different" is bullshit. Get a real answer.

-If I told you I wanted to get down tonight, how would you fuck me? This will make any man squirm, even a Mack because no woman returns fire like this so randomly on the first date. You are, as the internet would say, "Trolling" him to shock him into speaking his mind. A normal guy would be stumbling all over the place trying to understand who the hell you are. A Mack, would try to keep his cool and play up the role he's been taught by the Pimpology peddlers. If his follow up is some dating show answer about how he would take you back, lay you on his Egyptian cotton, and lick on your belly button, then keep trolling him. Ask him if he eats ass, likes to take a finger in his ass, or if he's had a golden shower. Your job is to see if he ever breaks character. These men are not sincere, they read a script and stick to it, once you throw them off it, they will keep trying to get back to what they know. His refusal to be real proves what kind of person he is and saves you the trouble of getting to know this loser.

-*Why are you Gaming me*? This is the final question. After he's done trying to recover, keep it real and let him in on the secret that you know he's just spitting game trying to get you open. He'll play like you're crazy and stick to his authenticity, but don't buy that. Let him know that it's okay, he can be real. Again, he will stand strong in the pocket, but this is where your Ho Tactics come into play. Defuse his anger and aggression about being called out by stroking his hand. Put him back at ease, and ask him about how he usually operates. *Is the way he picked you up normal, does he come to this place often, how much pussy does he get with this act?* You have gone from prey to friend over the course of dinner and he will warm to that after the embarrassment wears off. This goes back to men liking to talk. Why is the mafia nearly dead? Because men like to talk about their hustles much more than the old school guys did. You aren't exposing him, you're coming with the Tactic of, "teach me, oh wise one!" and he'll brag all night.

Step 5: What Flaw Did He See In You

At the end of the night, ask him one last thing. What flaw did he see in you? When he approached you, was it the looks, was it the way you were dressed, or was it just his own ego that made him try to run Game. At this point, if this guy is a real dude, he'll keep it 100 and tell you why he chose to go at you and not the next woman. It may have been as simple as you were the first girl he saw that day or it may be revealing like, you are a little on the chubby side and those are the women he runs game on most successfully. **The reason you ask is so that you can take a closer look at what you project in your day to day life and improve.** The next time someone who goes to the same

Pick-Up Artist forums as this guy or has read the same Mack books he has studied, tries to approach you it won't take but five minutes to recognize his hustle. Even the best Dick Tactics will fail if you know how to take a man off his script. Some of you may think this is a simple exercise, but when it comes time to go on a date, and go left into the realm of random questions like those I laid out, you will be afraid.

Women freeze up when trying to apply Spartan techniques from *Men Don't Love Women Like You* and this is no different. In order to expose these male Hos you have to be willing to open your mouth and challenge them. If you try to hint, beat around the bush, or freestyle what I just wrote to create a less direct method, you will FAIL. Most of you are involved with men whom you can't figure out. No matter if it's date one or date five, throw this monkey wrench in his machine and watch how he responds. It's better to aggressively expose a man and let him prove your suspicions wrong, than to keep your mouth shut and get worked like a mark.

#22
Using Ho Tactics to Save Your Relationship

It's time to take these tactics out of the realm of tricks, treats, and sponsors and turn them inward on your current relationship. All relationships hit rough patches where someone feels unappreciated, bored, or as if a distance is starting to build. For those of you with partners, the idea isn't to suck them dry then move on; it's to establish value or create a spark. I don't care if you've been together for nine months or nine years, the dates should be exciting, the birthday gifts should blow you away, and the sex should always be phenomenal. Here comes the but... BUT, most women who come to me for relationship advice have endless sob stories.

He would rather play video games then come to bed at night. He jumps to go hang out with his friends but drags his feet at date suggestions. He buys himself whatever he wants with no budgeting, then penny pinches on birthday or Christmas gifts for you. When he does get in the mood for sex, there's no foreplay, no creativity, he just goes in with a semi-hard dick, and finishes just as fast he started. Who wants to live life like that? Being able to brag about having a "man" means nothing when you aren't doing shit but growing bored together. It's time to stop holding on to mediocrity and start Hoing Up!

Why Doesn't He Take You Out?

A man in a relationship is more likely to take a new girl he meets on the side out to an expensive restaurant than a woman he's been with for years. Why? Because one he has to impress to fuck, the other he doesn't even want to fuck. Your goal is to get your man to see you in the same light he used to when you first started dating. For those of you who have never been taken out or treated to nice things even at the start of your relationship, this isn't for you. If you're coming from a history of a man never showing you value, then it's already over, and I suggest you switch to *MDLWLY* to hit reset. For those of you that were treated with value at some point, who allowed a man to win you over through actions, not words, continue.

Look at yourself in the mirror. One of the first rules of Ho Tactics is to look good enough to want to fuck yourself. When you get into a relationship you're no longer on the hunt; you don't do as much clothes shopping, get your hair done as much, you stop working out, and settle into home-cooked meals or take out. All of these things effect your physical image. You went from sexy and looking to committed and plain. Once again, look in the mirror. Do you still look like the woman he first met? Do you still turn yourself on to the point where you stare in the mirror and think, "damn, I should take a picture," or has your look become blah? Men are liars. They won't tell you that you've put on weight, that your hair is a mess, that your fashion sense is lacking, or anything that will cause an argument about the sensitive topic of a woman's appearance. He will keep giving you lip service, he will keep telling you he loves you, but his actions prove what he's really thinking. He's not going to take a woman he no longer thinks is sexy out on weekly dates or even monthly dates because you lost your trophy aspect.

The new girl that he's eyeing at work or the front desk chick at the gym, he'd take her to the moon just to see the looks on the aliens faces when he walks in with a bad bitch. You're no longer that in his eyes. More importantly, you're no longer that in your own eyes. Ho Power is dependent on sex appeal. I don't care what your excuse is; you had a kid, you work long hours, you're trying to save money, fuck all of that, you have to bring your sexy back. The easiest way to start transforming yourself back into a sexy beast is to start doing your hair. Go big, don't just switch the ponytail position or wear bangs, literally change up the way you wear your hair. We men don't notice much, but anytime a girl changes her hair we'll think, "damn, she's looking good." Won't know why until she points out she went from brown to red, but it doesn't matter that we couldn't pinpoint the change, the magic is that internally we felt a shift because a woman's hair quickly turns her into something new.

The next step is to upgrade your wardrobe around him. This isn't about going out and buying new clothes for work, it's about when you two are in the same space, put on a show. Those old sweatpants or faded shorts that he's seen for months if not years, toss them. Buy cute little things that highlight your body type. **You don't want your man to be on the couch, watch you get up to go get some water, and think, "There her flat ass is in that Victoria Secret Pink crap again."** You want him to look over and say, "My baby's looking good in those leggings." Stop being ordinary and switch it up. Loungewear is inexpensive, it's the effort that costs. Go out, try things on, accentuate your positives and he will notice. Things like losing weight and gong a dress size down take time, but if you looked in that mirror and feel as if you've let yourself go to the point where you're unhappy, it's worth it to lose the weight. Regardless if you look like old Kelly Clarkson or new Kelly Clarkson, the first two steps will get you to where you want to be quick.

Don't fuck him. Remember that this is Ho Tactics, you get more by not giving a man what he wants too fast. Your new hairstyle will make him want to get it in that night. Wearing new sexy clothes around will make him want to push you against the kitchen counter and get it in. There can be no sliding of the panties! But don't push him off with the standard, "I'm tired," routine. Use your Ho Power and seduce his hard dick. Kiss him, touch him, pretend you're down, then pull back. When you're in a relationship, you aren't going to hurt your man's feelings by saying "maybe if you're a good boy." The idea is to rev him up by coming off like new pussy. If you give in, he'll cum, and you'll go back to being normal. Give it a day or two, of him trying to get some, then you hit him with the death blow.

The common mistake women in relationships make is telling a man to take them out instead of inspiring a man to take them out. Telling a guy you want to go to Ruth Chris may get you to Ruth Chris that once, then he'll put his feet up like his job is done for the rest of the year. So at this point, with him full of lust over this new you, show him a dress you want. Doesn't matter if it's an expensive one from Saks or a Fashion Nova clearance, go sexy, and tell (never ask) him that you want to wear this on your date. "What date?" exactly! He's taking you out and didn't even know it, and now he's about to buy you this sexy dress with his debit card. To dismiss you with, "when I get paid" means that he's not getting sex and you're going to keep looking sexier and sexier each week. If he plays dumb about a date, same routine. The point is to lead this horse to water. You're looking good, you're going to be wearing a sexy dress, he isn't getting any lately—that's incentive to not only take you on a date but to take you on a nice one. Once you get this one date, the Ho part of the hustle ends, and the relationship part begins as you, as his woman, must have a legit talk about what you expect going forward.

Why Doesn't He Trick on You?

Men spoil to impress. The guy at the bar that buys you and your friend drinks without asking for your number or trying to hit on you, he's not doing it for sex—he wants you to think highly of him. Older men with money are notorious for giving away thousands of dollars to young women even after their dicks stop working. Tricking isn't about sex, it's about the male ego. For those of you in a relationship, you'll fall into two categories, men that don't trick because they don't have it and men that don't trick because they don't need to impress you. You know your boyfriend or husband, you know how much he makes, how much debt he has, and how much he spends on himself. If he doesn't have a pot to piss in, then you're not going to get much nor should you try because taking from him is like taking from yourself.

If your man has a surplus of money and isn't paycheck to paycheck, then you have a right to get in his pockets. One email I received wasn't even Ho Tactics related, but it showed the power of other women. A married woman of two years found out that her husband had been seeing his best friend's little sister, some cute little 22-year-old. The affair wasn't what broke her heart, it was that her husband had spent over a thousand dollars on Christmas gifts for this girl. What did he buy her that year? $50 gift card and some Walgreens $20 gift set of JLo perfume that still had the discounted price sticker on the bottom. Why would her husband treat the Rugrat better than his wife even after he had spent months fucking her? Because he wanted to impress that little girl with the idea that he was a big shot that could take care of her.

To get tricked on you have to roll over and play the game of male ego stroking. You don't do that because you want to be an equal, a partner, someone that brings something to the table. As I explained earlier in this book, that independent woman shit doesn't excite a man nor endear him to spend on you. It tells him that you don't need him. "I shouldn't have to ask," or "I can buy it myself," doesn't get you spoiled. "Daddy, can you please buy me this," does wonders no matter what level you're on. Women hate to ask for things because they hate rejection, they hate to seem weak, they hate to come off as needy. The other woman plotting on riding shotgun in your man's car and fucking him in your bed doesn't have a problem submitting to get what she wants. It's all an act! You can still be a strong woman, you're just pushing buttons to manipulate a man into thinking you need help. Seeing as though you do want more than you're willing to buy yourself, is this such a bad game to play?

The first step is to humble your attitude and dial down your independent streak for a few weeks. Start small. Things around the house, ask his help instead of being Diana Prince. That jar you can open yourself—ask him to do it. That cabinet you can tighten yourself—ask him to do it. The laundry you can carry yourself—ask him to do it. Then it's in the way you ask. Pout, frown, speak low, and always invade his personal space by hugging him or resting your head on his shoulder or chest. Make him feel as if you need him for small things. This is priming him the same way Maria primed her mark. Remember, you have to know what works and what doesn't. Starting small allows you to perfect your acting skills and determine what works given your man's personality type.

The coup de grâce comes after you figure out how to pull his strings to do things for you. With the working knowledge of what he can afford, you push him to 50% of that. **Some of you who are in relationships for love and not money may date men who toe the line of poverty. This tactic will work and has worked even with poor men, and I'll prove it!** If your boyfriend is making $15 working a 40hrs a week, after taxes and normal expenses in a non-coastal city, he can still afford that Xbox game or pair of Jordan's because that's within his budget of $200 left over as disposable income. Your job is to get at least a $100 gift to prove that he does care enough to give what he can spare. The more money a man has, the higher that goes, obviously, so if your man is making 80k per year, you raise the cost of the gift. If he doesn't spend the money you know he can afford, when you see him spending it on himself, then you need to reconsider the relationship you have. If he does spend, then like any good trick, he'll spend again. This is where you begin to train him like a Smart Ho.

The purpose isn't to escalate your gifts, this is your boyfriend, not someone you want to put a strain on. Even at $15 an hour he can afford to pick up a $50 a week expense of getting your nails and toes done, so that's what you ask for next. Make it his bill. Even at $15 an hour he can afford the $70-100 phone bill you have. Ask for that. Once you break him into being a giver, start getting what you need from the relationship be it bills paid, beauty maintenance, or even monthly shopping money. Don't feel bad. He's going to blow that money on dumb shit he wants anyway, so why not finesse him into spending it on you? Alternatively, if you're worried about his future, then maybe the money you ask for is for you to put in the bank under the cover of a joint savings account. A reader took this advice and asked her man for $75 every two weeks that would go towards a vacation. The truth was there was no vacation, she knew her boyfriend was bad with money. Over a year later they were in a bind and that two thousand dollars she got him to trick over time, saved them from being evicted.

Poor people don't save! You know this, they see an extra few hours of overtime as throwaway money they can spend at the bar or on food, and don't put anything away. This way, if he does lose his job or has to get his car repaired, you have that money plus interest ready to give back. Regardless if you're being a team player or getting your needs met, you shouldn't be in a relationship where you aren't getting anything out of your man! If he's working, he should be giving. If you're working, he should still be giving. Ho Tax.

Why Isn't the Sex Good?

Deep into a relationship, sex should be electric lovemaking that puts even the nastiest ratchet novel to shame. Your man knows what you need to climax and you know what makes him react to thrust harder and deeper. Role-playing, shit talking, daring each other to whip it out in public, nothing is awkward because you two are comfortably in love. That's the perfect world. **The reality laid at my door is populated by hundreds of women who hate the sex they're having.** You used to go rounds, now it's more like half a round. You try to spice it up, but he doesn't seem engaged. Watch porn, put on wigs, wear lingerie, and his dick still doesn't get as hard as he used to the first time you offered up a blowjob. Even on a good night, you're not having an orgasm, you're reaching for the pillow with thoughts of smothering him because you can't remember the last time you got to finish first. Your man doesn't need Viagra, the sight of crotch-less panties, or for you to do a British accent... he needs new pussy. How do you upgrade an old vagina that's always there? Unlike the previous section on getting back with an ex who hasn't hit in over a year, you aren't going to withhold sex for that long. So what now?

Psychology is your friend, so the first step is to analyze who your man is and what drives him sexually. A mistake I witness consistently are women who think on the level of ME ME ME. What is it about me that he doesn't like? As self-less as women can be, few rarely take time to look at scenarios from a man's POV. Therefore she thinks sex is about what she's lacking, not what he's searching for to rekindle his libido. You can turn a man on, you can change physical things to fill him with lust, as proved in the example above. Nevertheless being aroused isn't the same as being able to perform well in the bedroom. A man's penis isn't like a finger, he doesn't control it at will. What he does do is pile on stress and anxiety to the point where it blocks him from being all he can be. Again I say—psychology is your friend. The same way we went over phone sex with strangers in terms of testing the waters of dominant versus submissive, talking vs. moaning, etc.. you have to pre-plan your Ho attack by getting a handle on what your man needs as opposed to what you've been giving him.

The next time you have sex talk to him like you're directing a scene. He's your actor, you have to motivate and lead him to put on an Oscar-worthy performance—or just cum. This first session is all about cause and effect. You talk—he cums. I don't care about what he says back to you or what sounds he makes. I need you to pay attention to one thing. What did you say right before he came? For example, if you're on the bottom and he's pumping away, don't say all that stupid "oh babe, you feel so good," bullshit. Direct him! Tell him to choke you. He'll oblige. Tell him to choke you harder like the little whore you are. If he gets into it and cums twenty seconds later, it wasn't your vagina, it was the idea of dominating you and being able to fantasize that you're some closet freak. Let's say you're riding him nice and slow, don't just rub your tits, he's seen that act, it's played out. Go the opposite direction and call him a "little boy" tell him that you're going to get a real man to come over and finish up after he's done. If he returns fire, talks his own shit, cool, but that's not what we're looking for. If that belittlement makes him cum within a minute of saying it—you're on to something. That's the research portion of this initial planning stage.

Communication is next to bat. This is a relationship, you can't change a weak sex life with spontaneity alone. Couples don't talk about sex unless it's to complain. One woman told me how she had enough and told her boyfriend of three years he needed to put in more work in the bedroom. He broke up with her. Telling a man he needs to please you is like telling a cat to go shit in the toilet. Men don't know what you want. They have been having sex the same way for 10+ years—same stroke, same tongue tricks, same aggression level, and it's gotten them this far. If you can't communicate in specifics what you need, then you're basically just telling him his dick is weak sauce and that's the ultimate insult to a male. The communication I need you to lead with isn't about "I want you to do this twist motion my college boyfriend used, he had me climbing walls!" You need to communicate by way of schedule. Men are nothing but grown little boys. What excites boys? Games! Every Saturday night will be fantasy night where you two get to be as nasty as you want. Nothing is off limits when you're in the bedroom.

Each week you switch off fantasies—his turn, then your turn to lead. What this does is make him look forward to something new. It's still your vagina, but mentally it's rebranded. The first time you do this, go without sex for at least five days prior, really make him want it. When it's his week, do whatever he asks, submit to his game. If he cums quick and the entire build-up seems lost, keep at it. It's not one session it's the entire night. Stay in character. If he had you being a sexy nurse, even after he finishes, remain that sexy nurse. Keep yourself warm while he recovers, and unlike normal when he goes to sleep, he will be ready to go again because his mind is uplifted by you being this other character. When the next session comes the following week, aim your fantasy at what made him cum during the research stage. Why should you make this all about him? Because you're restarting his sex drive, not yours!

This is Ho Tactics, which means you give a man what he wants only to get what you want. By the second week, you will notice a change in his sex drive. He wants to go more often, he's always giving you that look, and his erections will be stronger. You've given him something to get excited about, something to look forward to, and that spreads to his subconscious, that part that actually controls what makes him hard and what makes him soft. Once you have his dick on a schedule, he's a slave to using it just as we were as teenagers masturbating multiple times a day. At this point, you can start pushing him to do things on your fantasy list, as his body is primed to need sex on that day.

If the chemistry starts to die out, use the "early morning special" technique. A man's penis has the most blood flowing to it in the morning. Why? Because the body is not in the process of digesting food. To break down what you eat, blood flows to the stomach. In the morning, on that empty stomach, the blood flow is abundant, not preoccupied. In ratchet terms, you're going to have a rock-hard dick to bounce on during this window. Take it without warning, be a wild woman, and unlike other times when he's just getting off work, has a headache, or his team just lost a game, his focus mentally and physically will be ripe for you to have great sex minus the gimmick of fantasy night. This instills confidence in him. He doesn't need you to talk dirty or set a scenario up, in the morning, crust still in his eyes he can still renovate that pussy by laying strong pipe. For the rest of that day he's going to walk around with a renewed swagger because he gave it to you like old times, no weak dick, no short burst, he was a stallion and he blew your back out. That's the key to this, instilling confidence.

Men are people too, they know when they're not giving it their all sexually, and it's a point of shame. Instead of correcting it, they just hide behind apathy, and the bad sex continues. By using your Ho charm to rebuild his self-esteem, to make him out to be this stud that has you turned out, clears his mind and boosts his sex drive naturally.

***

Relationships require constant rejuvenation or both parties become bored or complacent. It's not enough just to point out the problems or wait for the other person to fix it. If you notice it, you handle it, that's love. There are so many things Hos do that revolve around other women's boyfriends or husbands, and it's not about lack of love, it's about lack of inspiration. Be inspiring, hijack his mind in the same way these Hos do, and you can get anything you want from your man—better gifts, date nights, good sex, and the list goes on. You can't be too prideful or too shy to exercise your feminine wiles over your man because if you don't mind-fuck him with love, another woman will mind-fuck him with the fantasy of something new.

#23

How to Become A Sugar Baby Without Giving Up Sugar

Are you a Sugar Baby or are you an escort? Are you Hoing in the ways laid out in the first half of this book where you have yet to take off your clothes, or are you still living in the dark ages where a man comes to you with cash and hand, fucks you, and you brag that you just got paid. Secret arrangement sites are not *Ho Tactics*, they're fancy forums for prostitution. Having some fat guy eat your box in a hotel for tuition money isn't being a Sugar Baby, you're pay for play. If the only way you *get* is to *give* sexual favors than you're not using this book right. Any woman that is down with her back against the wall can use these steps to dig herself out in less than a month—fact. However, you must separate real life hustle from internet fantasy. "Girl, I got a friend that pays just to eat dinner with me every two weeks, step your game up."

Basic Bitches love to embellish and make the art of trading sex for money sound fancy by claiming the romantic title of being a Sugar Baby, but few of them are actually sugar babies, they're escorts or side chicks that must perform for that money or risk being cut off. They use their bodies, not their minds, which goes against the core of this book.

Google the term "sugar baby," and you'll see hundreds of hits for *"how to be a sugar baby without giving up any sugar."* Most of you aren't against being given things by men you don't like, so why not actually get what he has to give instead of daydreaming as if working these tricks is out of your reach? Because you don't have the confidence that you can pull it off without crossing a sexual line—but you can! **"I'm about to be a stripper," why does that cross so many minds?** Because the art of dancing naked for money, no matter how moral or high class you are, seems like an easy hustle when your education, paycheck, and the broke guy you're in love with fails you. You don't have to be in the best shape, you don't have to know how to dance. All you have to do is smile and rock to a beat, occasionally crawl to the guy tipping the most, and eye fuck him like he has a shot so you can squeeze an extra twenty out. That's the two fantasies—*I should strip,* or *I need to find a Sugar Daddy.*

Fuck the fantasy, Ho Tactics is a legit way to earn without having to dance, suck, or get touched. Each one of you can use this book to make more than the strippers that floss trash bags of money online or the fake sugar babies that fail to reveal what they're really doing for Grandpa millionaire. I don't care if you currently dance for money or let your former best friend's dad feel you up for Coachella tickets, there is always time left to reset and revamp your methods and exercise your power over these tricks. You're a Goddess, not some wealthy man's prostitute! This chapter will help any woman that's ever been disappointed with her bank account balance and thought about going to the dark side. Using examples I've gotten since *Ho Tactics* was first released, I'm going to show you how to be a Sugar Boss without giving up a fraction of what these rookies give up.

The Sugar Baby

Men will pay for company, they will pay for a trophy, they will pay for the energy of youth and excitement that you provide. We've established that earlier in the book. The snag some of you may hit will be when a man uses Dick Tactics under the cover of being a Sugar Daddy. He will give you a taste of his money at first, no strings attached because he likes you. He will flatter you. He will behave himself. He will seem like the answer to all your financial problems because he's showing, not telling you, that he doesn't mind helping you out just to keep you around him. The second phase of his plan comes after you get your hopes up, and what started out as some guy with money that didn't mind tricking transforms into a dependency. Allow me to expand by using an example that came to me last year.

Her Hustle: A Young woman living in New Jersey with a toddler needs money to pay for childcare, pay for community college classes, and to survive the cost of living in the Tri-State area. That's not asking for much right? 20-30k hustle which is nothing for any woman that can get a hold of a New York mark. She begins working in a restaurant as a hostess. The owner, a man 30 years her senior, begins pursuit. Although his wife also works in the restaurant, she sees this as her chance to get paid. She begins to return fire, and it works. She gets cash "tips" in addition to her check for the first few weeks. She comes to me as she doesn't know how to escalate this to more. I direct her to test his pockets like any Smart Ho would with an emergency need. She goes to him before work with tears asking for 3k to pay off a medical bill that may lead to pay garnishment. He gives her the money, in cash, at the end of her shift. Cha-Ching. I leave her to with a warning, *no matter what, don't fuck him and don't fall for him*. Did she stick to this? Let's find out…

His Hustle: Men in power, such as restaurant or shop owners, fuck their employees. Not every pretty girl that walks through the doors, but the ones that seem open to it. These men are always married, always older and established, and even if they aren't the most handsome, being a boss makes them attractive to women in their 20s who have Daddy issues and dreams of being spoiled. This guy most likely fucked the last few hostesses, which is why this would-be Sugar Baby was hired in the first place. Despite my warnings, she fell into the trap of him being nice, him giving money for free, and his game of "My marriage is just something we hold on to for the business and our children," aka male game that makes naïve women feel they have a shot at becoming *Mrs. Restaurant Owner*. Papa Player ended up fucking this young MILF a week after he gave her that three thousand. This led to more tips with her paycheck, more promises that she was different from other women he had affairs with, and of course more and more sex. Suddenly, the hustle of getting money out of a mark turned into her writing me a few months later with, "I think I love him and I know he loves me." She wanted to know how she could turn this from *Ho Tactics* to something deeper—predictable Basica response.

Epic Fail: The wife found out, as wives always do, and Ms. New Jersey was laid off until business picked up. She waited by her phone for over a week—nothing. She finally called Papa Player asking to borrow money to pay her rent, and the owner played dumb, asking if she had a family member or boyfriend that could help with this as it wasn't his responsibility. Once again, she came to me asking what happened, and I quickly went back through the entire story. Everything I said not to do, she did. Even a few weeks before she was laid off she was bragging about how it felt good to be taken care of by her "Sugar Daddy," and that her friends were jealous. The truth of her story, like many so-called Sugar Babies, is that she was never in control. She was the mark that fell in love with her male ho. She was reduced to a prostitute who was there to please him for a few extra dollars with her check. She ended up being laid off with no money to show for herself, unable to pay her bills and take care of her toddler because she lost control of the hustle and fell for the fantasy.

How She Could Have Won: When sizing up a mark that you work with or work for, you have to let them chase. Take the extra they give without asking, reward them with flirting and the idea that they're winning you over. Like Ms. New Jersey, always do a trick test where you see if he's small potatoes or if he's willing to go big. In her story, the test wasn't headphones. He was a business owner, so the test was a good chunk of cash that she knew he had to spend—it worked, he gave her the three thousand dollars. The follow up would have been to thank him by letting him get a little closer. Kissing, intimate hugs, words of praise, even some sort of sexting or phone sex would have been smarter than having sex. An old trick with money wants the chase more than the pussy. He doesn't know this, but all the research I've done proves this. The exhilaration of winning you over keeps him spending and doing more. There is one woman that writes to me with TWO authentic Sugar Daddies, she earned more in the first two months of working them than she says her mother made all year as a school principal.

The more you push old tricks away then pull them back in, the more they feel that all they need to do is spend more. The more they spend, the more you buckle. That's proof that they are winning (in their minds), but you still don't go all the way. That kind of torture gets men off. Remember, these aren't young, impatient millennial men that get mad that you didn't fuck them after buying you AMC popcorn and a large soda, and cut their losses. These are married men, widowed men, divorced men, all lonely or bored and looking to tap into some much-needed excitement. He's not fucking like a machine anymore, he's not trying to swing from the chandelier, his joy won't be your vagina it will be the conquest of your mind, soul, and body. Instead of falling into the trap and becoming his personal whore, you drain him dry. He'll get pissed, he'll give you the cold shoulder, then he'll come back because not too deep down he likes that you're a tease. Only when he proves that his sponsoring is sustainable and that you are in control do you even entertain the idea of having sex. It should be a strategic move, not something done because you now love him or because you fear he'll cut you off. A Smart Ho would have milked that restaurant owner, teased him by not wearing panties to work, accidentally rubbed up against his dick at the hostess stand, and had that old trick giving her access to the business credit card. Ms. Jersey couldn't do that because she wanted a man's love more than his money. That will always get you outfoxed.

The Stripper

Stripping is acting, it's a character, it's not who those women are, but it gets them fast money with little effort. The psychology of *Ho Tactics* and being an upper echelon Stripper are similar, but they aren't the same. The women who I've given advice to have either kept stripping or they've retired after snatching a mark out of the club and milking him dry. The difference between the girls that have to keep dancing and the ones that use it as a springboard for bigger and better things is that one doesn't comprehend the endearment part of this book. I correspond with so many women that dance these days, and the one thing 90% of them have in common is that they want to rush the process of bonding with a mark. Which of course makes them come off fake and ingenuine. You can be sexy, you can be charismatic, but the earliest chapter told you how important creating a bond was. He may be in a strip club, but he's not dumb enough to believe you actually like him just because you had breakfast the next morning.

Some people still think Pro Wrestling is on the up and up, and some people think a stripper having a conversation where she reveals her real name and calls him "baby" is real. For the rest of the population, we're all in on the showbiz aspect. Walking into a strip club is like walking onto a car lot, you know you're going to be sold—but you're down to be sold if it's something you want. When you get two people that are in on the hustle both trying to negotiate while still wearing masks, it's all about who's the better bullshitter. Ho Tactics trumps Dick Tactics, but only if used right.

Her Hustle: Cute little blonde from Kentucky who bombarded me with a bunch of pictures to prove that she's built for Ho Tactics was dancing in a club in Florida. She didn't have any aspirations for her money, she simply saw the number of men that would come in and spend an insane amount on drinks and dances and wanted her piece of that. There were a handful of men that would come in and ask for her by name, and they would always be generous. Now it was time to take this from the club to real life and get a sponsor who would pay her to breath air and look cute.

Her target was a Middle-Eastern Trick, he was some sort of consultant and would come to town once a month to decompress. He would always invite her out and was very respectful, saying he just wanted to learn more about her, that's it. After declining a few times, she asked me if it were a good idea. The plan she used was to have breakfast with him the morning he was to fly out. She would wear sweatpants, little makeup, and show him the other side. The conversation would be like any Ho recon, ask him about him, flirt, invade his space. Our game plan worked, and the breakfast date went so good he threatened to miss his flight just to keep spending time with her. By the time he landed, he was blowing her up with texts sounding and being thirsty for more. While he was overseas, he had gifts mailed to her PO box. He would ask if she needed any cash. And took an interest in what events led her to dance in the first place.

His Hustle: All kinds of men go to strip clubs, therefore, it's hard to pinpoint what a man's weakness is until you take him out of that club and Ho check him with conversation. This Trick was a foreigner who went for the most Americana (blond hair, blue eyes) looking woman in a diverse strip club. That tells you he has a fetish. He was persistent in coming in the club and trying to win Ms. Kentucky over, which told me that he was a bit of a nerd. Months earlier she had taken his business card and googled him, he was who he said he was and while he may not have been in the 1%, he was rich enough. This was going to be an easy guy to work if done properly…then Ms. Kentucky let her ego take her off course, and I didn't hear from her for weeks.

By the next time she reached out, she told me how she had agreed to have sex with Middle-Eastern Trick for 10k. He gave her two thousand of that and promised the rest later, but it never happened. When he later showed up at her club, he pretended not to notice her and was now giving another stripper his attention. This mark wasn't as dumb as this little girl thought. He lusted over her, he tricked gifts, but it wasn't real, he was allowing her to act out her role. This was WWE, he suspended his disbelief and played along, got worked up, but he never lost track of the fact that she was fake.

Epic Fail: The ability to cut your loses after making a mistake or running into a brick wall is priceless. Ms. Kentucky didn't adhere to this advice either. She started to reach out to the Middle-Eastern Trick anytime she was drunk cursing his name then asking to see him. When that failed, she started to feud with the other dancer. This messy behavior distracted her from getting money, and they moved her to a day shift—a death blow for a stripper. She quit and started at a new club that was ratchet and she blamed her decline in income on that trick.

I thought it was all over, then she reached out saying he sent a text and she went to his hotel to get closure—which is a code word for cry on his shoulder and get fucked. He gave her $80. Yes, you read that right, and told her that he would help her out the next time he was in town. The total amount of actual money she squeezed out of this Middle-Easter Trick: $2080.00. The amount she had gotten just dancing for him over the months before taking it out of the club was triple that amount. The mark got his wish, after wasting money in pursuit of this Hitler Youth looking piece of pie, he ended up having sex with her twice for a bargain price.

How She Could Have Won: Pretty girls grow on trees, stripper flirting is transparent, and men will play along in hopes you fuck for free or fuck for a set price. If you're not using the strip club to prostitute and you're not trying to fall in love with the guy tipping you, then the only way to come away a winner is to mind-fuck a man by breaking the fourth wall. The fourth wall is a term used to describe when a movie stops its actions and lets you in on the fact that this is a movie. The most famous of this would be *Ferris Bueller's Day Off.* This is how the hustle work: The moment you agree to see a guy outside of the strip club, you own up to the fact that you're a hustler trying to get money. There's no more "daddy," talk, you speak normally, and you share your life story with him and tricks of the trade. Tell him about the guys that come in, the bouncers that try to fuck you, all under the umbrella of "secrets." What you're doing is taking this man from sucker in the audience that thinks this is real, to an insider. Once you put your cards on the table and strip away the fake seduction, you become real.

I had Ms. Kentucky strip away the gloss for her first date, and it worked. In her case, the trick was smitten and proved his infatuation with long distance gifts and offers. She ruined that by entertaining his, "how much for one night," tease. Never ever talk numbers or take the bait of private dances, private meet-ups, or offers to pay you to not go to work. That allows a man to buy you, and confirm that you're just another sad bitch dancing for money. Never downgrade your value! He's a friend, not your client. Bad night at work, text him. Need someone to cheer you up, call him. This hustle can go on for weeks or months, doesn't matter. He's attracted to you, he's in lust with you from the club, but this process is making him like you as a person removed from that, not an object. By the time you sink your teeth in with the tactics laid out earlier in this book, he won't think you're fake or putting on an act because he feels different from just another guy you dance for. This is how you win over a strip club mark—time, patience, and shared experiences.

The Normal Women

Men with money won't spend it unless you give them a reason. As you witnessed in the examples above, guys are willing to give away the frosting, but it takes effort to get the cake. Nerds, grandpas, married men, unattractive men you meet on POF, no matter who it is you're only going to scratch the surface of gifts and money unless you give them the sugar…**plot twist, the sugar doesn't have to be sex.**

The sugar you give a man to become his sugar baby can be your personality, your charisma, even your backstory. Let's say you're just a normal woman who works answering calls for an insurance company. What would make a wealthy man want to give you money? Your sugar! You're no longer Jane Boring, you create a character that reflects mystery and sex appeal. When you know how to flirt like Jessica Rabbit you don't have to look like Jessica Alba.

Let's say you're just some poor college student stuck on campus with a bunch of broke jerks, how do you get to the money? Your sugar! A woman's best weapon besides her smile is her phone. Instead of scrolling through Instagram, use that phone to bring the marks to you using the trap of your youth and innocence! I took you through a few stories that went wrong to prove a point, but many of the girls I really invest my time in win at this game. Their stories aren't as juicy, truthfully, they're boring because it's very by the book. Still, I'll share with you a few real-life examples of what happens when you aren't hard-headed, impatient, or thirsty for love.

THE COUCH SURFER: A woman having a quarter-life crisis came to me for help because she had been told by her best friend that she could no longer just lay about on her couch now that she had a boyfriend. She had less than a month to move. No car. No job. No real money. All she had was a few bins of clothes and a willingness to try anything I suggested. For three days straight, she went out by herself hunting for marks. On the third day, leaving some hotel bar that was dead on her way to the next, she spotted a nicely dressed man getting out of an Uber. "I saw a briefcase like they have in the movies and went for it," were her exact words. She interrupted the man and asked was his Uber driver any good. He stumbled over his words, clearly liking the dolled up little Irish girl he was seeing and gave his approval.

Using a bullshit story about how she was just asking because she was going to call an Uber, she managed to get this man to engage in a ten-minute conversation where they exchanged numbers. A few days later they were on a date. A few weeks later he had given her money to move out of her best friend's apartment after she called him crying about how her Bff's boyfriend had tried to talk to her in secret. That was it, no crazy story, nothing very creative, she saw an opportunity and "Got her Maria on."

THE SOPHOMORE: This girl wasn't even old enough to drink and had a long-time boyfriend when she first decided to use Ho Tactics for extra money while on campus. Her school was in a college town, so she had doubts about how to pull it off given that any local with money was probably an Alumni. I told her not to worry about the "what if" aspect and just give it a try. Her big idea was to pretend that she was a dog walker, which gave her an excuse to go to an area of the town where the affluent lived without seeming like a creep. Her hair in two puffs, sweatpants, and a shirt with the school's logo on it that had been cut to reveal her belly button. That was her sexy look in her eyes, and she bet the bank on it.

The second door she knocked on got her a second "no thanks" but as she was leaving the man of the house was parking. He hurried out of his car and asked what she was selling. She later told me that the look in his eyes made her shake with nerves because she knew he was going to be the one. This couple didn't need a dog walker, they didn't have a dog. But this husband was quick to ask if the girl wouldn't mind helping him clean out his basement…his way of helping a fellow **** earn extra cash. That side job turned into a trick affair where this bored husband set the sophomore up with a bank account in which he deposited a weekly allowance. Even when this college student decided to move it to sex, it wasn't to keep getting things, it was her own hormones just wanting dick. Even though she's young, I tell her all the time that she's extremely wise in the Ho side of the force.

THE GIRL ON IG: Older woman looking to start a clothing company for curvy women but was stuck working a dead-end administrative job. Using Instagram to post work out pictures or samples of the kind of clothes she would one day sell she amassed tons of followers. She had an inbox filled with thirsty men but wasn't sure the first step in making any of them into income.

Her friend introduced her to *Ho Tactics* but never actually used it, she just found it a fun read. **In reality, this friend was not practicing Ho Tactics she was using IG like an escort service.** When the administrative job did layoffs, it led to IG girl having to work more hours on the same shitty salary. Like most adults with dreams they can't reach, she sank into depression and considered being an escort like her IG role models, but only a few times, to create a surplus. It was during this internal debate that she finally read this book all the way through as opposed to skim over it for laughs. She began to write me literally every week to the point of annoyance, showing me her IG messages, all the celebrities that were on her, but still unsure of how to use *Ho Tactics*.

That story about being one step away from prostitution upset me. The last thing I want is a woman to feel she has to sell herself for money. When I happened to be in her city, I had lunch with her and gave her a pep talk: *Why sell yourself for BackPage prices to guys who have real wealth when you can get so much more without even removing your bra?* She agreed and went to work researching some of the guys that would message her.

This woman, over thirty, admittedly not the baddest chick on the 'gram, used her weapons—a banging body to lure a mark who I didn't even know was a mark. This man wasn't just rich, he was also a major power player behind the scenes. The same way Imani worked that baseball player in the example, Ms. IG worked this Mr. Big. The catch was it took her four entire months of bonding, flirting, falling back when he tried to get controlling, all of the tactics. Not only did Mr. Big begin to respect her, but he also began to like her. Her IG page used to be pictures of her in a cubicle crying about "Getting back to the money," she was typical and broke, trying to make the best of her life.

Now she's always on vacation, and her brand is starting to take off. She used Ho Tactics at each point. She took a mark that was just trying to hit and turned him out mentally. Even when he tried to use the push and pull technique, she did exactly as I wrote earlier and fell back. So many women run towards the money man with this "oh my god, I'm going to lose out if I don't chase him," fear. <u>Not this woman.</u> No more cubical, no more breakroom depression, no more sitting up at night thinking of a get rich quick scheme because she turned some random guy in her inbox into a true Sugar Daddy.

***

Whenever I hear a woman tell me that they aren't good enough, I think about those three women and dozens more who win using their minds, not this idea that they have to come with a certain ass size, waist size, complexion, or social background. Remember that the sugar isn't in the sex, it's in selling yourself as indispensable! You don't feel pretty, you don't feel sexy, you don't feel confident in your skin, then start building! The same way you create a fake name to be written on your Starbucks' cup, create a persona and breathe life into her until she's as real as the money that's about to be in your bank account! Commit to that character, embrace that confidence, and your universe will bend to your will, and place opportunity after opportunity in front of you. If you rush, you fail. If you have the patience and courage to bank on yourself, you win—it's that simple.

#24
Using Ho Tactics On Rich Millennial Men

*T*hese new school men don't like spending money.
Correction, they don't like spending money on your
ass! Every cute girl thinks she can finesse, but the
moment you put a wealthy man in front of most, they fumble
the bag. Winning is work, yet you egotistically expect guys to
throw bands because you're pretty and flirtatious. Old men who
see your attitude as exciting and your youth as exotic, may trick
with little effort required, but the males you crave aren't
married grandpas. You want the rich, under 40 guys to put you
on the payroll, but why would they? Younger men with money
aren't impressed by your butt, boobs, and vapid Instagram
captions. You bring nothing to the table that he hasn't seen on
his IG explore page. The simps online or the broke locals may
label you special, but High Value Men pass on you because the
stench of your basic bitch aroma is overpowering.

If you pay your own rent, don't brag as if you're a
finesse queen! The world is filled with tricks, but have you
gotten 20k without giving out pussy? Explain to me right now
what you could do on a date (with your clothes on) that will
make a man want to invest in your ideas? The Tactics in this
book will always work because men who have it to trick will

<u>always</u> trick. The question is, are you patient, disciplined, and savage enough to use the secrets I'm about to share on men around your age?

Social media changed the game for men with disposable income. Every type of woman is a direct message away, and all it takes for these men to get a reply is to have a page that shows off that he's paid or has a high follower count. Men without money *Ho Bait* the most, meaning they flash money or cars online in order to seduce shallow women. If a broke man with a leased G Wagon can get pussy from trophy type women, imagine the attention that men with actual riches get online on any given day. My point is you can't sit on social media and wait to be DM'd by a wealthy young mark; you must do what the rest of these low IQ Hos aren't doing—using male psychology against them! The game has evolved, and these men are prepared for your finesse attempts. Their game is to mind fuck you, sleep with you, and toss you to the side before you can put your plan in motion.

If you don't possess confidence and dick discipline, then don't try Ho Tactics on younger men! Wealthy millennials know they can get everything you have to offer for cheap. They don't trust you, they see through your basic attempts to use these tactics, and they dangle enough money to make you thirsty. This results in you being used before you have a chance to use them. **Let's get this straight, you're fucking a man with wealth, and all you can get out of it is dinner, petty cash, or cheap jewelry?** You left money on the table because you were too afraid to follow my tactics or thought that you were smarter than this book and could do your own thing. In the end, the male hos with money are making you their marks, and it's time to reverse course.

This chapter is a crash course on positioning yourself as a one of one. Men spend money, chase, and hold onto women who can't be found elsewhere. Your job isn't to be like the random thots on social media with cosmetic appeal. Your job is to challenge him mentally and tease him sexually. I don't care if you meet men by DMing them online or in airport bars between flights. The power isn't in the introduction. The power is in what you do after that first connection that will make you stand out.

Fear Factor

Reading about Maria's Ho-Conquest, your adrenaline spiked, your mind raced, and you felt a form of indirect confidence. Your intuition tingled because you now know that **feminine power is God power**. Everything that you want can be yours. No man is above your charm. You are undeniable! That isn't an affirmation. That's a spoiler. The anticipation you have to go out and try Ho Tactics is so great that you don't even finish the book! "I read enough. I'm securing the bag this weekend." ...or so you thought.

Flirting with men on dating apps is easy. Going after old sugar daddy type doesn't require confidence because you don't want them on a real level; thus, they don't intimidate you. What about the men that look good and talk even better?

I've advised dozens of women who were great at Ho Tactics for a month when it's all a video game. Then they come across someone who's handsome, or an ex tries to come back into their lives, and they fail miserably. The reason it's so easy to get three thousand dollars from a guy you just met off Bumble is because you're not emotionally invested enough to be scared of his rejection. The reason why you can't look your boyfriend in the eyes and tell him you'd like him to pay for your hair and nail appointments from now on is because you are emotionally invested and are terrified to hear "no" or "I'll see."

Ho Tactics and fear can't coexist! You claim you're not afraid of anything, then confess that you hate being told "no." Go deeper! Why do you hate "no" to the point where you would rather do things for yourself than ask? Because you're afraid of what that "no" means. If it's a new guy, that "no" means he isn't impressed enough by your looks to give you what you want. He sees you as "mid," and that hurts your ego. If it's someone you're already dealing with, his "no" means that this man doesn't love you enough to give you what you want even though you are willing to do the most for him.

Be honest, failing to get a man you put on a pedestal to give you something makes you feel like a loser. All these ratchet rap chicks talk about how easy they get Chanel bags, and you can't even get a pair of headphones. All these basic blonde girls with their oversexualized podcasts talk about how they get flown to islands, and you can't even get reimbursed for an Uber. That. Shit. Hurts! I don't expect you to destroy your ego overnight, but I want you to realize this "I don't want to hear no" shit is a wall that's blocking you from pulling off these tactics.

Do you believe you're pretty enough to be spoiled? Do you think you're confident enough to seduce a man? I know what you're capable of, I know you are power—but if YOU don't believe, then anytime a younger man pops on your radar, you'll end up letting him get away with murder. Are you built to mindfuck men, or are you just a boy-crazy romantic who just wants male attention? You can read this book every month, you can become a pro at doing your makeup, you could even go get your body done. None of that matters if you're mentally soft when it comes to men. Do you know what men think of you while they're smiling in your face, liking your pictures, and making false promises? *"She can read all the dating advice, but in the end, she's still a ditz with daddy issues. She can go get a BBL, but in the end, she's still an insecure little girl who no one paid attention to. Watch how easy I run through this dumb bitch."* It's time to prove these men wrong!

Affirmation: No man is bigger, smarter, or better than me. There is no way he can reject me because I am secure in my power. There is no way he can make me chase him because I am confident in my ability to manifest someone better.

Declaration: From this day forward, fear will not exist when I am dating. I will take comfort in the mission and gain strength in the knowledge that I Am That Bitch.

Trust Factor

I advised a woman in Chicago who was looking to get money to start her cosmetic business. She set her intentions on 50k in three months to launch by the summer. She was dating two guys, a wealthy Nigerian man and a blue-collar maintenance worker who owed his own window cleaning business. Both men were in their late 20s and a bit flashy, which is how they caught her attention on Instagram. The Nigerian guy would take her out to random parties and introduce Ms. Chicago to all of his friends, then they would chill at his house. Blue Collar would take her out on actual dates, and they would talk in the car for hours afterward. She told me that she liked Blue Collar the most but wanted to focus on the Nigerian as he was worth millions, spent freely on bottle service, and would most likely provide her 50K faster. I advised her to go after Blue Collar, as he was more emotionally invested.

Ms. Chicago disagreed with me and doubled her efforts on The Nigerian, trying to create a fast bond. Finally, she tested The Nigerian by telling him that her rent was due, and she had spent her paycheck helping her mother out a week earlier. The Nigerian gave her the rent money, which was less than 2k. However, when she came over to get the money, he was more aggressive than usual. She told him she wasn't ready for sex, and he did what most men do, he explained, "We don't have to go all the way."

She wrote upset that what was supposed to be a quick money test ended with her giving the Nigerian head. He even left extra money for her afterward, basically treating her like a prostitute. By the time Ms. Chicago told him about her business idea, he had shot it down as a bad investment but offered to give her some business advice when they met up again. That advice cost as The Nigerian basically lured her over, pressured for sex again, and this time they went all the way. For the next month, Ms. Chicago basically became a sex toy that got a few thousand here and there. She could pay her rent, but at what cost?

My initial advice to Ms. Chicago when she first emailed me her prospects were to focus on Blue Collar as clearly, they were building a deeper bond. In her mind, if a man is blowing 10-15k on liquor, strip clubs, etc… he's an easy mark. She failed to realize that women like Ms. Chicago are a dime a dozen in the Nigerian's circle. She did nothing to distinguish herself as a real option. He met her on IG because he was attracted to her looks, and he knew that she would be attracted to the pictures of his cars and lavish lifestyle. The Nigerian was "Ho baiting," and Ms. Chicago didn't realize that the hunter had become the hunted until it was too late.

That blue-collar business owner valued her enough to take her on official dates, not this "hey come hang out with my crew and pop bottles" bullshit. He wasn't in a race to take her back to his place; instead, he kept the conversation going in the car. He was primed to trust Ms. Chicago enough for her to work her tactics. However, the thirst for fast money got in the way.

I received a flood of emails from women I once advised during the pandemic, but none proved my point better than Ms. Chicago's last update. She informed me that although she ghosted that blue-collar guy, she continued to stalk his movies on social media. Last year, blue-collar had a massive wedding with "this bitch who doesn't even look half as good as me," as she put it.

Ms. Chicago fumbled the bag with a man who had a lot more money than she thought and who would have invested in her business. This is what happens when you get impatient and choose flashiness over connection! <u>You always want a trick to like you more than you like him.</u> A man who has a million dollars in the bank but doesn't trust you will never spoil you as hard as a man with 200k in the bank and thinks you're special. The net worth means nothing. It's about how much you can net based on the worth he sees in you!

"He thinks I'm pretty and wants to fuck me, so why not focus on the guy with the most money," Earth to Basica! Trust is everything when dealing with younger men! Those with extreme wealth are the least trusting. If a man managed to make a fortune before he turned 40, then that means he's intelligent, talented, or really good at picking lottery numbers. Let's assume that he's relatively smart, then his lust alone won't make him trust you enough to do more than small tricks. He'll spend to fuck, as in pay to play, but he's too up on *Ho Game* to blindly trust you and label you the wifey type.

In the past, women could manipulate men with money relatively easily because the idea of "she's smarter than me "was the male's Achilles heel. Look at the famous Hos throughout history. The men they made their fortune or fame off didn't see it coming because of their own egos. *"She wouldn't use me for money, she's not that smart… she wouldn't have a baby with me to get the child support, she's not that savvy… she wouldn't marry me after all these years just to divorce me, she's not that forward-thinking."* Long before the age of Housewife reality shows and Instagram influencers, there were women who knew how to get to the bag, drain a man, and move on with their lives.

Men aren't more intelligent now; they're just more aware. Women snitch on themselves by posting about their sugar daddies. The current ladies of hip-hop talk about scamming men out of money excessively to the point where finessing is a mainstream concept. **What happens when secrets get out? It fucks up your ability to move in silence!**

We live in the information age where men can educate themselves on how others have been played and adjust. There are forums, message boards, books, and YouTube videos about how to spot gold diggers. The idea of "watch out" has even trickled down to broke men whose only assets are sneakers and Xbox games. These men would rather meet up for coffee dates because they don't trust your intentions. Think about that, "ho fear" is so great that even broke men are careful. So, imagine how distrusting a man with real money has become in the past five years?

Coach Deion Sanders invited my friend, the infamous and brilliant Brittany Renner[19], to speak with the players of Jackson State about how they will be targeted by women if they happen to make it to the NFL. After Brittany's speech, Coach Sanders remarked, "If I had been sitting in that room at Florida State and I had her come and lay it out like she laid it out… I would be at least $20 million richer."

Recognize that men are now on high alert and will continue to be skeptical about you. <u>The only way to counteract suspicion is to earn trust.</u> Lazy effort will never lead to trust. "Babe, can you help me out with a bill," after two dates is transparent. "I don't understand why we have to split the bills when you make more," in a relationship where you haven't seemed concerned about money will make your boyfriend or husband think you're up to something sneaky; maybe trying to save money so you can get your own place and leave him. The point is, you can't just put in half of the work, hold your hand out, and expect a man to give it to you.

Why do men with money spend on strippers, escorts, or take on mistresses? **There is no trust needed in transactional relationships!** That man paying for a lap dance and trying to negotiate an "after the club" price knows that dancer is working him. That British man in New York for a week will happily call up an escort to have dinner with him before he tries his luck on Tinder. He's paying for a woman who understands what "company" means, not trying to solicit a connection with someone who has ulterior motives. Married men, especially as they get up there in age, would rather buy a condo for a woman who he knows will keep her mouth shut and be at his beck and call rather than take his chances sneaking around with someone

---

[19] Brittany Renner is a social media influencer whose book, "Judge This Cover" detailing her various high profile romantic relationships, I highly recommend.

who would try to blackmail him or want him to leave his wife for her.

Transactions don't require trust, it's clinical, and the rules are understood. At the same time, the man will always be in control of these situations. You're getting hundreds from someone with millions. You're getting a house that he can take back. You're getting negotiated down to what he thinks you're worth because, in his mind, you're beneath him, a sex slave. Ho Tactics, where you actually get a man to trust and need you, will always net more money and a better lifestyle than a transactional relationship, as you, the woman, set the rules. However, as I just laid out, fear and trust are the locks that must be removed to gain access to his mind. How do you gain trust without spending years "faking" a relationship? Easy, you put yourself into the shoes of your mark, discover his vulnerabilities, and attack!

The Empathy Factor

Who is this man you're after, and what will make him see you as a trophy? Go ahead, list everything you bring to the table. That's what every woman does, but you're missing the mark. The first part of that question was, "who is this man." If you don't know men in general, let alone specifics, how will you know what will attract him, lower his guard, and let you in?

Putting yourself in a man's shoes doesn't mean you just transfer what you see as ideal and put a male twist. As a woman, you most likely value security, someone who is employed, a high earner, and eventually wants to settle down. Men don't value security in the same way as women! This is why they gamble, race cars, and jump out of airplanes at much higher rates than their female counterparts. Men live in the moment and take risks. If you've ever said, "men are stupid," or "guys are so weird and confusing," then you have yet to identify, let alone empathize, with the male mind to the point of comprehension. There can be no Ho psychology without first understanding the mind of your mark and what makes him tick.

Identify: When you go on a date, you're doing reconnaissance on where this man comes from in terms of family structure and economic background and how he's moved up in life. Is he a suburban kid with two parents and a bit naïve when it comes to the world? Was he an inner-city youth who was raised by his grandma and has a need to prove himself? Is he a first-generation son of immigrants who has strong, old school, gender beliefs? Did he go to college or go into business without a degree? Was his money inherited, or did he have to grind? Is he stable or someone whose fortunes are split between many partners or dependent on deal after deal?

9 out of 10 guys you meet won't be athletes or entertainers whose information you can google. It will be on you to ask questions that give you intel on this man's origin story.

"He took over his father's business, I think his parents are divorced," isn't what you should leave a date with! Men with money often have egos, and egotistical men usually overshare about everything positive to prove how smart or destined they are. Identify his true-life story, and from there, you categorize him into a box based on statistics, not assumptions.

Categorize: Is he a party boy who works too hard and has to overcompensate by drinking and drugging all night? Is he an introverted nerd who is still uncomfortable in his own skin or with his success? Is he an emo narcissist who feels like no one understands him or cares about him outside of his money? No man is "mysterious" if you're doing your job.

Shut your mouth and open your ears. A man disarmed by his attraction and lust for you will snitch on himself. The reason younger men with money prefer crowds or having you meet them out with friends is that they get to keep it flirty and fun without exposing themselves to questions and deeper conversations. Don't allow a man to blind you with drinking and jokes. As I laid out in the earlier chapters, you have to isolate them to gain information.

Some men will rush to get you back to their place to fuck you and give you basic crumbs, talking for hours about exes or work problems that frustrate them. Centering the conversation on other women who didn't live up to his expectations or career talk keeps you away from identifying what makes him tick and who he is, and this is done intentionally. Recognize when a man is deflecting and talking about "them" instead of "him."

When dealing with a self-made man who grew up poor, he may harbor resentment towards women because he knows they didn't want him until he had money to offer. When discussing inherited money, it usually comes from a father who wasn't good to his mom. To expose his past is to reveal his thoughts. That could be his ugly duckling phase, the dad whose shadow he's stuck in, or the mother he resents for being a weak bitch who stayed for the money. Childhood traumas are the best way to pinpoint a man's vulnerabilities, but you must first get that guard to drop. How do you drop it quickly? By exhibiting empathy.

Empathize: If a man tells you about how his ex-girlfriend cheated on him, how do you receive that information? If you're on the first date and that man tells you how his best friend stole money from him, what's your follow-up? You're ego-based, so most likely, your response is to point to your own life and say, "I know what you feel like," and then switch the topic to how your ex-boyfriend fucked around on you or how someone you trusted also stabbed you in the back. That's not how you endear yourself!

Stop trying to bring everything back to your life story. This man does not give a fuck. If he's opening up about something in general, it's because he is feeling comfortable enough to vent. You must respond by milking him for more details of these stories. Instead of, "My ex was a serial cheater," ask, "How did you find out she cheated? Did you have any clue that was going on?" Just like the *Date Like A Spartan* technique of turning questions into stories, you pump him until it's all out on the table.

The most you ever tell him is that you're sorry he went through whatever it is that he went through and make him feel better with a physical show of affection: a hug, hand rub, etc... Remember, your goal is to be a sexual fantasy, best friend, and little sister. The sexual part is easy. The "I need you" aspect of being like a little sister isn't hard to grasp either. It's the friendship aspect that you all fuck up at, because you're not being empathic to a man's story. Listen, act like you care, and allow him to release himself. Guys don't get to open up to other men in this way. By being engaged in what he's saying when other women are quick to bring it back to themselves will make you stand out as an empathetic figure.

Assimilate: Once you identify where this man comes from, categorize the kind of male he is, and crack his story open in a way that makes you empathetic. The final step is to assimilate, meaning become a part of his life based on the intel you gathered. Suppose you're dating an actor who is really just a theater geek who fell into money and still has insecurities about not being good enough. In that case, you become the ultimate compliment to that lifestyle. You lean on the nerdy and geeky shit he still loves to create a bond and get him to feel even more comfortable around you as if you're a kindred spirit. It doesn't matter if you don't know anything about his world, you can learn by asking him questions. Ask him to tell you the plot of his favorite movie. Ask him to break down something and be engaged. This is how you make men feel heard! When you're having serious talks, bring up the things he's told you about growing up, ask him more high school stories so he can vent about how he's winning, and they're all losers now.

When it comes to assimilation, the final nail is to tell this man your own war story that echoes his own. This isn't in a "let me talk about myself" egotistical way that I warned about. It's more of an admission that he's earned. Let's say you finally agree to a house date, you know he's going to try for sex, and at the moment where you put your feet in his lap, you finally tell him a deeper story about how people treated you or how you had it hard. You say this under the cover of, "You remind me so much of myself, and I've been afraid to admit what I've gone through, but I feel I can trust you at this point."

What happens at this point is that he sees you not as pussy, but as a human, a part of his tribe, a like-minded spirit who he's now happy to have met. To endear yourself to a man in a way where he feels that you are on the same frequency drops his guard and opens him up to trusting you.

Patience Is A Virtue

Do you want to rush a man to give you money because your car note is due, or do you want to take your time and sink your hooks into a man to the point where he will need you on his team? Younger men expect you to ask for shit, so they don't give you shit, but lies, excuses, and only break you real money when you're exchanging it for sex. However, when you have the patience to identify, categorize, empathize, and assimilate into his life over a few months, you become "different" from the rest. The young thots online just want their boobs or ass done, so they fuck whoever has money, get a few dollars and call it a finesse. No! That's prostituting. The difference between you and those kinds of women will be wisdom, strategy, and patience! Never put yourself on a time clock to get money from a man if it will compromise the steps.

I hear it often, "Should I go in for the headphone test now? Did I wait too long for the headphone test?" You're so worried about being on a schedule that you're not feeling these guys out. When a man is falling for you, when he's putting added pressure when you guys are crossing boundaries into more sexual talk, that's when you know he's primed to start asking for small things. Energy is real. Vibrations are science. Feel it. Don't chase it. When he's falling for you, it will come with more attention. Sometimes it'll come with jealousy as he becomes territorial or fear as he tries to push you away before he falls too hard. It doesn't matter how he's reacting; it only matters that you feel a change in how he's treating you. A millennial man who begins to get emotional over you is one who has been softened up for the kill shot.

Hoexample

Let's check in with Maria to see how she sinks her teeth into a new school man and drains her mark without him being wise to the fact that she's a seasoned Ho. Maria has been dating her Millennial Mark for a few weeks, doesn't like the pace of their dates, and must now adjust her tactics.

This Millennial is "cool rich," he's not an entertainer that's known to a lot of people, but he's not a tech sector nerd either, just a guy in his mid-30s who made his money from investments. With money comes entitlement, and this guy wants to go out on his schedule, which is usually last minute and rarely anywhere chill. Maria has had to put her foot down about going out on actual dates, not in a bitchy, "Well, call me when you're free." Kind of way, but more of a flirty, "aww, you're the boss, make some time for me, baby," kind of way that stroked his ego and got him to take her to some upscale places. Millennial Mark isn't fake busy. He has multiple phones, always seems distracted, and openly talks about his exes being too clingy. Maria identified this mark as your typical new money asshole who has a chip on his shoulder and is running from commitment. Why does he have a chip on his shoulder? That's Maria's job on the next date.

The flirting and seducing are taking hold, but this is a man who Maria can tell is sleeping with at least one other woman. Any smart ho knows that when a man is getting pussy regularly from a more convenient option, he comes off cocky and unbothered. Unlike a guy in a drought or not used to top-tier women, he's not in a rush to shower attention and romance. Millennial Mark doesn't need Maria, he likes her, but he will not be hurt if they stop talking. Maria realizes that the connection isn't there yet, so she isn't going to rush her headphone test. She's going to spin the block and break this clown down even more.

Young, entitled, and misogynistic, this is clearly a man who didn't get female attention until he was older, and he is clearly resentful. Still, how do you know without assuming? For the next date, Maria will use flattery to get this millennial to open up and snitch on his past. By asking him if he was always entrepreneurial or something his father taught him, it will give him a chance to revisit that past. If this mark didn't have a dad in his life, he's going to be offended at the thought that some guy who wasn't there was responsible for his success. If the mark's success was influenced by a mentor type, the chip on his shoulder wouldn't come out there, and she'll have to pick a new topic to delve into, like his parent's relationship.

Maria knows that 99% of wealthy men who achieve success at an early age are narcissistic. They have a burning desire to divulge their success story in the same way a supervillain has to tell Batman his entire plan before he kills them. Ego reveals all! Maria finds out the mark started off helping a family friend with their business and learned to be money-minded. He brags that while all his peers were chasing girls, he read books like *Rich Dad Poor Dad* and thought of the bigger picture. Maria understands that this Millennial Mark isn't telling her this because he trusts her. He's saying it to brag about how different he was from the kids in his school. Maria keeps egging him on, asking him about his first business idea, if his parents believed in him, and that's where her first clue came from. This mark gets a little testy, and he raises his voice recounting how his mother thought he was wasting his time and needed to finish college.

Maria is picking up on the wounded vibe, and what does a Ho do when a man gets emotional? She becomes his bestie by holding his hand for comfort. The mark then discusses how it was hard early on, and all of his money went into the business. Maria asks seemingly basic things like what part of the city he was living in and if he had a car at the time. The mark says he had a crappy blue Camry and shared a room with a cousin. This was a trap, as Maria asked about superficial things to open the conversation up to women. If a man had it bad, then he either had zero women chasing him, or he had one "day one" chick in his life for emotional or financial support. Maria comments about how he must have had all the bitches with his Smurfy ass Camry. Of course, the mark laughs and goes into how he wasn't really dating at the time, focused on the money. This is bullshit. There's never been a man business-minded or not who was not consumed by chasing pussy. Maria pushes, "there had to be some girlfriend during this period." Finally, the mark opens up about a girl who he liked, but she would play games then eventually ghosted him. Bingo! **Family trauma and girl drama.**

This Millennial Mark had a mom who didn't believe in him. When he did open himself up for love, a female rejected him. Now that he has money, he uses it to run through women, avoid commitment, and keep any and every female in the "all bitches do is lie and leave you" box. In short, this mark doesn't trust women.

This psychological disorder is why Maria couldn't crack him open over the first few dates and why he hasn't been applying pressure like other marks. Now that she knows what kind of man she's dealing with and why he won't trust, she can begin to place herself in his shoes and empathize with his plight. This date is no longer about seduction and setting someone up for a headphone test. It's about showing the mark that you give a fuck about him, not the watch on his wrist or his job title, but him as a person. Maria is going to go left where other girls go right into the "My mom was overbearing too" lane.

By the end of the date, it's been all about the Millennial Mark venting and telling his rise to power, with Maria simply being an active listener. It's the third date, so it ends with heavy kissing and light neck sucking. The mark doesn't trust Maria, so he's trying to leave his mark on her neck, and she doesn't stop him, as he's the richest man on her roster, and a bitch knows how to use makeup—*suck away, clown.* Maria does the same trick on the mark's neck, but he pulls back, says he has Zoom meetings and doesn't want his partners asking personal questions. More bullshit. This mark probably has a sneaky link scheduled for the next night and doesn't want to upset his other bitch.

Maria isn't here to be his girlfriend, so she isn't going to get mad that he pulled away; instead, she closes the deal with, "thank you for opening up to me tonight." She doesn't say this just because it's to put in his head the revelation that he dropped his guard, and it didn't hurt him. If anything, it was fun. This is called "positive reinforcement," rewarding a man when he opens up in order to get him in the habit of sharing. Maria is a student of the game, and the game dictates that men are so bottled up because they don't know where to start when it comes to sharing. Maria made his confession feel as casual as discussing favorite TV shows.

On the next date, Maria initiates and even suggests they meet at his place. In the mark's mind, this is a dick appointment, but Maria is going to come with two things—an excuse as to why she has to leave by 11pm and a heartfelt confession of her own.

During their house date, Maria drops the bomb about how she had this business idea and even had money in her account to start it with, but her Dad called it stupid and forced her to go to college. She tells him that while she likes her job, she knows she could have been in a better position and that she's struggled with depression because of "what if" in terms of losing out on her own dreams of being an entrepreneur. Of course, the mark will tell her that she can still follow her dreams, but this isn't the time for Maria to pitch this mark on an idea he can invest in. Instead, she stops talking about herself and brings it back to him. Thanking him for sharing once again because of what he told her last date, she finally felt comfortable sharing the story about her own parents with someone who "gets it."

Are you paying attention? This is what men want! To know that they are appreciated and different from every other man you're dating. Maria has faked her own vulnerability to make her mark even more vulnerable while engaging this narcissist's ego at the same time. This is proper Ho Tactics!

Over the next week, Maria will finally initiate phone sex and then jump into the headphone test. It took her a few extra dates to do these steps, but it doesn't matter. <u>The goal of Ho Tactics isn't to be fast or locked into a schedule. The goal is to secure a man's trust!</u> You can do the second date headphone test and get a $400 pair of Apple headphones. It doesn't mean that he's invested, just that he likes you enough to trick. If you want to truly embed yourself in this man's brain, understand that the younger they are, the more suspicion stands in your way. Take your time to crack them open, and only move when you feel a clear connection has been formed.

Maria will now be able to take the foundation she started with and lead this man into investing in her old business idea or finesse him in other ways. Even as a man in his mid-30s who can get other women, he recognizes that Maria is more than just pussy. She's an experience, she's a confidant, and that kind of woman is rare in his world. Maria used patience, didn't give up, didn't panic, didn't give up sex to keep him, and adjusted her strategy to allow more time to work her tactics.

Ho Tactics is work, but it's easy work, the only hard part is committing to the mindset. Once you embrace it, the lessons in this book will flow, trust me! You must be willing to face the challenge head-on with patience and wisdom. If your mark isn't doing things on schedule, relax, utilize this chapter, and take baby steps to assimilate into his life. Slow and steady secures the biggest bag.

#25
Using Ho Tactics
As An Introvert

Are you awkward, shy, or prone to moments of uncontrollable anxiety when you're forced to deal with high value men? If so, pulling off Ho Tactics could seem impossible. How can someone lowkey and quiet compete in a world filled with aggressive women and win over domineering men? Stop doubting yourself and realize that there is a power that comes from being introverted that any woman can tap into.

My favorite success stories have come from introverted women who sought me out with basically the same question, "How can I get the things I want from men when the thought of asking terrifies me?" Throughout this chapter, I will break down precisely what I told these ladies and how they were able to internalize my advice, put it into practice, and secure the luxurious life they deserved.

Quiet Hos Are The Most Deadly

To break a man down, you must first understand what turns him on and off and then anticipate his moves based on this information. What kind of woman is universally loved? Feminine women who come off as easy to attain. What constitutes "feminine" in the mind of the average male?

The ideal woman is soft, quiet, and allows a man to lead. In reality, being introverted doesn't mean you're any of those things, but on the surface, males will assume that it's all connected, and this is the information you use to mindfuck them.

Think of the film stereotypes you've grown up on. Cinderella, the humble and meek peasant girl who pops into the prince's life for one dance and snatches his soul without saying a word. Ariel the mysterious yet quirky dimwit that pops into the prince's life and charms him despite being unable to speak. Who wrote those movies? **Men**. The patriarchy trains women to be the kind of women they find desirable—pretty and silent. Shut your mouth, show him attention, and you'll become his princess.

Culturally the stereotypes are even more heinous. Asian women are often lusted after by men of all races because of this belief that they're quiet and submissive. Latinas and black women are painted as masculine because they tend to be more vocal; thus, they're generalized as less feminine. This false belief system that wrongly labels women based on cultural perceptions is also paper-thin. Put glasses on that same black woman or put that Latina in pigtails, and it softens them instantly in that man's mind. By becoming a "nerd," that angry black woman stereotype fades. By styling hair to look younger, the "spicy" and crazy image is replaced by a more sensual one. My point is no matter how you look, the right combination of clothing and being naturally quiet and reserved, especially in a room filled with more verbal women, will catch a man's attention based on his own misogynistic cliché of "silent means soft, soft means submissive."

Getting Men To Approach You Without Trying

The token Caucasian businessman who stops by a hotel lobby to grab a drink and check his emails will come across a multitude of women. Nevertheless, he won't approach the prettiest woman. He'll go after the one that falls into the category I'm describing. He's not looking for the powerful woman in the pantsuit that may be his equal. He's seeking out that woman who is sitting alone, dressed in a feminine way, and awkwardly minding her business. Note that if you're the one approaching him first, none of this matters. As I've pointed out earlier, men rarely get unsolicited attention and will jump at a chance to talk to any type of woman who shoots her shot first, but if you're looking to be chased, there is a quiet sexiness that all men look for.

I mentioned "dressing in a feminine way," and many of you still don't understand what that means. On dates, you have to dress like sex, as exhibited by Maria's story, but when you're simply out and about, dressing sexy is more of a vibe. As I mentioned earlier, hairstyles can make you look younger, and jailbait looks work 99% of the time. Many of you wear glasses but keep them in the house or pop in the contacts. You fail to realize that looking like a dork disarms a man. Your glasses will forever be seen as cute. Instead of "she's out of my league," his mind will go to "she's a look geeky, maybe I have a shot." Obviously, glasses don't reflect personality, but the cliché and stereotypes that men grow up with will get you chosen.

In terms of clothing, of course, you want to wear fitted clothes, bright colors, and bring attention to your best assets, being either your boobs, butt, or face. The X-Factor that's often overlooked are feet. There's a reason foot fetish pages make a killing on OnlyFans. Men like feet. A nice pair of fitted jeans, your hair in a side ponytail, and a pair of sandals that showcase your freshly manicured toes will make a man introduce himself faster than a miniskirt, heels, and a full face of makeup. Why? Because guys, even the wealthy ones, are intimidated when they think a girl is too high maintenance. Understating your appearance makes you seem like low-hanging fruit but in a good way.

Men gawk at the sex kitten because they want to fuck that woman on the most basic and barbaric level, but the women they take care of, who they spoil, and who they see as delicate trophies are the ones that have this silent sex appeal. This has nothing to do with the brand of clothing. It's an energy. High school movies take the glasses off a nerd girl and reveal her to be prom queen material because that's the male power fantasy. The adult film industry makes billions off the barely legal category of porn because that's the male power fantasy. Everything you've consumed since the time you could read and write has hinted at what the male ego craves—power over docile women, so present yourself as if you're that kind of chick.

"I don't want attention, it makes me uncomfortable, so I try my best to hide when I go out." I don't care how shy you are, there must be an effort to pull people into your orbit, and the easiest way for those of you who don't want to be verbal is to present yourself as eye candy. The changes are as simple as this, stop covering yourself with hats, stop wearing baggy clothes, sweatpants, and yoga pants, and put a bullseye on you by feminizing yourself in the ways I just mentioned. I understand that attention from unwanted men can be awkward, but the more eyeballs you can put on yourself in public, the less work you will have to do on social media or dating apps. Ease into a new look over the next week, go out to nice areas when you have to do errands or when you want to grab something to eat, and see the results for yourself.

Why They Fall In Love

Take a moment to soak in the stereotypical thinking of the patriarchy. Now, realize the gigantic flaw it created that will now allow you to manipulate and mindfuck men. As a naturally introverted woman, you are more equipped to lower a man's defenses and earn his trust than your extroverted counterparts. *Ho Tactics* takes a bit of acting or a lot of acting. When you're naturally shy, the role-playing is small because you don't have to play the part of being bashful or humble; you really are about that life!

An extroverted man and an extroverted woman can have a passionate and torrid love affair, but that energy will turn chaotic unless someone compromises and submits. An introverted man and an introverted woman can have a very loving and thoughtful relationship, marry, raise kids… but unless one of them is willing to go against their nature from time to time and speak up on a litany of topics, it'll be a relationship of repression and resentment. Every relationship requires balance. Most men who you try Ho Tactics on will either be geeks whose brains made them wealthy or high-energy go-getters who grabbed life by the balls and made themselves a success. It's important to know how to turn yourself up or down depending on the personality of the mark you target.

The Mind Of An Extroverted Mark

The extroverted male wants to break you out of your shell. He wants to get you to laugh, smile, and feed off his energy. Think of it like a toddler who throws a toy and hits someone in the head. If the parent gets mad, the toddler cries. If the parent chuckles before scolding, that toddler realizes that doing something bad gets a funny reaction. So even though you told them to stop, they'll do it again. Males crave attention, and what's more encouraging than someone who doesn't say much, lighting up at each story, joke, or opinionated take?

As an introvert, you're happiest in your own head. You are truly comfortable alone, but that comfort can seem like a cage to others. That's why extroverts try so hard to open you up. These personality types see your silence as a sign that something is wrong. "Let loose, drink some more, turn up, have fun!" You are having fun, but not in a way they want you to. Since extroverts are always blabbing on, oversharing, and needing to be around others, they can't conceive of a thought process where chilling out feels good. If you've studied Ho Tactics, then you get where I'm leading you. Men have to want to save you from something. In this case, it's your shyness that will make them work harder.

The more you seem like a damsel in distress, the more he'll feel a need to spring into action! The businessman at the bar will come over and ask your name because you seem lonely, you seem lost, you seem like you need a white knight. Understand that quiet is feminine! The male ego convinces itself that life isn't worth living without him there to entertain you. As you begin to date and you're not being overly talkative and allowing him to lead, that quiet is taken for submission. He feels he's teaching you things, enlightening you with his long stories, and without doing much, you've already won this man over. You're now Ariel wowing Prince Eric!

Getting gifts and things from extroverted men becomes child's play. Your lack of a big reaction makes him feel like he has to do more. You understand that it's possible to be having fun without always smiling. You understand that you can like a man a lot without feeling the need to be overly touchy. You understand that you can enjoy yourself and just leave it at a simple "thank you" or "that was fun." Again, your mind is foreign to the extrovert. They want the ego stroke that comes from doing something nice. When all of your reactions are lowkey, what does that do to this extroverted mark's mind? It casts doubt!

How does he get you to smile bigger, hug him tighter, or show real excitement? I repeat—he does more! A man buying you a "just because" gift is him seeking your approval. Mind you, this isn't about impressing you enough for sex. It's deeper. For an extrovert, especially one with money, he's used to having his ass kissed. **He's used to women blowing up his phone and being clingy. By being chill and unbothered, you confuse him and cause him to find other ways to stand out.** This is the psychology at play that you can organically tap into without memorizing seduction techniques, so keep this at the front of your mind when you come across this kind of mark.

The Mind of An Introverted Mark

I pointed out that a relationship between two introverts will require one half to take the extrovert role if balance is to be had. When your goal is to acquire value from a man, you must be willing to embrace what I refer to as "**selective aggression**." Even if he has money, an introverted man may not be outgoing enough to walk over and buy you a drink. He may not want to message you first on a dating app. He may not even want to make eye contact if you two are introduced by a mutual friend. This isn't due to a lack of interest; some men just aren't good at talking to women no matter how old they are or how successful they become.

As an introvert, you must be empathetic instead of offended. "Men are supposed to make the first move," not if that man is socially awkward and anxious. **Recognizing a fellow introvert should give you insight, not make you fold your arms like, "nope, he has to speak first."** 90% of other women will sit and wait for an introverted man to make the first move, which never happens because it isn't his style. To be a part of that 10% that recognizes that he's shy, not uninterested, then goes after him will put you ahead of the game. Think of all the wealthy men who aren't flashy or outgoing. They're sitting there waiting to be hooked up by their friends, paying for matchmaking services, or simply recycling exes, because new women aren't brave enough to socialize with him first.

How do you connect when you're introverted? You find your comfort zone. Conversations about something you're passionate about are the key. I had a reader match with this young wealthy Indian American man. He was boring, barely responsive, and she didn't want to go on the actual date. However, the idea of not going for it with a rich, handsome guy just because he was awkward didn't sit right, so she came to me.

My advice was to find common ground, stop asking him about work and get him to share his passions and hobbies. On that date, she recognized that he was a soccer nerd who knew way too much about the clubs. She didn't know shit about soccer, but she kept asking him to tell her more about the game and the rivalries. This led to her comparing soccer feuds to her interest, reality TV. This broke the ice, and he began to open up about TV shows he watched, and from there, the conversation flowed.

The lesson she learned was that this man wasn't a weirdo. He was just afraid to open up for fear of judgment. The safe space of talking about a hobby, a book, a show, places you've traveled, etc., will cause any man to relax more and more. If you're strategic enough to keep him talking and link other interests, he will go from reserved to excitable. The same way women think, "Men won't care about the girlie thinks I like," men feel the same way. Most successful introverts are geeks who didn't fit in school, watched anime before it was cool, didn't play traditional sports, and are still under the impression that "pretty girls" won't think they're cool enough. Having money doesn't stop a man from being corny, so these guys tread lightly even when they like you.

The moment you realize his personality isn't that of an extroverted go-getter, you have to flip that switch. **Even as an introvert, you must still have the confidence of a Spartan when engaging with men.** Your mouth can't stay closed if it risks you fumbling the bag. I have a good friend Mariya who came on my podcast and told me how she met her husband. She's extremely introverted and soft-spoken, but she had a crush on this guy she went to college with years earlier. Once she found herself single, he came to mind. She's more of the type to secretly stalk a page than to shoot her shot in the DMs, but knowing this guy from college to be very quiet and reserved himself, <u>someone had to make the first move</u>. Mariya used *Selective Aggression*. She went against her norm to get what she wanted. "I'm never too shy to go after something I want. It can be overwhelming, but it's paid off in my career and, of course, in my relationships."

In terms of getting gifts from introverted men, it becomes no different from extroverted men. They're deep thinkers. They want to keep you around because forming connections is hard, so they'll begin to gift you what you think you should have, which opens the door to getting them to gift things you actually want. Understand that the ends justify the means when it comes to finding true love or climbing the ladder of a career. There will be times when you must bully yourself out of your shell, and I want you to keep this idea of Selective Aggression in your mind as push yourself out of that comfort zone when opportunity knocks! Now that you understand the psychology let's get into the practical aspects of getting things from men as an introverted woman.

The Type of Women Men Never Spoil

Trusting a woman requires a leap of faith. If a man is dating a woman who seems cool, oozes sex appeal, but then asks for something out of the blue like help with getting her car fixed, it raises an eyebrow. Asking for a monetary loan or financial favor casts doubt. "Is she working me? Does she think I'm stupid? Or is this a legit need?" The problem with impatient women who rush through this book and try it out because rent is due is that they never gain a man's trust. I'll take you through two scenarios that demonstrate my point.

The Impatient Scammer: This kind of woman has gone on three dates with a man then hits him with a favor that will cost $500. That amount doesn't mean much for a man with money, but it's not about the money. It's the timing. The Scammer goes with a sob story about how she'll pay it back and that she's really in trouble and has no one to go to. Her mistake is that she hasn't created and shared a life story where she would need this kind of help. She hasn't gotten this man to be vulnerable enough to buy into her as a potential trophy or girlfriend. She's asking because she doesn't have time to wait, and that rush makes her tactics sloppy.

The Impatient Romantic: This kind of woman is not looking to scam money fast; she's looking to lock down a wealthy boyfriend or sugar daddy that can take care of her. Her thirst is "the luxury life" that she sees on social media. To test this man, she'll try to use something like my headphone test but will go overboard. Three dates in, and instead of letting him choose, she will specify a gift that she thinks proves she can get big things. The Romantic doesn't realize by making high demands on this man, she's ringing the alarm in his head that she's not here for him.

The Suspicious Man Vs. The Scammer: Most men assume that the majority of women are gold-digging whores, so he will be suspicious from the jump. Your choice to rush through Ho Tactics and only build a surface-level bond or play the sexual teasing game makes keeps him on the fence with his guard up. If the scammer asks for $500, he counters in one of two ways.

1) He will give her the money, but she has to come and see him. Once she sees him, he will basically make her prostitute herself for that money.
2) He will inform her that he's unable to help out with the money based on a bank issue or promise to give it to her when he sees her again (but he doesn't).

The Suspicious Man Vs. The Romantic: You think that because you aren't asking for money, just something like a pair of $400 shoes, you're not going to upset him, just test him. By telling this man exactly what to get you, it takes the joy of spoiling out of the equation and destroys the surprise aspect that would allow him to impress you on his own. Furthermore, when a woman comes to a man with a specific demand, that request seems premeditated. You've been wanted what you're asking for, and in his mind, you think you found a sucker willing to actually buy it. Here's how he'll deal with you.

1) He'll buy you this luxury gift, but again you have to come to get it, or you have to see him before or soon after as again he's going to pressure you for sex.
2) He'll pretend as if he's going to buy it when he gets the chance but never does but continues to pressure you to see him knowing that he can use that gift as bait for sex.

Most women fall into these two categories. I've gotten too many, "I asked, and he ghosted," and, "I asked, we fucked, and he gave" stories. Suspicious men will always use a woman's impatience to get fast pussy or as an excuse to cut her off. Rushing through Ho Tactics only works when you come up against a thirsty man who isn't too smart. Even then, you're still leaving money on the table by speeding through the connection.

"I just want men to give me money fast. I don't want to go on all of these dates and get to know them," says the woman that got fucked for rent money and never got anything else.

"I met a married guy who I know is worth 8 figures, so why shouldn't I ask for a condo down payment after a month?" Asks the Basica who will fuck up a good thing before it has a chance to maturate and pay off for years.

Throughout this book, I've walked you through male psychology, and the secret to getting will always depend on coming off as a woman who needs but doesn't want to ever ask. Now let's break down how you can use your shy nature to train a man to spoil or sponsor you for as long as you want.

Training A Man To Spoil

Introverted women pretend everything is fine. They don't want to bother anyone with their problems, making them ripe for being "saved" by men. When you first start dating, it'll only take a date or two for him to realize you're shy. The more you connect with him in terms of conversation and forming that bond, the more infatuation sets in. Ho Tactics dictates that you allow him to take you out, then suggest your own type of date to train him to your taste. What has he learned from you? That you don't speak much, that you're lowkey, and a "good girl" who he can probably get to be bad. From the male POV, how does he now get this shy girl open enough to fuck him, admire him, and possibly want to be exclusive? He goes into his bag!

Because you don't demand or ask, he will begin to try to impress you on his own, and because you showed him on that second date that you like luxury things, he now must pay attention to that cue. Taking you to a place that's even better than where you suggested. Bringing you flowers, giving you money for gas because you drove yourself, or buying you some random fashion accessory because he was shopping for himself and thought about you… these are male-centric gifts women get when a man is starting to really like her. The more generous the man, the better the gifts will be, but that's not your aim, is it? You don't need random you need specific gifts or money which directly benefits your Ho goal.

The average woman isn't in the habit of talking about what she prefers, so she has to ask directly, or a man has to guess and assume. Going forward in your Ho journey, you must mentally prime a man by dropping hint after hint about your tastes. The way you suggest date places is training him, and the headphone test works because it's a man giving you what he thinks you deserve based on those dates. I showed you how to do things more directly as Maria did. As you go forward, more tests can be created to see if a man has been paying attention to what you like and if he sees you as a long-term investment. If you've done a successful headphone type test, then use the second month of dating (dates 4-8) to use these subsequent two tests that will help you get what you want without having to step too much out of your introverted nature.

New Venture Test: Tell your mark how excited you are to start something new such as your own online business or something as simple as a new gym glass. Organically the things you have to do to succeed at this new venture will be a topic of conversation. Instead of demanding something, you mention what you're lacking. You're stressed shopping for cute gym shoes. You're searching for a new laptop for your business. Innocently mentioning these things without dwelling on them will give a man an opportunity to offer. If you've done your proper date bonding, flirting, and sexting, this man will offer up his help. If he only suggests a brand of gym shoe or a model of computer that he likes without going that extra mile and telling you that he will buy it for you, then he's not as into you as he should be.

I repeat, if he has money and sees you as a trophy he must acquire, then he will spend without hesitation. Do not continue to date men who have money but show you they're cheap. Do not try to test men who you've slept with or given oral to, as they are no longer in chase mode. Women keep testing men who keep failing when the object of ANY test is to pass. You're rewarding bad behavior when you don't cut a man off and move onto a new man on the roster. The headphone test shows how much he values you early on. The New Venture test shows how quick he is to offer without asking. Now let's break down the test that will solidify that this man will trick on you for the foreseeable future.

The Ownership Test: Whether you're dealing with a single man or has a girlfriend or wife, the biggest spending will only come once he feels like he has ownership over you. A bachelor who doesn't want a traditional relationship but wants to keep you exclusive will only buy you that car when he feels like you're "his bitch" for lack of a better term. Meaning no other man can embarrass him by saying he's dating you or sleeping with you. That married dentist will only put you on the payroll until he feels like you're his full-blown mistress who understands her role and who will not blackmail him or reveal the secret. The male ego thirsts for Hos because it's a fantasy more than a serious emotional investment. A fun time girl who he doesn't have to commit to but will be loyal, and at his beck and call, that's what wealthy men want—to have their cake and eat it too. As cold as that seems, emotions are needed when spending large sums of money to keep that woman happy. By playing the role of the quiet woman who doesn't ask for much, flirts hard, and doesn't stress him about a commitment, you're proving yourself a valuable asset, one that now can negotiate her wroth.

So how do you gain this level of loyalty and get into the deep bag without becoming someone's actual girlfriend? Fake submission! The first dating level broke him down with flirting, shared experiences, and stroking his ego until he became smitten. The second level, the stage where phone sex or sexting has been introduced, where you're okay with house dates. This is where he's trusting you more. You're willing to spend more time because he's passed the initial Ho Tests, and he sees that as you falling for him. The third level, meaning sex has been introduced, or you're on the cusp of sex, will bring an opportunity to mindfuck him.

Guys joke about "other men" often, playfully asking about who else you're dating. This is done in jest, but it's a sign of insecurity. They don't want you out there fucking other men or even dating them, but they don't want to lay claim to you as an official girlfriend either. Most women looking for normal or "square" love would say something like, "If you don't want other guys talking to me, then you need to claim me." You aren't trying to be his girlfriend in title, only in spirit; therefore, the commitment talk must be dismissed with submissive reassurance.

If a mark questions your other options, you calm him down with an ego stroke. "You know I'm yours, babe." If a mark starts in on future talk and acts like you'll get tired of him, laugh it off with, "I'm yours for as long as you want me." Any instance of questioning your loyalty must be stomped out with words of affirmation. Women seeking genuine romantic relationships don't submit in this way. They argue, demand, and fuss because they're not after money. They're after respect and love. Fuck that! This is Ho Tactics, not Marry Me Tactics.

"I don't want this to ever change," "Even if you were ever to cut me off, this pussy would still be yours." "We don't need titles. I know who I belong to." Again, square women don't speak in these terms because they're too independent and strong-willed. Even when dealing with married men or guys in relationships, other women treat the wives and girlfriends like the opposition. As a savage with her eyes on the prize, his other women aren't mentioned because your job is to be his peace, not make him stress or feel guilty. These things lead to you being seen as "different." A suspicious man will now begin to relax as he has multiple reasons to believe that you're genuine. He's taken you out on various dates, spent money on dates you suggested, bought you a small gift during your headphone test, and even offered you help with the new venture test. In his mind, he earned your obedience. He doesn't know it's a mind fuck at all!

Words of *Ho Affirmations* should be layered in whenever you two get into deep talks. A month or two of you telling him how great he is or encouraging his moves, even if you've yet to have sex with him, will eventually endear you to him. Once you feel that he's u he's emotionally invested, you spring the test.

As an introvert, you will always need alone time. If not, you'll suffocate under the weight of always having to be "on" for the benefit of others. This is a real-life trait, not something you have to "act" like. Once you're embedded in this man's life in the ways I outlined above, take a page out of my book *Men Don't Love Women Like You* and go missing from his life. Get too busy to see him. When he texts, don't respond with long sentences, be short and busy. If he calls you, ignore and text that you'll have to get back to him when you get home—you don't.

Think about what this does to him mentally. You're his fantasy girl, you're becoming a best friend, and he's been looking over you like his little sister. What man would want to lose that out of the blue? **Males with status or money don't take well to being ghosted, it's a power dynamic they're not used to, and it will drive them to the edge.** Therefore, for you to take away his favorite new toy right when he thinks he's about to have sex, or right when you just started to have sex a week or so before, he's going to get deep into his feelings.

Allow him to blow your phone up, try to hunt you down, curse you out via text, whatever. But the entire time, you have to no-sell it. Earlier in the book, I told you not to give a man too much access to your real life, so even if he knows where you live at this point, he still shouldn't know your friends or family members to the point where he can go hunting you down. Thus, his only choice in terms of communication is to wait for you to respond or wait for you to make more time to explain yourself.

2-3 days should be all it takes for his anxiety to reach its peak. Don't be afraid that he's mad and going to cut you off for good; you're too valuable! Reach out to him as if you weren't being weird over the past few days. He's going to agree because he's like a junkie needing a fix at this point. When you finally talk, use what you've established about your character and backstory. Explain to him that you got overwhelmed with other things in life and didn't want to bother him with your stupid problems, so you just went dark to clear your head.

A man who is infatuated and just had a "maybe she doesn't like me anymore" scare, will not call bullshit on this excuse of needing a mental health day or two. He'll be pissed off that you don't trust him enough to talk about what was going on in your life. Remember how Maria shared secrets with her mark and then went to him with her big problems? You are doing the same thing indirectly. By using your disposition as an introvert, you're forcing him to come to your rescue without asking.

The natural follow-up to your ghosting him and having mental health issues will be, "what can I do to help you." This is when you go in for the kill shot. For example, if you need a lump sum of money, then this is where you explain the amount the reason and throw in, "I would never ask you for this on my own, but if you really are open to help, then here's what I need."

Let's say this is a man of means who has a wife and kids somewhere, and your goal is to be a kept woman. You hit him with, "I'm overextended, and I'm not able to do anything I've been telling you about. I want to move out and not worry about anything, just focus on my business. Do you think we can get a place to share for a few months? I don't expect you to be there all the time given your situation, but it's the only thing I can think of that can take me out of this dark place." Bringing in your stress level and positioning the new place to live as a shared space where he can come and go hits him from all angles. He gets access to you whenever and gets to save you from your demons.

Finally, if you just want to extend this into a deeper romantic relationship so you can keep getting spoiled and tricked on, then the conversation is you submitting to him with a, "Sorry, daddy, I didn't mean to scare you. I'll make it up to you." And if you haven't fucked him yet, this is where you blow his mind with that 24k coochie. The combination of thinking he lost you, followed by nasty passionate sex, attaches you to him in ways which simply saying "we go together" can't. The power over men with money comes in knowing that you are invaluable to them. They can buy all kinds of material things and get attention from all levels of women, but they can't replace you.

Proving that you can walk away from him shows him that he can't walk away from you. That's the power dynamic that most women fail to attain. **Understand that "ownership" isn't him owning you, but you now own him by becoming irreplaceable.** If he passes this test, then know that anything else you need you can ask for and get. If he fails and allows you to ghost him without chasing you down and offering help, then you didn't embed yourself deep enough. Don't beat a dead horse or try to squeeze money from a stingy man. Cut this mark and try again with a new one, but this next time, follow the steps I laid out. This has NEVER failed when a woman does these steps properly.

***

Don't let your shy nature stop you from being a powerful object of desire. The more you come off as a quiet woman who just likes to have fun and flirt a little, the more he will be drawn to you as a woman he can mold, turn out, and dominate. In reality, he's not turning you into his little submissive freak. You're turning him into your debit card. There will be times when you must use *selective aggression* to show him you're genuinely interested, but for the most part, you're silently leading him to spoil you by coming off as unimpressed and low maintenance. By the time you're into the three stages of testing, headphone, new venture, and ownership, you should be comfortable enough to get what you want from this man without the anxiety of "what if" crippling your mission. The beauty of perfecting Ho Tactics is that you can have a roster of men with whom you try it multiple ways.

If you're an extrovert reading this section, you can play one guy in a more laid-back manner as described in this chapter and another in a more aggressive way, as demonstrated by Maria in the earlier chapters. The key is to winning is understanding that men are suckers for submission. Whether that's submitting by being silent and unassuming or submitting by being forward and using sexual undertones, that's up to you. This chapter was written to show all the women who have written me over the years that being introverted is not an excuse! No matter what personality type you possess, there is no reason why you can't seduce these men and get what you want out of them.

#26
More Questions & Answers

A week has yet to pass where I don't get at least a dozen questions about Ho Tactics. There is no way I can cover every scenario you may find yourself in, and I shouldn't have to, as the point of this book is to use the understanding of what you now know about psychology to make these tactics yours. The previous chapters can be tailored to fit nearly any situation if you think it through and use your Ho IQ. Nevertheless, I will answer some of the more precise questions you may have, starting with the most popular question I received from women who discovered Ho Tactics during the pandemic.

Q: *I didn't read this book until AFTER I started dating my mark. Is there any way to hit reset, or did I already screw up?*

A: People read books for which they have an immediate need. Many of you will grab *Ho Tactics* after you've already had a few dates with a rich guy who's being cheap or after you've already had sex and given away your power. Regardless of where you are in the process, you can usually hit reset.

Let's be logical and not panic, and logic dictates that if this is within the first 90 days, you can readjust. I don't care if you told the mark your entire life story. You can reinvent yourself by adding in new details and showing new sides to yourself. For example, if you've gone out a few times and he hasn't really taken you anywhere upscale, you may think that it's game over, you can't do what Maria did and pick your own places and see how much he's willing to spend. Wrong! <u>Chapter 7: How To Seduce The Ho Way</u> shows you how to get the dates you need to see if he's worth your time. You failed to get those kinds of dates, so pull back and get too busy for him. **Remember, you have to seem like your time is limited to build a demand for your attention.** Most of you hate to turn a man down and refuse to make up an excuse as to why you can't see him when he wants to see you. Stop being afraid of losing this man!

Things aren't working out for you, so ghost him and make him miss you and respect your time. You can respond to his texts or calls, but when he tries to schedule a date or have you come over, that's when you become too busy. Make up things that you must do in advance, which are airtight. You have to help a friend or family member late into the night. You're taking online classes and need to study (which could help set him up later if you're looking to get money for your company out of him). You just found out someone you went to school with died, and you're just going to take a mental health break this weekend. Be creative but more importantly, be stern. You must reframe this relationship as one where he's chasing you.

Once you cool him off for a week, then pick up with the steps I broke down in Chapter 7 but in terms of the "plan your perfect date," meaning that you tell him a place you want to go and why. "I want to go to this sushi restaurant because I hear the chef is amazing, and I actually follow top chefs." You over-explain because you already fucked up with the first impression. You can't suddenly go from UberEats & Chill to luxury dining and get that each time out. You must establish that you were compromising for him. Now you want to show him how you roll. Talk about other places on that first "Do over date" and let him take notes. If he doesn't suggest a good place for the next do-over, ghost him again. It's all about training these men. The women who aren't afraid to risk the bag have the best success stories. "What if he gets interested in another woman while I'm playing this game," get your head out of your ass! If another woman CAN take him, it will have happened with or without you showering attention on him. Other women aren't your competition. You are! Show him you don't need him, then pull him back in.

If you've already had sex, ghosting may not cause him to beat down your door. Pussy is power, and you gave it up. You chose to have sex with this man without establishing your value or getting spoiled in advance. I won't crucify you, but I won't bullshit you either about your odds. Post-sex tricking can be a lot harder, depending on how good you were in bed. Don't sit there and say, *"My diamond-encrusted pussy had him shooting on accident like Alec Baldwin,"* He may have cum quick, but he hasn't spent real money, so your vagina talk is all hype!

At this point, you must use reverse psychology on this mark to make him see you as special again. If he's gone cold on you, warm him back up with verbal seduction techniques. Be nastier when you text or when you talk. Since you've already did the deed, use specifics about what you've already done, then promote what you're going to do next time.

For example, if he thinks your pussy was mid, or if he hit it a few times and the lust is gone, make him think you have a new pussy waiting for him. I'm not talking about another woman. I'm talking about the fantasy talk that makes him believe that you held back until now. "I've been watching Pornhub a lot, practicing something I want to do with you." He responds with, "Really? What are we going to do exactly?" That's when you coyly drop, "I can't tell you, I want to build you up for this, daddy." Remember, voice inflection and mystery can bring out the teenage pervert in any man, no matter how cool he may come off. Sex with you is a notch on his belt. Another woman is more enticing because that's another notch, but by teasing him, you entice him to come back.

By sexting him or having phone sex with a new attitude or flavor, he's surprised and assuming that you're coming with something amazing for the next session. His ego inflates, and his brain cells drop off because you feel like new pussy again! At that point, you ask for your kind of date. If he agrees to date you on your level, then he's still thirsty for you. If he doesn't want to take you out, just come and fuck you, then obviously you didn't make an impression, or he's moved on to a new pussy on his roster. If you came upon Ho Tactics late, my ultimate advice is to re-visit Chapter 7 and remember that everything starts with you making sure he's willing to take you to a high-value place and invest money on the date level.

Q: *You touched on strippers and webcam girls but is there a way to use Ho Tactics on sites like OnlyFans? Also, in terms of business, is there a way to mindfuck a boss for a promotion?*

A: Ho Tactics can be used on anyone you can make a personal connection with, and they take a vested interest in you. In terms of subscription sites where men pay to access you, it's about selling a bond, not sex. A person pays to see you naked or in skimpy clothes, big deal. What makes them come back for more? It's not your body at that point; it's your ability to make them feel seen. Paying marks are still marks, meaning they require attention and affection. The pages that fail are run by women who thought they could just post provocative photos like it's Instagram and collect money without having to interact with the "weirdos."

The women I know that have made upwards of 40k in one month work their messages, post captions that entice even the introverted men to comment and handle the fragile male ego with kid gloves. That's where your success comes from, the messages that make them feel like they know you and thus want to take care of you. In terms of using Ho Tactics to climb the corporate ladder or gain career advantages, I'll break that down in a future entry.

Q: *I'm not "Ho Pretty," is there a certain type of man I should look for who isn't overly concerned with flawless beauty?*

A: When I wrote that any woman could upgrade herself to appeal to any man, I meant it. There is no one type of flawless beauty that wins over another. Under the hood of every man is an engine fueled by turn-ons that he won't share with homies on the internet or his friends at the bar. You can point to what men say they want or what kind of women guys on TV have on their arms, but in reality, men are turned on by a wide variety of looks, shapes, and, most important, personalities.

When choosing a mark, you can't let your mind be bogged down by basic thoughts like, "will he like the way I look?" You must not assume that you look good enough to get any man; you must BELIEVE. Belief in your attractiveness will come across when you're face to face with your target. Will you land each mark you go after? Of course not, nor will you land each job position you apply for. There will always be incompatibility in life. The key is not to be defeated and understand that the percentages will always be in your favor the more you put yourself out in front of these tricks.

Q: *When I approach men, they think I want sex right away, and they become very aggressive. How do I hold them off?*

A: Understand that men aren't used to women coming on to them; those pursued by women have most likely had the groupie experience. This experience is where a girl is so impressed by looks, money, or fame that she just gives herself away. Do not worry yourself about what he thinks he's going to get out of you. Focus on what you're going to get from him. Go back and read the chapter on being Dick Disciplined, and realize that you must be comfortable weathering the storm for any of these tactics to work.

A man's goal is to say and do anything to get between your legs. Say, "We'll see" instead of "No," for starters. Avoid being alone with him and always have an excuse that keeps him believing he's one date away from hitting that. A man will get aggressive; he will pretend to be done with you, or he will guilt you into giving it up. You must call his bluff through all of this because that's all it is, male manipulation.

Q: *You said that three dates are enough to research him, but what if things fall apart after the first date with a guy I know has money. Should I give up or chase him?*

A: Never get thirsty! When looking for love, I drill into heads that there is always someone else out there, no matter how perfect the person that you break up with seems. When it comes to Hoing, the key to winning will always be your ability to abort your mission, reset, and go after someone new. This man could be a multi-millionaire who doesn't mind spending, but you have to walk away if you get red flags. Alternatively, if you get off on the wrong foot during the research phase and he cools on you, don't get desperate and try to make things right. You must walk away. What happens is that these male Hos rely on bitch checks and reverse psychology. If he distances himself and you come running, then he knows that he has the power over you going forward. Never give a man leverage over you by acting as if he's the only trick in the world.

Q: *How many marks should I have on my team? I usually talk to two or three guys when dating, but this seems more time-consuming.*

A: You should take on as many as you can handle. Realistically your life is filled with things like work, school, etc… Hos are always on the clock, but they don't spend 24-7 doing Hotivities. In a perfect world, you would have two of the three. That means one treat and one trick or one treat and one sponsor. Finding a sponsor doesn't mean you kick your feet up.

That sponsor's investment in you upgrades your way of living, meaning that you can now have access to men from lifestyles that you couldn't reach before. By "handle," I also refer to your mental capacity for juggling men.

Not all women can date multiple men, and not all women can work multiple marks. Don't get greedy! If you're comfortable with one and are really trying to nail this guy, then work him and him alone. The point isn't how many marks you can have on your roster; it's about learning how to perform these tactics effectively.

Q: *I'm horrible at phone sex. Is it okay to keep it at sexting?*

A: Sexting is very effective; a man can get off by reading just as fast as talking. However, things can get lost in translation during texts in general. Therefore, to master this man's likes and dislikes, the phone is superior because it leaves room for error and recovery. For instance, if you text him something about eating his ass, and he's not into that kind of thing, the sext convo may slow down or come to a halt. You don't know what's going on; you're just waiting for the next reply. However, on the phone, a misstep like that can be laughed off, and within seconds you are back to testing out other freaky things that get him off. Whether you hate your voice or aren't that good at it, you must graduate to the phone sex stage.

Q: *I can fake interest, but I don't like to lie about things like sex trauma. What other excuses can I make to not have sex?*

A: I understand that trauma can be hard for those who have experienced it for real. Rape and molestation aren't joking matters, but trauma is the most effective tool for keeping a man from crossing the line when he's tired of hearing wait until next time. There are only so many times you can fake a period, so the alternative is to tug on a different emotional string—fear of failure.

Tell him you're just not ready yet. The key is to keep him interested but not feel as if you're playing games, so the reason for your apprehension should be all about you and never about him. Men don't trust women, and since they see sex as natural and nothing to be afraid of, guys get easily frustrated when you keep them waiting. Therefore, your excuse has to be a bulletproof reason that hits that same idea of emotional fragility.

You don't want to get attached to him too quick after sex because you have a history of doing that. This isn't tied to trauma, just hurt. Throw in that you're currently seeing a therapist about it if he's not buying it, and he will believe you. Sell this like it's a condition that is about you, not him. Finally, you can pull out what I call "limited religion," which means that you aren't practicing celibacy, but you are going through a cleanse and are a month away from being done. Men don't argue with God, so if you say you need four more weeks to get your soul pure, he will wait.

Q: *Oral sex, giving or receiving, isn't real sex for me. Should I use this as a seduction technique early on?*

A: Absolutely not! During college, I learned that blowjobs will tide you over and drive away lust almost as quickly as having vaginal sex with a girl. Men can live on head alone, so you don't want to get into the habit of going down on him just to keep him interested. What will happen is that when it comes time to get in his pockets, he won't be as hard up due to the fact that you've already given him the release he was looking for.

In terms of him going down on you, it's a slippery slope because you know the only reason he's trying to eat your box is to beat your box, and when you're in the moment with a man that has the material things you want, you may give in. It's better to avoid mouths being put anywhere below the waist until you start milking him.

Q: *I live in a small city where everyone talks. Should I try this elsewhere in case word gets out? Is there a specific way to go about being a small town Ho?*

A: Refer back to the chapter on Exit Strategy. The brilliance of the Smart Ho lifestyle is that no one will tell unless you open your mouth. To land a mark, even in a town of 10,000 people, is still something that he will keep private. When you go out to date, people may see you and assume you're having sex. However, it's just assumptions and gossip. When his friends ask him what's going on, he isn't going to ruin his fun time by telling your business or his business because rival men plot on New Pussy. Women tend to get caught up in the drama of "people are talking behind my back," but Hos do not care.

When it comes time to move on to the next man, you won't have a reputation because you hold something over his head, the fact that he was tricking on you. A man would rather say, "We're still cool, that was just my friend," than "She's a gold-digging Ho" because that makes him look like a small town sucker who got taken in by a small town Ho.

The positive thing that can come out of this is that you get to be seen with someone known as a winner in that small town. Men want what other men have. Why do you think celebrities date and even marry cast-offs of other celebrities? Even if a guy only heard you used to go out with an old mark, he will want to know what a man with money or power saw in you. Men don't run from Hos; they chase them, even when the chasing is subconscious. No matter where you live if you start with that foundation of loyalty and build it into leverage, that mark will never sell you out.

Q: *Can gay men or women use Ho Tactics? Are lesbian women least likely to be sugar mommas than men?*

A: Ho Tactics is LGBT-friendly! Men can be Hos and women can be Hos, so there is no real difference except in the gender aim. Gay men, in particular, have been known to master the art of being sponsored better than females. In Los Angeles, I've heard several behind closed doors stories of famous directors or producers tricking on up-and-coming pretty boy actors and even assistants. A friend told me how simply giving the "Boyfriend Experience" to this older man without any sex or sexual acts paid for his first year in Hollywood. When it comes to women, we all know they are givers for the most part, which means to gain the affection of a lesbian who is sweet on you, can work the same way as if it were a man. In this recent explosion of bisexual women, I've seen former Hos be out Hoed because they weren't used to a woman's manipulation the same way they were used to a man's.

In the past year, I've gotten some amazing stories from lesbians that proved beyond a shadow of a doubt that "sugar mama" women make better sponsors than straight men! Being gay or lesbian can be a lonely existence; coming in and being his or her friend, lover, and confidant in a world where they're being judged makes you extremely valuable. Thus, they will go above and beyond to keep you on their team. In the end, it's all about the process of endearing yourself to a human being, and that can be done no matter their orientation. Hoing is equal opportunity.

Q: *I don't have much money to go out or to put on appearances like Maria did. How can a poor Ho-In-The-Making, do this on a budget?*

A: You don't need red bottoms or Gucci bags to attract wealth. You don't need to have a luxury car or even a car at all. Most importantly, you don't need to live in an upscale community. Women's fashion can be extremely cheap. From thrift stores to Forever 21 and fast fashion sites like Fashion Nova, you can find a pair of jeans that hugs your ass and a blouse that flatters your top. What was the foundation of these tactics? To look sexy as fuck in your own opinion. If you can't master the art of putting together a cheap or already worn outfit that inspires a smile when you twirl in the mirror, then you will never have the confidence to do any of these tactics.

There was a woman who thought that every question I made her ask a mark would be shot back to her—*where do you work, where do you live, etc...* and based on her being poor with a boring job, she would stumble out of the gate. Wrong! Men will ask just to be polite, but they don't care. Make being poor a part of your story. If you have to, exploit your life! You live in a low-rent community because you're saving while paying off school loans—that makes sense to any man. You live with your parents because they need extra help—that makes sense to any man. You have to call Ubers to and from dates because your car was totaled a month ago—*oh that's so sad, how can I help*! Remember, these men will grow to love you, and if you come saying that you need money to pay off an unexpected bill or need a co-pay for your mother's medicine, he will be more inclined to help because it fits your life story of being in the struggle. If you want a car, doesn't it sound better to be without one and dependent on ride shares when you finally ask "daddy" to lease you a whip? Take your burden and weaponize it, don't be ashamed!

Q: *I'm afraid of a man seeing through my Ho tactics and doing something to get me back. How can I safely cover my tracks?*

A: Never reveal that which may come back to haunt you. Throughout this book, it never says you have to bring him to your home or even give him your real name. Again, refer back to the chapter on Exit Strategy and build evidence against this man in case things go south.

If your mark begins to show signs of anger or frustration, walk away immediately. The same way you research his finances, research his temperament. A man that's constantly angry drops hints about doing violence to others or gets even a little rough when you tease him, trust that he has problems. Do not ignore or stay the course because you're money hungry. Safety aside, you must safeguard your assets. Even if you end up dealing with someone who buys you a house or a car, you must protect your interest if the bottom falls out. If the home is in his name, make sure you talk him into putting you down as co-owner or siphon enough money from him that you have rebound money if he does kick you out.

One woman shared how her sponsor started running into money problems and wanted her to return the car he bought with the promise of getting something new. She agreed without fuss, then quickly asked for a large lump sum of money to go on a shopping trip. The underlining message was, "I'll only give you this car back if you pay me." This guy never got her another car, but she came away with enough to go put a down payment on something new. In the end, she may have lost that mark, but she ended up with what she wanted. Always be financially stable enough to walk away and savvy enough to get a little extra on the way out.

Q: *I seem to attract marks that are long-distance or very busy, I've done my research, and they aren't fake busy. It's real. How do I use Ho Tactics day to day with a man that's not able to see me?*

A: I developed *Ho Tactics* to be a time-saver, hence three dates to see if a man is down to spend, so you can walk away and move on to the next. However, there are scenarios where *Ho Tactics* will take more time and patience. I currently advise a woman that dates a musician who tours with one of the biggest pop stars in the world. This guy literally couldn't go on three dates over three weeks, nor was he always available for phone calls. Her hustle became more of a side hustle.

She had another guy she was seeing, but she kept up appearances with the band guy by being sure to show him attention each day. Texts when he was in new cities. Pictures randomly. Sexting as a reward. And most importantly, she found out his interest outside of music, studied it, and when they would have time to text back and forth, it was her having something fun to say about shit other than "how's the tour."

It took over a month, but he arrived with a gift for her by the time she had her official first date. He flew private to take her on a second date a few weeks later, and she gave him a small gift of her own. She used the limited time together to endear herself by explaining her backstory—family drama, not finishing school, she exploited her life for his empathy. She became his friend/lover/sister within two months, and by the time he was done touring, she tested their bond. Her new venture test was for him to get "them" an apartment in the city where she could live, take care of him when he's in town, and do work on her career goals. To this day, she lives there rent-free and barely sees him.

Long-distance relationships require patience, but they're better suited for Ho Tactics than regular love. Women who meet guys in other cities get tunnel vision; they want attention, to know that he's not dating local women, and of course, physical touch that can't be had until someone visits. These Tactics are all about making a man wait to have you. Butter him up with sweet talk on the phone, grow that bond by sharing stories, and don't be in a rush to see him. At the same time, have other men on the roster so you won't start to over-invest in a long distant mark.

The idea is to not obsess over a mark and feel a need to rush through the steps if he's unavailable. Slow and steady is about chipping away; not swinging for the fences is key. The longer you take, the more he trusts you, the more he trusts you, the more you will get when he does finally get to see you.

Q: *I love the idea of Ho Tactics, but I want love from a man that's also able to provide, someone who I don't have to see as a mark but as a true partner. Should I stick with Ho Tactics, or should I just invest my energy searching for the right romantic option?*

A: The empowerment that you get from Ho Tactics can be intoxicating! It's like wearing leather or tall heels; it makes you feel dangerous. However, Ho Tactics is not for Cosplaying. If you only want to use this book to rebuild your low self-esteem or to dominate men out of revenge, then stop. In my book *The Unicorn Delusion*, I talked about the lies women tell themselves that block the blessing the universe has in store. If you really want true love, then date with an open heart, don't see this man as a mark or a bag. See him as a human worthy of your time, as that's the only way you can give or receive genuine love.

90% of my work is about Spartan power and finding your perfect match who values you and respects you. Ho Tactics has many of the same principles, but it does require acting and manipulation. The game of love is about being trusting, vetting, and testing to see if that person is worthy of your love. The game of Ho Tactics is about seducing, gaining trust, and testing to see if he's willing to spend. As I wrote earlier, you can fall in love with your mark, get married, and he'll never know. I know three Hos that quarantined with marks during the pandemic and then came back outside engaged or pregnant. You can always change your goal and turn that mark into your man.

Nevertheless, I want you to focus on what you want in the long run, not what you think you need based on a temporary situation. **Intentional thoughts give way to intentional living, so make a genuine connection your primary goal if you want love.** However, if you feel like love can wait another few years, then put that sappy stuff out of your head and get to the money. These marks are practically giving it away these days!

#WhatWouldMariaDo

The great thing about *Ho Tactics* is that no matter if you meet your trick in Best Buy, at a wedding reception, or online, it all goes back to the basics of confidence, seduction, and manipulation. Once a man likes you, even if it is only a lust for quick sex, you immediately have power over him. Truly understand the concept of power, don't pretend, and try to freestyle these lessons. Power over men is not this cartoon concept of heart-shaped eyes and zombie-like following. Power is under the surface but supremely binding. He will follow wherever you want to lead this man because he wants something from you. **The catch is he doesn't even know he's being led; he thinks he's doing the leading.** The more you tease sex, the more he wants to fuck you. The more you come off as "Let's go get drunk," good time girl, the more time he wants to spend time with you. The more you talk to him privately as a friend, the more he will cherish your company.

Ultimate power comes in the form of separation anxiety. Unlike the jump off he fucks after a week, the girlfriend that loves him more than herself, or the platonic buddy that relies on his friendship, you have no desire to be in his life. Think back to Pussy Value and how your ability to cut him off becomes a turn-on. The average girl can't cut a man off, which is why they get exploited. Once you give him a taste of this fantasy living, then threaten to pull it away, the tables turn, and you become the exploiter because you are uniquely special, and he must have you in his life!

Ho Tactics isn't about tricks or games. It's about insight! Male psychology makes you a living weapon. You're not a Ho, you're Ho Conscious, and no matter if it's a mark, your boss at work, or a teacher at school, all you have to do is concentrate and think about what people want to hear, then sink into your character to make them melt in your hands!

I repeat for the fifty-leventh time, it's not tricking if you got it! Men with money blow paper on all types of hobbyist things or ego-stroking trinkets. To be his fantasy woman that has made him full of both lust and love means that you will get anything you want because making you happy means you will continue to make him happy.

This is the Gold Edition, my ultimate update of this book, so I can say with even more confidence that everything written has worked when used by women just like you! Every race, the old and the young, middle class and lower class, single women, and those in relationships have gotten far more than headphones. Nothing is holding you back but doubt—kill that noise! Study this book… highlight this book… and refer to it often until you understand the power a sexualized personality has over men.

No matter if you're looking to get your boyfriend to treat you better or a single lady who is ready to turn to the Ho side of the force, you will not be denied! Right is a direction, and Wrong is an opinion. Men have been manipulating women since the dawn of time, study these tactics, apply these techniques, and even up the battle between the sexes until you get what you deserve.

I want you to win! So, if you get stuck at any point in your Maria journey, you can sign up for personal advice via **SolvingSingle.com**

Ho Tactics: The Audio Book
Also Available On Audible

Listen to episodes of the G.L. Lambert Podcast @
FarFromBasyc.com

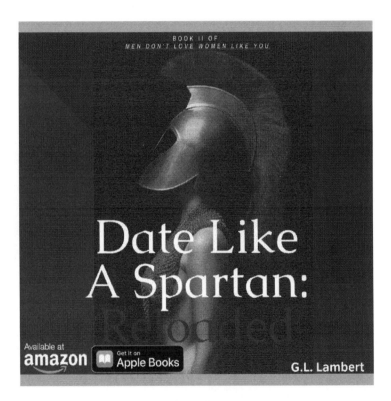

Date Like A Spartan…

Learn to take your power to the NEXT level.

<u>On Sale Now</u>

Made in the USA
Las Vegas, NV
12 October 2024

f83c2cdb-47f4-4e79-ba63-ba1e24204888R01